SERIALS IN THE PARK

Proceedings of the NORTH AMERICAN SERIALS INTEREST GROUP, Inc.

NASIG

18th Annual Conference
June 26-29, 2003
Portland State University
Portland, Oregon

Serials in the Park has been co-published simultaneously as *The Serials Librarian*, Volume 46, Numbers 1/2 and 3/4 2004.

SERIALS IN THE PARK

Proceedings of the
NORTH AMERICAN SERIALS INTEREST GROUP, Inc.

NASIG

18th Annual Conference
June 26-29, 2003
Portland State University
Portland, Oregon

Patricia Sheldahl French
Richard Worthing
Editors

Routledge
Taylor & Francis Group
NEW YORK AND LONDON

Serials in the Park has been co-published simultaneously as *The Serials Librarian*, Volume 46, Numbers 1/2 and 3/4 2004.

First published 2004 by The Haworth Press, Inc.

This edition published 2021 by Routledge
605 Third Avenue, New York, NY 10017
2 Park Square, Milton Park, Abingdon, Oxon OX14 4RN

Routledge is an imprint of the Taylor & Francis Group, an informa business

ISBN 13: 978-0-7890-2565-4 (pbk)

Cover design director: Thomas J. Mayshock Jr.

Front cover logo and image designed by Kerry V. McQuaid

Library of Congress Cataloging-in-Publication Data

North American Serials Interest Group. Conference (18th : 2003 : Portland State University)
Serials in the park : proceedings of the North American Serials Interest Group 18th Annual Conference, June 26-29, 2003, Portland State University / Patricia Sheldahl French, Richard Worthing, editors.
p. cm.
"Proceedings of the North American Serials Interest Group, Inc. 18th Annual Conference, June 26-29, 2003, Portland State University, Portland, Oregon."
"Co-published simultaneously as The serials librarian, volume 46, numbers 1/2 and 3/4 2004."
Includes bibliographical references and index.
ISBN 0-7890-2564-7 (alk. paper) – ISBN 0-7890-2565-5 (soft cover : alk. paper)
1. Serials librarianship–Congresses. 2. Libraries–Special collections–Electronic journals–Congresses. 3. Electronic journals–Congresses. I. French, Patricia Sheldahl. II. Worthing, Richard (Richard L.) III. Serials librarian. IV. Title.
Z692.S5N67 2003
025.3′432–dc22

2004005754

NASIG Officers and Executive Board

2002/2003

Officers:

Eleanor Cook, President, Appalachian State University
Anne McKee, Vice President/President-Elect, Greater Library Western Alliance
Bea Caraway, Secretary, Trinity University
Denise Novak, Treasurer, Carnegie Mellon University
Margaret Rioux, Past President, Woods Hole Oceanographic Institution

Executive Board:

Marilyn Geller, Information Management Consultant
Daniel H. Jones, Southwest Foundation for Biomedical Research
Mary Page, Rutgers University
Robert Persing, University of Pennsylvania
Kevin Randall, Northwestern University
Joyce Tenney, University of Maryland, Baltimore County

2003 Program Planning Committee

Co-Chairs:

Kate M. Manuel, New Mexico State University
Charity K. Martin, University of Nebraska, Lincoln
Sherry Sullivan, University of California, Los Angeles

Committee Members:

Eve J. Davis, EBSCO Information Services
Sandy Folsom, Central Michigan University
June Garner, Mississippi State University
Kit Kennedy, Blackwell, Inc.
Lee Kreiger, Rensselaer Polytechnic Institute
Pat Loghry, University of Notre Dame
Emily McElroy, Loyola University Health Sciences Library
Lanell Rabner, Brigham Young University
Connie Roberts, Hamilton College
Rose Robischon, United States Military Academy, West Point
Steve Savage, San Diego State University
Gale Teaster, Winthrop University

Consultant

Lisa A. Macklin, Georgia Institute of Technology

Fritz Schwartz Serials Education Scholarship

Lyudmila Shpilevaya, Long Island University

NASIG Conference Student Grant Award Recipients

Dana Antonucci-Durgan, Queens College, University of New York

Lisa Bowman, Emporia State University

Fang Gao, University of Illinois at Urbana-Champaign

Rebecca Soltys Jones, University of North Carolina at Chapel Hill

Jacalyn Spoon, State University of New York at Buffalo

Horizon Award Winner

Sarah Sutton, Texas A & M University

Mexico Student Conference Grant

Pablo Carrasco Renteria, Escuela Nacional de Biblioteconomia y Archivonomia

ABOUT THE EDITORS

Patricia Sheldahl French is Head of the Serials Department at the University of California, Davis, Shields Library. She held several previous positions at the California State Library including reference librarian, bibliographic systems librarian, and state documents cataloger. She holds a BA in French from Occidental College in Los Angeles, an MA in Art History from the University of California Davis, and an MLS from U.C. Berkeley. She has been a frequent speaker on cataloging electronic resources and a contributor to three previous NASIG proceedings. She is co-founder and chair of the California Digital Library Shared Cataloging Program. She co-authored the recent publication "One for Nine: The Shared Cataloging Program of the California Digital Library," *Serials Review* (v. 28, no. 1, 2002).

Richard Worthing received his MLS from U.C.L.A. in 1980. He is the Serials Cataloger at the California State Library in Sacramento, California. Rick is editor and publisher of *Classic Baseball*, an alternative view of Major League Baseball standings which he distributes occasionally to a small circle of friends.

Serials in the Park

CONTENTS

Introduction 1
Patricia Sheldahl French
Richard Worthing

President's Greeting at the Opening Banquet 5
Eleanor Cook

PRECONFERENCE PROGRAMS

The "Seventy Percent Solution": Assessing Criteria for Model Fund Allocations 9
Claudia Weston, Cyril Oberlander, Mary Ellen Kenreich, Don Frank, Sarah Beasley, Presenters
Marcella Lesher, Recorder

Cataloging Survival for Non-Catalogers, or You Thought You Would Never Need to Catalog Again 17
Karen Darling, Presenter
Siôn Romaine, Recorder

PLENARY SESSIONS

Content Industry Outlook 2003: Asteroids That Are Changing the Information Landscape 27
Leigh Watson Healy, Presenter
Reeta Sinha, Recorder

Town Hall Meeting 33
Christa Easton, Facilitator
Jerry R. Brown, Recorder

There Is No Forest, We're Only Hugging the Trees: Nontraditional Ways of Acquiring, Providing Access to, and Managing Serials 39
Jill Emery, Rick Anderson, Adam Chesler, Joan Conger, Ted Fons, Presenters
Debra Skinner, Recorder

CONCURRENT SESSIONS

The Information Resource Matrix: A Revolutionary Method to Present Relationships Among Online Serial Objects 59
Carol Casey, Mark Jacobs, Lihong Zhu, Presenters

Serial Aggregations, Multiple Versions, and the Virtual Union Catalog: The California Digital Library Catalog, SUNY, and Ex Libris Experiences 69
Michael Kaplan, Presenter

Finding a Better Trail Through the Journals Forest 83
Timothy Gatti, Heather S. Miller, Presenters

Expose Yourself to Electronic Journals 99
Jill Emery, Claire Ginn, Dan Tonkery, Presenters
Kevin Petsche, Recorder

The Digital Preservation Conundrum, Part 1 107
Abby Smith, Presenter

The Digital Preservation Conundrum, Part 2: Preservation and Electronic-Archiving 115
Eileen Gifford Fenton, Presenter

How Electronic Journals Are Changing Patterns of Use 121
Peter Boyce, Donald W. King, Carol Montgomery, Carol Tenopir, Presenters

Usage Statistics: Taking E-Metrics to the Next Level 143
Oliver Pesch, Presenter

Seeing the Forest and the Trees When Developing a New Acquisitions System 155
Shelley Neville, Presenter

From Tiny Acorns to Great Oaks: Taking a Nationwide Approach to Library Cooperation 161
Pauline La Rooy, Presenter

Helping Manage the E-Journal Forest: Do You Need an Agent Any More? Part 1 173
Philip Wallas, Presenter

Helping Manage the E-Journal Forest: Do You Need an Agent Any More? Part 2 179
Stephen Bosch, Presenter

Hot Topics 191
Keith Courtney, Miriam Gilbert, Michael Markwith, Kim Maxwell, Presenters
Jerry R. Brown, Recorder

WORKSHOPS

Case Studies in Electronic Serials Cataloging, or What Am I Supposed to Do With This? 203
Steve Shadle, Workshop Leader
Holley R. Lange, Recorder

Branching Out: The Importance of Networking in a Library Landscape 209
Jeff Slagell, Workshop Leader
Mykie Howard, Recorder

Web-Based Trails and Cross-Campus Partnerships 215
Sharon Elteto, Maggie McVay-Lynch, Workshop Leaders
Elizabeth Parang, Recorder

From Catalogers to Ontologists: Changing Roles and Opportunities for Technical Services Librarians 221
Nathan Rupp, Workshop Leader
David Burke, Recorder

Copyright Law: Fact or Fiction? 227
Janice M. Krueger, Workshop Leader
Karen Matthews, Recorder

Electronic Content: Is It Accessible to Clients with "Differabilities"? 233
Cheryl Riley, Workshop Leader

Planning for New Growth in the Forest: Cultivating New Serialists for the Future 241
Selden Durgom Lamoureux, Workshop Leader
Susan Davis, Recorder

When the Rug Comes Out from Under: Managing Change, Technology, Information, and Staff 245
Althea Aschmann, Workshop Leader
Gail Julian, Recorder

Tools for Tenure Trailblazing: Planning Productive Paths for Green Serialists 253
Claire Dygert, Markel Tumlin, Workshop Leaders
Marsha Seamans, Recorder

Policies and Procedures Manuals in Technical Services: The Forest, the Trees, and the Critters 257
Stephanie Schmitt, Workshop Leader
Sandra Barstow, Recorder

Paving the Way for Print Repositories Through Electronic Access 263
Mary Jo Zeter, Jeanne Drewes, Workshop Leaders
Michael A. Arthur, Recorder

Reinventing Acquisitions with a "Forget-to-Do" List 269
Ann McHugo, Carol Magenau, Workshop Presenters
Jeanne M. Langendorfer, Recorder

Electronic Resource Management and the MARC Record: The Road Less Traveled 275
Paula Sullenger, Workshop Leader
Anne Mitchell, Recorder

From Survival Hike to a Walk in the Park: Training Guideposts to Lead the Way 281
Rene J. Erlandson, Workshop Leader
Robert J. Congleton, Recorder

Starting with an Empty Map: Benchmarking Time and Costs for Serials Operations 287
Nancy Slight-Gibney, Mary Grenci, Workshop Leaders
Lisa S. Blackwell, Recorder

Is It Working: Usage Data as a Tool for Evaluating the Success of New Full-Text Title Access Methods 295
Joanna Duy, Eric Pauley, Workshop Leaders
Wendy Highby, Recorder

Using the Library's OPAC to Dynamically Generate Webpages for E-Journals 301
Kathryn Paul, Elena Romaniuk, Workshop Leaders
Daisy T. Cheng, Recorder

Keeping the Connection: Maintaining E-Journal Subscriptions 309
Bill Kara, Christine Stamison, Workshop Leaders
Sarah E. George, Recorder

Providing a Table-of-Contents Service to Faculty 315
Madeleine Bombeld, Lynn R. Shay, Workshop Leaders
Rebecca Sheffield, Recorder

Poster Sessions 321

18th Annual NASIG Conference Registrants 329

Index 345
LadyJane Hickey

Introduction

On June 20, 1803, Thomas Jefferson wrote a letter to Meriwether Lewis containing detailed instructions regarding the proposed Corps of Discovery. Thus was launched the historic 18-month-long journey across the continental United States to find the mouth of the Columbia River at the Pacific Ocean. Two hundred years later, the North American Serials Interest Group issued instructions to NASIG members and serialists everywhere to travel to Oregon for the 18th annual NASIG Conference. Fortunately, it did not take this group nearly as long to make the journey as it did Lewis and Clark. By June 26, 2003, NASIG's own Corps of Discovery–more than 600 serialists from North America, Europe and the Caribbean–had arrived in Portland, ready to explore new territory in the world of serials. There, comfortably installed on the campus of Portland State University, in the heart of downtown Portland's tree-lined South Park Blocks and near the banks of the mighty Columbia, exploration took place NASIG-style.

A look at the Table of Contents will show that many presenters found rich metaphorical possibilities relevant to serials work in the conference theme of "Serials in the Park." The mysteries of the uncharted forest, the sprouting and branching of new growth, the need to blaze the trail by creating new maps, and the importance of seeing the forest through the trees–these themes and others worked well to frame the conference's focus on the challenges and quandaries of managing serials in 2003.

Two pre-conferences began this years' exploration of serials issues. The first presented a model for reallocating funds among academic disciplines within a university. The second pre-conference offered an over-

[Haworth co-indexing entry note]: "Introduction." French, Pat, and Rick Worthing. Co-published simultaneously in *The Serials Librarian* (The Haworth Information Press, an imprint of The Haworth Press, Inc.) Vol. 46, No. 1/2, 2004, pp. 1-3; and: *Serials in the Park* (ed: Patricia S. French, and Richard Worthing) The Haworth Information Press, an imprint of The Haworth Press, Inc., 2004, pp. 1-3. Single or multiple copies of this article are available for a fee from The Haworth Document Delivery Service [1-800-HAWORTH, 9:00 a.m. - 5:00 p.m. (EST). E-mail address: getinfo@haworthpress.com].

http://www.haworthpress.com/web/SER
Digital Object Identifier: 10.1300/J123v46n01_01

view of serials cataloging for the non-cataloger, with some emphasis on the rule changes that took effect this year.

In the first plenary session, Leigh Watson Healy went beyond the theme of trees and forests, suggesting instead that everyone who is involved with information content needs to look out for incoming asteroids–cataclysmic changes in the information content industry that will reshape our work in the future. The second plenary session truly explored new territory within NASIG itself, offering for the first time a Town Hall meeting for NASIG members to share their thoughts about the future directions of the organization and the annual conference. And the final plenary offered a wrap-up of views on the changes taking place in the serials world–thoughts from representatives of libraries, publishers, and integrated library system vendors.

As has been the case at several recent NASIG conferences, many presentations focused on electronic journals–how to order and manage them, how to catalog them, and how to figure out whether and how people are using them. The concurrent sessions were a potpourri of topics on serial aggregations, preservation, the role of the agent in the new acquisitions world of electronic journals, usage patterns for electronic titles, library cooperation in New Zealand, and the planning process for designing a new serials acquisition system. This year's volume also includes a concurrent session entitled "The Information Resource Matrix," which was inadvertently omitted from the published 2002 conference proceedings.

This year the nineteen workshops were divided into two topical groups. The Issues/Skills set included topics related to the practice of serials librarianship and personnel issues. How do we prepare people to take serials jobs? How do we provide training on the job? How do we prepare ourselves to succeed in tenure reviews for promotion and retention? How can we work with staff to manage change in the workplace and document evolving procedures? Are there traditional serials management tasks which are no longer necessary or relevant as our collections become increasingly electronic? Which activities can be dispensed with in the context of shrinking budgets and staff support? What kinds of partnerships can we cultivate within and outside the library to tailor services that effectively deliver new services and improved access? How can we support each other through networking, and what will be the role of the technical services librarian of the future?

The Research Set offered seven workshops which described innovative or experimental projects designed to foster new uses of data and access to electronic information. Two workshops reported projects that extended the use of data stored in the MARC record to new purposes including creating dynamically generated Webpages and managing access restrictions and content of electronic journals. One workshop dealt with use statistics for full-text journals via an in-house Cold Fusion search tool. The remaining workshops reported projects to benchmark the cost of staffing serials operations, provide a table-of-contents service to faculty for electronic journals, train staff, and manage subscription maintenance tasks.

Veterans of NASIG will know that the highly successful annual conference is the result of volunteer efforts by many hardworking NASIG members dedicated to working together for professional growth and collaboration. The Executive Board, Conference Planning Committee and Program Planning Committee begin work on the annual conference at least two years in advance. Speakers and presenters answer the call for program proposals approximately one year ahead. And the published proceedings comprise papers written by volunteer recorders who attend the sessions and author the reports. As editors, we gratefully acknowledge the efforts of all these individuals. Special thanks go to the authors who, as a group, answered the call to contribute to the proceedings, met their deadlines conscientiously with short turnaround times, and produced high quality reports suitable for publication. They made the editing job painless and enjoyable. Thanks also go to our Executive Board liaisons, Mary Page and Kevin Randall. And, lastly, thanks to the helpful and professional staff at Haworth Press who provided support and guidance to two fledgling editors in training.

Pat French
Rick Worthing
Editors

NOTE

The editors regret that the concurrent session, "The 100% Communication," was not available for publication at the request of the presenter, Mary Devlin. Mary's session was participatory in nature and drew an enthusiastic response from attendees. It was, by its nature, not conducive to being recorded in a static written report.

President's Greeting at the Opening Banquet

Eleanor Cook

Welcome, welcome!

You all don't know how GLAD I am to see you!

What a white-knuckle year for conferences this has been.

So–here we are, and we have a GREAT conference planned! There will be something for everyone, and plenty of time mixed in for networking and socializing. I hope everyone gets a chance to experience the beauty and diversity of Portland and Oregon while you are here.

Since I have a few minutes to bend your ear before we eat, let me make a couple of observations:

- NASIG is entering an exciting period of its history. As I have alluded to in my President's column in the NASIG Newsletter, we are embracing change like never before. Our draft strategic plan is in the hands of the Board and soon you all will get to review it as well. We want your feedback and ideas in order to keep our future bright.
- With change comes controversy. Not everyone will like every change we have made or are considering. And you have a right to say so! So please do! And don't forget to fill out those evaluations!
- You'll have numerous chances during this conference and afterwards to bring up burning issues that are on your mind. Our town

[Haworth co-indexing entry note]: "President's Greeting at the Opening Banquet." Cook, Eleanor. Co-published simultaneously in *The Serials Librarian* (The Haworth Information Press, an imprint of The Haworth Press, Inc.) Vol. 46, No. 1/2, 2004, pp. 5-6; and: *Serials in the Park* (ed: Patricia S. French. and Richard Worthing) The Haworth Information Press, an imprint of The Haworth Press, Inc., 2004, pp. 5-6. Single or multiple copies of this article are available for a fee from The Haworth Document Delivery Service [1-800-HAWORTH, 9:00 a.m. - 5:00 p.m. (EST). E-mail address: getinfo@haworthpress.com].

http://www.haworthpress.com/web/SER
Digital Object Identifier: 10.1300/J123v46n01_02

hall forum will be an interesting new venue for discourse and I encourage your participation. We also are offering a "Hot Topics" session that promises to add some sizzle to the conference.

- If you are new to the NASIG experience, we hope you'll benefit from this unique meeting. NASIG is a somewhat tribal experience–actually, some have compared it to summer camp–though staying in hotels this year will make it a bit less rustic–and–I hope–a bit more civilized. I do not expect to hear complaints this year about cockroaches, failed air conditioning or scrawny towels!
- Later this evening we'll be giving awards and recognizing many people who have worked hard in recent times and especially this year to make so many things happen. I hope you'll stick around for this part of the evening as these people deserve your rounds of applause.
- Of all the many people who have labored this year to bring us to this point–in particular, I want to mention the Conference and Program Planning Committees. Please thank these people over and over and over! If you have ever served on these committees, you know–so tell them that! Tell them you know what it takes!
- Finally, I would like to tell all of you just how much of a privilege it has been for me to serve you this year as your President. It's been a real honor for me–and in keeping with the metaphor of this year's theme, I want to observe that I have attempted to follow in the path of excellent leadership provided by former NASIG Presidents, yet I have also strived to leave my own footprints as well.

Thanks, and have a great conference.

PRECONFERENCE PROGRAMS

The "Seventy Percent Solution": Assessing Criteria for Model Fund Allocations

Claudia Weston
Cyril Oberlander
Mary Ellen Kenreich
Don Frank
Sarah Beasley

Presenters

Marcella Lesher

Recorder

SUMMARY. Portland State University Library's fund allocation committee presented information and practical advice on the process of developing a model to reallocate funding for library materials. After experimenting with funding ratios, they decided to use their model to reallocate 30 percent of the funds earmarked for discipline-specific materials while protecting 70 percent of each discipline's original allocation. *[Article copies available for a fee from The Haworth Document Delivery Service: 1-800-HAWORTH. E-mail address: <docdelivery@haworthpress.com> Website: <http://www.HaworthPress.com>]*

[Haworth co-indexing entry note]: "The 'Seventy Percent Solution': Assessing Criteria for Model Fund Allocations." Lesher, Marcella. Co-published simultaneously in *The Serials Librarian* (The Haworth Information Press, an imprint of The Haworth Press, Inc.) Vol. 46, No. 1/2, 2004, pp. 9-15; and: *Serials in the Park* (ed: Patricia S. French, and Richard Worthing) The Haworth Information Press, an imprint of The Haworth Press, Inc., 2004, pp. 9-15. Single or multiple copies of this article are available for a fee from The Haworth Document Delivery Service [1-800-HAWORTH, 9:00 a.m. - 5:00 p.m. (EST). E-mail address: getinfo@haworthpress.com].

http://www.haworthpress.com/web/SER
Digital Object Identifier: 10.1300/J123v46n01_03

INTRODUCTION

Presenters of the "Seventy Percent Solution" NASIG preconference gave attendees an overview of the process that was involved in developing a new funding model for library materials at Portland State University Library. Participants were also given the opportunity to work through parts of the process through group work activities. Claudia Weston introduced participants to program presenters and provided an agenda that outlined the program.

HISTORY

Mary Ellen Kenreich began with an historical perspective of funding at the library and a discussion of issues that led to the creation of a library committee to examine funding and make recommendations for change. Kenreich explained that materials funding had been divided into 300 fund lines that included individual subject lines subdivided by publication format including monographs, periodicals, microforms, and standing orders. Collection development was based on the library's architectural design, with each floor serving different academic disciplines. Because of this physical division, sciences, social science, humanities, education, and business were almost functioning as separate library units. The library had been working with two percent annual budget increases over a number of years. These budget increases had been traditionally divided into three percent increases for standing orders and microforms, seven to eight percent increases for journals, and stable spending for monographs. Money not spent by subject selectors in monographic lines was used to prepay for items for the next fiscal year. Eighty percent of the budget was being spent on serials.

Kenreich noted that in trying to analyze their own funding needs in the mid-1990s, the library had experimented with a funding model developed by Linfield College in Oregon. Based on the Linfield model, there were indications of over-expenditures in some areas and under-expenditures in other areas. The library used this model to distribute new funds across academic disciplines.

In 2000, after a library building and staff reorganization, PSU's collection development model was no longer based on the library's physical components. It was felt that an in-depth look at funding allocations was needed. This decision was based on factors such as serials inflation (especially in the area of science journals); a lack of flexibility in the existing funding model; and spending that no longer truly reflected PSU's enrollment or the research interests of students and faculty. Money was not being spent based on actual needs, but on what had been spent in previous years. A committee was formed to study and recommend a new allocation model.

CONCEPTUAL FRAMEWORK AND FORMULA COMPONENTS

Claudia Weston began her presentation by referencing an article by Charles B. Lowry.[1] She discussed the importance of recognizing the realities involved in institutional change–primarily the politics involved in any funding decision. She also spoke of equity and need as important components of change.

In developing the model, the committee began with an examination of the library's mission statement and collection development policy. The committee also looked at mission and policy statements of other libraries. Workshop participants were also given the opportunity to experience this process through group work in which each group was given a library mission statement, collection policy statement, or other relevant material. Each group was asked to develop the goals that they thought funding should achieve based on the mission statements of the various libraries examined. Participants discussed such issues as curriculum support, student diversity, and types of degree programs. These issues were targeted as objectives that many funding models would probably need to support.

In addition to the importance of goal setting based on the library mission, Weston noted that the committee also needed to understand the environment of the university. This was essential to establishing the formula components necessary to the allocation process. Committee members examined the local environment in terms of demands from clientele, research activity, and actual library usage. Quantifiable data were identified within these broad categories, such as number of faculty and students, courses taught, degrees conferred, research funding, monographic circulation, and faculty ILL requests. Supply issues were also quantified, such as numbers of books and serials titles by discipline, average cost of books and serial titles, and actual expenditures for these items. Weston noted that "The availability of data has a significant influence on which components are chosen."

Preconference participants were then asked to look at the libraries they had analyzed previously and pick the factors that they thought might apply to that particular library. Weston then provided a handout showing formula components matched with PSU library goals. For example, a PSU goal to "accommodate interdisciplinary/interdepartmental needs" was matched with a formula component to "establish subject clusters." A goal to "provide selectors with greater flexibility in determining format and type of materials to be added to the collection" was matched with a formula component that would "allocate to discipline without segregating by format."

PUBLISHING UNIVERSE

Sarah Beasley provided an in-depth look at how the supply side, or what she termed the publishing universe, affected how funding was to be allocated to the new subject clusters created in the funding model. For example, the number and type of degree programs were considered an important factor. To determine what individual programs or disciplines needed, book costs were examined using Blackwell's Cost and Coverage Studies,[2] as were serials pricing statistics published in *Library Journal*.[3] Discipline-specific titles were grouped by LC class and assigned to a subject cluster. Disciplines were grouped into one of three clusters–Science and Engineering, Arts and Humanities, and Social Sciences. Publishing statistics and cost statistics were then calculated for each cluster. Beasley discussed the problems inherent in the placement of certain titles in the allocation model using the example of law and health and medical journals that were interdisciplinary in nature. By using subject clusters, the team felt they could better deal with the interdisciplinary nature of many of the titles. Clustering was also used to protect against perceptions of overfunding for areas in which book and serial costs were truly overwhelming.

THE FORMULA

Cyril Oberlander presented an overview of how the formula was actually created. Creating the formula involved: (a) collecting, relating, and managing data pools, and (b) testing and synthesizing new data (using formulas, charts, etc.)

Data were entered into Excel spreadsheets and analyzed in a variety of ways. Oberlander presented "an evolving formula of ratios," in which various factors, such as percentage of faculty FTE and percentage of UG course hours, were given differing weights in the allocation formula. As the group worked with the data, various problems were encountered. Different weights and factors were applied to the formula in attempts to resolve various problems. For example, the first problem was that the formula distributed funds evenly along subject clusters without representative differentiation, so a department of five FTE faculty in the humanities cluster would be given the same allocation as a department of ten FTE faculty in humanities. This leveling effect was caused by the great impact of the publishing universe factors in the allocation formula. The solution to the leveling problem was realized by re-applying the formula to the cluster budgets; in effect, the allocation was first divided into subject clusters using the formula, then divided again into departments within the subject clusters using the same formula. This provided better differentiation between individual subjects or budget units within the cluster.

The next problem was one of severity of cuts. The proposed cuts and growth areas in the budget were considered too extreme by the budget task force. They continued to experiment with changing weighting factors to better understand the behavior of the formula. The solution was to recognize some of the historical budget as a factor in the formula by preserving 70 percent of the previous allocation budget, while re-allocating only 30 percent of the budget using the formula.

IMPLEMENTATION

The next stage in the process began with presentations to the campus community. Open meetings were scheduled to discuss the proposal.[4] Kenreich discussed some of the issues initially addressed by administration and faculty. The administration asked for information about what remained in the core budget. They also wanted to know about possible alternatives. A funding model used to allocate funds to institutions within the Oregon University System was suggested and run using the library's data. Allocations that would have been called for in this funding model were found to be remarkably similar to those in the library-developed model. Based on another suggestion, the number of credit hours and faculty data were pulled from three full school year terms instead of one in order to give a fuller picture of funding changes.

The Faculty Senate Library Committee also reviewed the proposal. This review resulted in a change of the Faculty Senate Library Committee's membership, making it more representative of the campus schools and departments. This change in membership was perceived as an overall positive outcome of the allocation review process.

And finally, while the intent of the budget formula was to make better decisions for growth in the collection, Kenreich noted that the library is facing budget cuts and the formula will be used to make some of those cuts.

Don Frank concluded the workshop by discussing some of the issues and problems the committee faced during this year-long project. He reiterated the interrelationship between money, politics, and turf, and how that affected the development of the formula. Frank surveyed subject selectors regarding their perception of the development process. Allocation through formula was perceived to be more fair than the previous model. Selectors wanted to be able to manage their own funds. There was also some sentiment among selectors that they should have had a broader representation on the budgeting team.

Frank noted that it was useful to look at the entire university system in developing formula components. The library was fortunate in having a very good relationship with university administrators. His recommendations for those considering taking on such a project included doing it in less than a year and involving selectors along the way. He also encouraged the use of open forums to obtain needed feedback and to make the decision-making process regarding allocations more clear.

CONCLUSION

This preconference provided an excellent opportunity for participants to experience a very holistic approach to budget planning. The presenters discussed issues ranging from the political realities of planning for change to the minute details of how funding models are put together, taken apart, and finally applied to a changing environment. This presentation highlighted the strategic, political, and practical implications of a budget allocation process redesign on the library and its surrounding environment.

NOTES

1. Charles B. Lowry, "Reconciling Pragmatism, Equity and Need in the Formula Allocation of Book and Serials Funds," *Acquisitions '90* (1990): 251-277.

2. Blackwell's Book Services, "U.S. Approval Coverage and Cost Study," http://www.blackwell.com/level4/coverageandcostindex.asp (31 Oct. 2003).

3. Kathleen Born and Lee Van Orsdel, "41st Annual Report Periodical Price Survey 2001: Searching for Serials Utopia," *Library Journal*, 15 April 2001, 53-58.

4. Portland State University, "Outline of January 6, 2003 Faculty Senate Presentation," http://www.lib.pdx.edu/about/budget_model/ outline.html (31 October 2003).

CONTRIBUTORS' NOTES

Claudia Weston is Assistant Director for Technical Services at Portland State University. Cyril Oberlander is Interlibrary Loan Coordinator at Portland State University. Mary Ellen Kenreich is Acquisitions Librarian at Portland State University. Don Frank is Assistant Director for Public Services at Portland State University. Sarah Beasley is Education Librarian/Collection Development Coordinator at Portland State University. Marcella Lesher is Periodicals Librarian, Blume Library, at St. Mary's University, San Antonio.

Cataloging Survival for Non-Catalogers, or You Thought You Would Never Need to Catalog Again

Karen Darling

Presenter

Siôn Romaine

Recorder

SUMMARY. This workshop was a basic introduction to the rules underlying serials cataloging. The intent of the workshop was not to train participants to be serials catalogers, but rather to provide them with an understanding of the rules, principles and terminology underlying serials cataloging. The presenter gave a brief overview of the development of standards, discussed the main standards catalogers work with, and reviewed recent revisions to chapter twelve of *AACR2*. *[Article copies available for a fee from The Haworth Document Delivery Service: 1-800-HAWORTH. E-mail address: <docdelivery@haworthpress.com> Website: <http://www.HaworthPress.com>]*

[Haworth co-indexing entry note]: 'Cataloging Survival for Non-Catalogers, or You Thought You Would Never Need to Catalog Again." Romaine, Siôn. Co-published simultaneously in *The Serials Librarian* (The Haworth Information Press, an imprint of The Haworth Press, Inc.) Vol. 46, No. 1/2, 2004, pp. 17-23; and: *Serials in the Park* (ed: Patricia S. French, and Richard Worthing) The Haworth Information Press, an imprint of The Haworth Press, Inc., 2004, pp. 17-23. Single or multiple copies of this article are available for a fee from The Haworth Document Delivery Service [1-800-HAWORTH, 9:00 a.m. - 5:00 p.m. (EST). E-mail address: getinfo@haworthpress.com].

http://www.haworthpress.com/web/SER
Digital Object Identifier: 10.1300/J123v46n01_04

INTRODUCTION

For most non-catalogers, it has been a long time since they read the cataloging rules for serials; many never had to read the rules. Cataloging rules are an attempt to bring order to chaos and to ensure that when a reference librarian (or patron) sees a record in the catalog, they have a good idea of what the item (tangible or intangible) will look like. Catalogers therefore often say no when asked to change data in a record because any inconsistency in applying these rules can create more problems. Understanding the rules catalogers use allows non-catalogers to understand why catalogers say no and also gives them an understanding of which rules can be bent and why.

HISTORICAL OVERVIEW OF CATALOGING

Darling noted that catalogs have been around for a long time. The first library in Alexandria had catalogs. Monasteries in Europe had handwritten catalogs for centuries. The Bodleian Library at Oxford had a catalog as early as 1620, while Harvard came out with the first printed catalog in 1723. The growing number of volumes held by libraries necessitated a new way of organizing library holdings. Catalog cards were invented, allowing records of new acquisitions to be interfiled in a logical order among the rest of the card collection.

DEVELOPMENT OF STANDARDS

No national standardized rules existed for cataloging until the ALA cataloging rules for author/title entries were developed. The author/title entry standards gradually evolved into *AACR (Anglo-American Cataloguing Rules*) and its successors *AACR2* (2nd edition) and *AACR2r* (2nd edition, revised). These standards are English-language centered although they are also used by many non-English libraries. They assume that the catalog is in English. Such things as title changes can be problematic in other languages. For example, adding a resource type to an English title may be considered a minor change in the English-speaking world, but may be more problematic for a French title, where filing is affected (e.g., *Communications bulletin* vs. *Bulletin des communications*).

AACR is the Anglo-American interpretation of *the ISBD (International Standard Bibliographic Description)*. For some countries, the *ISBD* is the main rule book; others, such as Germany and Russia, have their own code. Of the various cataloging rules in use around the globe, the Anglo-American code is the most widely used. It has been developed by a joint steering committee consisting of representatives from the Library Association, the American Library Association, the Canadian Library Association, and the Australian Library Association.

The 2002 revisions to *AACR2* chapter twelve bring three important changes for serials catalogers: (1) the definitions of a serial in three codes–*AACR2*r chapter twelve, the ISBN and the ISSN (International Standard Serial Number) manual–have been harmonized; (2) a broader definition of a serial that allows more resources to be cataloged as serials; and (3) more flexibility and provisions for minor changes so that fewer new records are required due to title changes.

DEFINITIONS

Bibliographic resources may be tangible or intangible. They may also be continuing (resources that are intended to continue forever) or finite.

A serial is a continuing resource made up of discrete parts, usually with numbering, that has no predetermined conclusion. A serial is described from the first or earliest available issue, and the convention of successive entry cataloging (see discussion following) is applied. A monograph is a finite resource and may be a work complete in one part or in a number of finite parts (a monograph set). Darling reminded the audience that finite resources such as monographic sets may look and act like serials and are often ordered and acquired through a serials acquisitions unit.

INTEGRATING RESOURCES

Integrating resources consist of updates that do not remain discrete, and can be either finite or continuing. They are described from the latest or most recent entry and are cataloged according to latest or integrating resource entry conventions. An example of a finite integrating resource would be the NASIG 2003 conference Website. Although changed on a daily basis leading up to the conference, the Website will be complete at the end of the conference.

Examples of continuing integrating resources include updating Websites (e.g., *CONSER Website*), loose-leafs (e.g., *LC Rule interpretations*), and databases (e.g., *Global Invasive Species* database). The convention of latest (or integrated) entry will be applied. That is to say, one bibliographic record is used for the life of the resource, with changes made to the one record. Added entries are used for previous titles, with dates if known.

LATEST ENTRY vs. SUCCESSIVE ENTRY CATALOGING

Latest entry cataloging uses one bibliographic record for both the current and previous title. The current title is the main entry; the older title is a note and access point. Darling commented that this method was problematic in the card catalog environment because the card had to be pulled out and regenerated each time a title changed. In contrast, successive entry cataloging uses a new bibliographic record each time the main entry changes. A linking note provides a reference to the earlier/later title. In the card environment, this meant that refiling was no longer necessary because a new card could simply be added to the existing catalog with a cross-reference to the earlier title. Catalogers still use successive entry cataloging for serials today, although it is less important in the machine environment. MARC tags and the online environment allow us to find a serial easily through many different access points.

The 2002 revisions to *AACR2* were developed to reduce the number of new titles or successive entries required each time a serial changed.

MAJOR CHANGES vs. MINOR CHANGES

The 2002 rule revisions to *AACR2* divide title changes into the categories of major change (requiring a new bibliographic record) and minor change (not requiring a new bibliographic record). If in doubt, one should consider the change to be minor. Darling stressed that a minor change still requires bibliographic maintenance, as catalogers still have to make sure the patron can get to the record. Minor title changes can be put in a 246 field, with volume/date information in subfield f; additional information can be put in a 500 field note. Darling again reminded the audience that there will be no ISSN change with a minor change, because the ISSN manual and *AACR2r* are now using the same rules.

These changes to the title are considered major changes:

1. Any change (addition/deletion) in the first five words, unless it belongs to one of the categories listed under minor changes
2. Any change after the first five words that changes the meaning of the title or scope of the serial
3. A change in the name of corporate body in the title (new heading required)
4. There is a generic title, and the issuing body changes its name, or a serial is issued by a different body
5. The merger of two serials or split of one serial

These changes to the title are considered to be minor changes:

1. One spelling vs. another (i.e., color vs. colour)
2. An acronym or initials are used instead of the full form, or vice versa
3. The addition, deletion, rearrangement of the corporate body name or substitution of a variant form, including abbreviation, in the title
4. An addition/deletion of the type of resource (magazine, journal, newsletter)

Other rule changes allow for a repeatable 260 (imprint) field, and the use of all fields for all formats (such as the 780/785 fields for monographs).

CATALOGING AT YOUR LIBRARY

Darling emphasized the importance of local practice when cataloging. If something isn't updated in OCLC by a CONSER library, catalogers don't have to wait to make the change in their own catalog. She added that the record in your catalog doesn't have to match a CONSER record exactly. She reminded participants that libraries will never have enough staff to make the catalog perfect. Instead, catalogers should have an idea of what their catalog could be and work towards that. Computer systems provide dozens of ways to access material and the job of the cataloger is to make it accessible.

In response to the question, "A serial has changed its title three times in three issues–how should I handle this?" Darling commented that if the title changed, but the masthead didn't, one could probably use one or two records. She emphasized that technically it should have three records, but noted that this was a good example of how knowing the rules allows one to bend them. A library which is not part of CONSER or a union list is free to do what it wants in its own catalog.

Similarly, when asked, "How do I tell my staff which constitutes the best record to pull from OCLC?" Darling said that it is up to the librarian to decide which records best suit the needs of their institution. The 040 or 042 field will indicate if the record is a CONSER record; however, non-CONSER records may be equally suitable for a local institution's needs.

DISCUSSION AND WRAP-UP

Darling ended her presentation by discussing the importance of the association or issuing body in accessing a serial. Public services staff often focus solely on the title because most serials are easily found by title. With a generic title like *Report*, *Annual Report* or *Journal*, using the name of the association or issuing body is usually the quickest way to find the serial.

Perhaps the liveliest part of the session was the chicken-or-the-egg discussion regarding whether it was best to shelve periodicals alphabetically by title or by call number. Those in favor of shelving by title felt this method made it easier for patrons to find items; those in favor of shelving by call number argued that frequent title changes provided ample justification for grouping all incarnations of one serial together in one place. The room appeared to be evenly split on this issue and no consensus was reached.

Exercises on MARC tagging and major/minor title changes were provided, as well as a glossary of useful terms for non-catalogers. Participants felt this session was very relevant to their current work, was logically planned and presented, and they enjoyed the opportunity to ask "dumb" questions in a supportive environment. Attendees left the session considerably more confident and better informed about *AACR2r* standards regarding serials and integrating resources and how to apply and adapt these rules to meet their own local needs.

RESOURCES FOR FURTHER READING

Hawkins, L. and J. Hirons. 2002. *Transforming AACR2: Using the revised rules in Chapters 9 and 12.* http://lcweb.loc.gov/acq/conser/aacr2002/A2slides.html (22 Jul. 2003).

Library of Congress. CONSER. 2003. *CONSER : Cooperative Online Serials.* http://www.loc.gov/acq/conser/ (22 Jul. 2003).

Library of Congress. Cooperative Cataloging Team. 2003. *Program for Cooperative Cataloging.* http://www.loc.gov/catdir/pcc/ (22 Jul. 2003).

Library of Congress. National Serials Data Program. 2003. *US ISSN Center.* http://www.loc.gov/issn/ (22 Jul. 2003).

Library of Congress. Network Development & MARC Standards Office. *MARC Standards.* http://www.loc.gov/marc/ (22 Jul. 2003).

CONTRIBUTORS' NOTES

Karen Darling is Head of Acquisitions at the University of Missouri-Columbia. Siôn Romaine is Serials Services Project Librarian at the University of Washington.

PLENARY SESSIONS

Content Industry Outlook 2003: Asteroids That Are Changing the Information Landscape

Leigh Watson Healy

Presenter

Reeta Sinha

Recorder

SUMMARY. Key trends and players are changing the information content industry. In her keynote address to NASIG, Leigh Watson Healy provided a "20,000-foot" view of the content industry past, present, and future. Drawing from her experience in the field of educational information and from research conducted by Outsell, Inc., a marketing and research firm focusing on all aspects of the information content industry, Healy invited the audience to challenge the assumptions presented, and encouraged NASIG members to think about the dramatic changes in store for vendors, buyers, and end users of information. *[Article copies available for a fee from The Haworth Document Delivery Service: 1-800-HAWORTH. E-mail address: <docdelivery@haworthpress.com> Website: <http://www.HaworthPress.com>]*

[Haworth co-indexing entry note]: "Content Industry Outlook 2003: Asteroids That Are Changing the Information Landscape." Sinha, Reeta. Co-published simultaneously in *The Serials Librarian* (The Haworth Information Press, an imprint of The Haworth Press, Inc.) Vol. 46, No. 1/2, 2004, pp. 27-32; and: *Serials in the Park* (ed: Patricia S. French, and Richard Worthing) The Haworth Information Press, an imprint of The Haworth Press, Inc., 2004, pp. 27-32. Single or multiple copies of this article are available for a fee from The Haworth Document Delivery Service [1-800-HAWORTH, 9:00 a.m. - 5:00 p.m. (EST). E-mail address: getinfo@ haworthpress.com].

http://www.haworthpress.com/web/SER
Digital Object Identifier: 10.1300/J123v46n01_05

Leigh Watson Healy is an executive-level advisor at Outsell, Inc., where she provides research and analysis related to the information content industry. She began her keynote address by noting the contrast between NASIG in 2003 and her first NASIG conference at Dennison University in 1987, when most of the membership fit into one room.

Answering the question that was on many minds, Healy explained that Outsell is the only marketing and research firm that focuses exclusively on the information content industry. It provides high-quality research, analysis, and advice related to successful product development and deployment to content vendors and buyers. Clients range from publishers and serials vendors to knowledge managers, chief information officers, and libraries. Outsell also actively looks at end users of information in the academic, government, and corporate sectors to determine how they use information. Using a tremendous amount of research, Outsell captures hot trends in the industry and, according to Healy, there are asteroids a-coming for anyone involved with information content.

THE INFORMATION CONTENT INDUSTRY

The information content (IC) industry is huge but largely invisible. Citing data Outsell has gathered, Healy pointed out that the IC industry is rarely featured in leading business magazines, despite the existence of 3,000 vendors with over 400 products that are sold to more than 2,000 global buyers who serve over 30,000 end users. It is an industry that lacks a unique identity and, for that reason, risks being overrun by information technology (IT) giants like Sun Microsystems, IBM, Apple, and Microsoft. This has become more apparent with the ubiquitous "e." Healy defined "e" as the union between technology and content, where IT and IC intersect.

Comparing past and present characteristics of the IC industry, Healy described the old IC world as one in which containers of information were print-based. Information flowed for the most part in one direction: from content creators and publishers to users who obtained information from libraries and corporate or governmental information centers. The online aspect of this process was limited to abstract and indexing databases that helped users find print resources.

Change came with the Internet, rapid advancements in technology and ubiquitous access to content. The new IC landscape is a complex flow of information between content creators, print and e-publishers, deliverers of information, libraries, portals and end users. Users are faced with a confusing array of content options, and content is everywhere. Once well defined, industry partners and competitors now play interchanging roles. All of this has led to what Healy described as à state of "content-spaghetti." The IC industry has also changed to one that is more market-driven, focusing on end users of all kinds–novices, power users and users who may also be content creators.

Unlike the IT giants who adapted quickly and frequently to changes in the market, IC companies have not fundamentally changed the way they do business. The IC industry lacks e-DNA–the technological savvy, innovation, and marketing expertise that many in the IT industry possess. Cultivating this e-DNA will be critical for IC companies that wish to succeed and survive in the future.

TRENDS, ISSUES AND CHALLENGES

Based on Outsell's research and analysis, Healy next listed trends and issues facing the IC industry. First, though it may not be readily apparent, the IC market is actually shrinking. Some segments, like the science, technology, and medicine (STM) content sector, fared better than others but overall industry growth decreased by almost 2 percent between 2001 and 2002. Outsell predicts that over half of revenue growth in coming years will be due to mergers and acquisitions in the IC industry. Consolidation of industry will continue, and Healy noted that most of this consolidation will occur among European companies.

Next, there is the increasing invisibility of the content buyer. Content providers are finding it more difficult to identify the buyer, not because libraries are disappearing but because of the changing roles and names of content purchasers. Both end users and those who deploy content now purchase content, as do information professionals and knowledge managers. IT and IC functions are now working side-by-side, if not merging, with the chief officer level becoming increasingly important. For example, librarians may now report to an organization's chief information officer or chief technology officer. Healy cited Sun Microsystems' Sun Library as an example. As part of Sun's corporate training entity, the library has a visible role within the corporation and is leading the development of the company's internal portal product. This trend may be more prevalent in the corporate world; the speaker invited the audience to tell her if this change was also occurring in academic libraries.

The top challenge facing the IC industry today is the shrinking budget within organizations for information content, something libraries have been dealing with for years. Outsell's annual survey of companies indicates the budget for content will decrease from 54 percent in 2002 to 47 percent in 2003. Other challenges that both vendors and buyers must contend with include decreased staffing and not enough time to meet the demands for information. In other words, doing more with less.

Changes in end-user behavior have also impacted the IC industry significantly. End users have moved almost completely to a self-serve model. They know what they want and when they want it, which is generally 24/7. Not surprisingly, this resonated with librarians in the audience. The knowledgeable IC vendor recognizes these changes in their markets and the high expectations users now have regarding information.

Results from an Outsell survey of 30,000 users showed that 79 percent sought information themselves and, of that 79 percent, 45 percent went to the open World Wide Web. Sixty-two percent of corporate users said they were satisfied with the information they found, as were 50 percent of academic users. Outsell also found that users were more willing to buy their information independently and that they viewed themselves as competent searchers. When asked about their concerns, users listed their top three problems as: (1) not having enough time to search for and find the information they seek; (2) not knowing where to find information and which sources to use; and (3) not being able to determine the accuracy/credibility of the information.

Outsell's findings indicate that users still prefer print content but want to find information online. Users also prefer to work remotely and, while they trust the library as a resource for content, users prefer the Internet for daily information use. At work, self-sufficiency is the new information paradigm. The roles users play within organizations and the type of institution they are in directly affect preferences and behavior.

META-ISSUES FACING THE IC INDUSTRY

Healy next discussed meta-issues, which she described as "Incoming Asteroids," facing the IC industry in 2003. These changes are not incremental but cataclysmic for all industry players. Healy predicted that those who recognize and adapt to these changes are the ones who will survive the asteroid shower.

First, content integration is everything. Knowledge workers are increasingly saying they want a single place to go to for information. They want it delivered to their desktop and to the applications they are using.

So content that is created within the firewall is now being integrated with content created outside the firewall and vice versa. Content integration has also produced a new breed of companies that may bypass the IC industry altogether as they exploit technology to create content and look at new ways to deliver information.

Examples of integration include some tools that are familiar to academic libraries. Ovid provides the technology platform for Kluwer's STM content. Blackboard, Google, and Yahoo! are now leading the way with institutional portals in the corporate sector replicating their success in the educational market. IT giants such as IBM and Microsoft are integrating content with existing software. For example, IBM's data-mining product, WebFountain, uses powerful technology to extract content-specific information, both licensed and from the World Wide Web, completely analyzed for the user. As the speaker put it, the product not only finds the needle in a haystack, it tells the user what the haystack looks like. Microsoft is integrating business and news information within its software so that licensed content from Factiva, for example, is available to the user working with Word or Excel.

Another meta-issue facing the IC industry is the e-content logjam created by outdated business models which create barriers between content providers and end users. The example that most frequently frustrates academic libraries is the practice of bundling pricing for full-text content. Vendors subsidize unpopular products by setting pricing for popular content in packages, while aggregators concentrate on creating value-added interfaces that ultimately provide little value to the user. To succeed, content vendors need to develop more flexible business models. Using Napster and the file-sharing phenomenon as an example, Healy said the IC industry could learn from the experience of IT companies. The success of Apple's iTune product demonstrates that if the price is right and ease of access is incorporated, users *will* pay for content they crave–in this case, online music.

In her final segment, the speaker provided tips for success to both groups in the NASIG audience–information professionals and content providers. First and foremost, both groups must know their users, understand how they use information and the roles they play within their organizations. Information professionals need to partner with IT professionals as solutions are developed for users. For example, Healy advised that the library make sure it is involved as Blackboard technology is implemented on the campus. Other recommendations for information professionals include developing marketing skills to promote services and products to users and periodic self-assessment to demonstrate the return on investment of institutional funding.

Content providers must develop new business practices and models based on changing needs of the user. Products must be easy to use, allow for self-service, and incorporate more granular content, such as content-specific information and objects. Vendors must offer simplicity and flexibility in pricing and packaging–content that is free *and* for a fee, for example, or payment options that are subscription *and* transaction based. Also, content providers must no longer view the IT department as a competitor, but a strategic partner. Finally, like vendors in the old IC world, they must still earn the trust of users and buyers.

In closing, Healy hoped the presentation provided food for thought. In response to a question from the audience about the announced acquisition of Springer, she replied that though a challenge to the deal was inevitable, developing alternative publishing and deployment models may be a more effective way to increase competition within the IC industry.

It was difficult to assess the audience's reaction to Watson Healy's address. One NASIG member wondered afterwards if the topic should have generated more questions and reactions. Perhaps it was the enormous amount of information delivered in the fast-paced presentation or that, as a profession, we may still not be accustomed to thinking in terms of industry trends and business models. Nonetheless, the keynote address served as a timely reminder to librarians that our success as key players in today's information market depends on our ability to develop business savvy and marketing skills. With Healy's address, NASIG provided an excellent opportunity for members to learn about an industry whose future we, as information content buyers, can influence tremendously.

CONTRIBUTORS' NOTES

Leigh Watson Healy is Vice President and Chief Analyst at Outsell, Inc. Reeta Sinha is Head of Collection Development, University Libraries, University of Nevada, Las Vegas.

Town Hall Meeting

Christa Easton
Facilitator

Jerry R. Brown
Recorder

SUMMARY. This Town Hall meeting provided an opportunity for the audience to ask general questions about the state of NASIG and the serials profession, and to discuss questions of interest and concern to the membership in a civil, collegial atmosphere. Note: Q = questions, C = comments, and A = answers to particular questions. *[Article copies available for a fee from The Haworth Document Delivery Service: 1-800-HAWORTH. E-mail address: <docdelivery@haworthpress.com> Website: <http://www.HaworthPress.com>]*

Christa Easton began by asking the audience to help set ground rules for the discussion. The following format was quickly settled upon. Speakers were to use the microphones, identify themselves, and participate in a collegial interchange of ideas via respectful discourse.

Easton suggested a topic to get the session rolling: This year we're staying in hotels instead of dorms. How do you feel about this change?

C: Staying in hotels has a lot going for it, but there is concern about losing the atmosphere inherent in being on a campus.

[Haworth co-indexing entry note]: "Town Hall Meeting." Brown, Jerry R. Co-published simultaneously in *The Serials Librarian* (The Haworth Information Press, an imprint of The Haworth Press, Inc.) Vol. 46, No. 1/2, 2004, pp. 33-38; and: *Serials in the Park* (ed: Patricia S. French, and Richard Worthing) The Haworth Information Press, an imprint of The Haworth Press, Inc., 2004, pp. 33-38. Single or multiple copies of this article are available for a fee from The Haworth Document Delivery Service [1-800-HAWORTH, 9:00 a.m. - 5:00 p.m. (EST). E-mail address: getinfo@haworthpress.com].

http://www.haworthpress.com/web/SER
Digital Object Identifier: 10.1300/J123v46n01_06

A: Another member gave some information from the point of view of a site selection committee member. Site selection is a long, agonizing process. When NASIG had only 300 to 400 members, many colleges/universities could accommodate the conference. It is very difficult to find campus venues that can host 700 or more at meetings and also have dorm facilities for about 500. Also, it is difficult to find a library director who is willing to give up some of their faculty for 18 months to prepare for the conference.

As you know, the wonderful part of NASIG is the committee involvement by the membership. Last year, Joyce Tenney and Stephen Clark did nothing but NASIG work for eight weeks before the conference began. In the past five years, many people have used the conference evaluation form to comment against using dorms as housing for the conference.

Attendees want convenience and comfort. The reason we're staying in hotels this year is that we had such a time finding a campus willing to host the conference. If you are planning a meeting, food is king. This year NASIG met 98 percent of the room reservation block. NASIG does not receive any of the hotel money. Our hotel next year is the historic Hilton Hotel in Milwaukee, Wisconsin. If we meet our reservation quota and have a meal there, the hotel will give us the use of the meeting rooms at no charge. Convention centers are set up to give visiting organizations help with many aspects of the event such as signage and local promotion of the event. Using hotels for housing gives us more options in choosing a location.

In 18 years, NASIG has met in the Midwest only twice. We're aiming to start looking at places that have been underrepresented as conference sites. Next year, Marquette University, the University of Wisconsin- Milwaukee, the Milwaukee Public Library, and Cardinal Stritch University are cooperating to host the conference. We're not getting away from campuses, but we must accept that we have grown. We are victims of our own success. Unless we want to limit participation in the conference, we have got to move on and explore different venues.

C: We are in three hotels this year and some of us are concerned that we have lost the collegiality of being together. It is important to encourage participants to maintain the NASIG tradition of community. That's what makes us special.

C: Most fiscal years end on June 30th and it is hard for some folks to leave at that time. Consideration of a slight change in the dates of the conference would be appreciated. Also, would the site selection committee consider a Mexican location for a future conference?

C: A member agreed and certainly understands that people like hotels, but urges keeping the unique NASIG atmosphere. Also, being in the same hotel and using the meeting rooms at the hotel can be claustrophobic. Is there a way to be creative and keep the environment conducive to the energy for which NASIG is noted? Also, please keep the NASIG dates away from the ALA dates.

C: A member really misses the long walks on college campuses, but has noticed that there are some NASIG members with mobility/breathing problems and understands that a single location would be much easier for those attendees.

A: A quick comment on the timing of the conference. The 2005 dates have been selected: May 19th in Minneapolis/St. Paul. Staying in hotels gives us more flexibility as to dates, so please use the conference evaluation form to let the Board know what dates you'd like for future conferences.

C: A member suggested NASIG hire a part-time paid executive secretary. As the membership approaches 800, volunteers can only do so much. The organization has grown and only a small percentage of the membership volunteers. It is time we have an office and phone, even if it means paying more in dues to pay for a staff.

Easton asked the group what they think about having paid staff.

A: The Board has talked about this. It may be much more expensive to hire a person than one might think. There is salary to pay and also benefits and the cost of office space and miscellaneous expenses. Perhaps we should have a referendum to see if the NASIG membership wants to go to a paid staff.

C: Concern was expressed regarding raising dues. The graying of the membership has been mentioned, but there are lots of younger members and they don't have the income to pay a lot more in dues.

C: There are many different models for managing organizations. There is no need to cede all authority to paid staff; a carefully written job description will give a paid position shape and set out the incumbent's authority, keeping the power with the president and board. We don't have to turn into ALA.

C: One person who has been on the Board for ten years said that this question [paid staff] was debated every single year. The Board wanted to use NASIG funds to support the community. Each conference made a small profit to subsidize membership fees. The budget was always over $100,000. Those funds support each conference committee, allowing them to hire a half-time person or a student to help with the work.

NASIG has had 600 to 700 members for probably the last ten years, and there are campuses that can support our numbers.

C: Should NASIG consider a graduated dues schedule based on salary?

Easton suggested a new topic: Is continuing education a value NASIG should support more? Should we continue to co-sponsor small conferences around the country in order to reach underserved regions? What would you like to see NASIG provide you with in the way of continuing education? What programs would you like to see at conferences or in your regions?

C: Even though the NASIG conference is inexpensive, not everyone who would like to is able to attend. It would be good to offer continuing education opportunities in various parts of the country that library staff can attend.

Easton noted that taping programs for delivery to paraprofessional staff helps get the information out to interested folks.

C: The North Carolina Serials Conference is sponsored by the library school in the region. It is a baby NASIG that is easy for those who don't have support for travel to attend. There are 100 to 150 attendees, and the conference is held over a day and a half, so attendees may choose to attend only one day and opt to not stay overnight.

A: There is more continuing education in other parts of the country. Some meetings are held via video conferencing, Instant Messaging, or shared via videotape.

C: NASIG has picked up the expenses for a speaker to regional library associations. Some conference presentations can be recycled to local groups so those who can't travel can benefit from them. The Continuing Education Committee is trying to support places that need help, but they need a local group with which to work. Let the Continuing Education Committee know if you want help in your area.

C: NASIG is negotiating with ALA to get a serials course online. This might be a way for NASIG to help library students by providing independent study opportunities via online courses.

C: Continuing education is needed for the commercial sector. This is an opportunity for vendors to host internship and independent studies opportunities for library students so they could see the non-library opportunities available.

Q: What happened to the Website?

A: The Continuing Education Committee is still developing the Website. If you're having workshops on your campus, you can have them put on the Continuing Education Website. We can work with you on a regional basis to bring in speakers and work with you on other projects.

Send the Continuing Education Committee your ideas and suggestions for local co-sponsors. A task force is working on a proposal for student outreach. There has been discussion of a mentor program for students. If you have Web courses you can share, we can put them on the Website. There will be a call for proposals and ideas from the NASIG membership as to how we want to support continuing education.

C: We need to do a better job of publicizing technology workshops and making continuing education opportunities accessible to all those interested in attending or sharing the information via online resources. Perhaps a library could sponsor a grant for someone on staff to attend a technology conference and make a presentation on it to NASIG.

C: I didn't find out about NASIG or student grant opportunities as a student. A co-worker told me about them after I got my first job. We need to do a better job of promoting the grants and NASIG membership to the students in library school.

C: There is some concern when vendors are present at meetings. How do the other members feel about vendor involvement at meetings?

C: NASIG is a group of individuals. We need to find ways to diversify our membership. We need to talk to trading partners and vendors, not just other librarians.

C: I've always loved the fact that we're librarians, publishers, vendors all together.

Easton asked that all Board members stand so everyone can see who is who. She suggested that this conversation needs to continue in the larger group.

C: A first-time attendee and public librarian commented that he had really enjoyed himself at the conference. He liked having the chance to talk with vendors on an individual basis and build collegial relationships with them.

C: The Voice of History–NASIG was organized on the founding principle of providing a level playing field where discussion could occur in a non-confrontational way. It was a deliberate choice that NASIG not be a policy maker or lobbyist. We want to encourage vendor/publisher participation. We need ideas from those areas and the opportunity to network and discuss developments in our field in a civil, non-confrontational manner.

Easton thanked everyone for attending and sharing their thoughts. She asked that everyone be frank on the session evaluation and that constructive criticism on the format would be appreciated.

CONCLUSION

This was an interesting session. It was a pleasure to witness such a wide-ranging discussion of serious topics without any observable rancor or displays of temper that can sometimes mar such occasions. As a new member/first time conference attendee, I was impressed by the efforts of everyone concerned to comply with the ground rules established at the beginning of the meeting, especially to "participate in collegial interchange of ideas via respectful discourse."

CONTRIBUTORS' NOTES

Christa Easton is Head of Serials and Government Document Serials at Stanford University, and a former NASIG Board member. Jerry R. Brown is Instructor of Library Services at Central Missouri State University.

There Is No Forest, We're Only Hugging the Trees: Nontraditional Ways of Acquiring, Providing Access to, and Managing Serials

Jill Emery
Rick Anderson
Adam Chesler
Joan Conger
Ted Fons

Presenters

Debra Skinner

Recorder

SUMMARY. The whole serials industry has been in a state of transition from print production and management to the electronic dissemination of information for about ten years now. We are no closer, however, to having a handle on the new ways of doing business and managing these resources than we were when the first e-journals began to appear. What has been proven is that traditional management techniques do not suffice with the production, workflow, or access of scholarly works. The panel-

[Haworth co-indexing entry note]: "There Is No Forest, We're Only Hugging the Trees: Nontraditional Ways of Acquiring, Providing Access to, and Managing Serials." Skinner, Debra. Co-published simultaneously in *The Serials Librarian* (The Haworth Information Press, an imprint of The Haworth Press, Inc.) Vol. 46, No. 1/2, 2004, pp. 39-56; and: *Serials in the Park* (ed: Patricia S. French, and Richard Worthing) The Haworth Information Press, an imprint of The Haworth Press, Inc., 2004, pp. 39-56. Single or multiple copies of this article are available for a fee from The Haworth Document Delivery Service [1-800-HAWORTH, 9:00 a.m. - 5:00 p.m. (EST). E-mail address: getinfo@haworthpress.com].

http://www.haworthpress.com/web/SER
Digital Object Identifier: 10.1300/J123v46n01_07

ists addressed the fundamental tenets that need to shift in order for the serials industry as a whole to better address the current electronic environment. *[Article copies available for a fee from The Haworth Document Delivery Service: 1-800-HAWORTH. E-mail address: <docdelivery@haworthpress.com> Website: <http://www.HaworthPress.com>]*

SURVEYING THE LANDSCAPE

Jill Emery

It's been a hell of a year so far. One of the major serials vendors is felled by fiscal collapse. One of the electronic journal management system players leaves the field and, in its wake, we find three new transplants. There's talk of one major ILS being up for sale while another ILS vendor experiences a leadership shake-up. Out on the horizon, it looks like we're about to see the merger of two major academic/STM publishers into some new hybrid. To top this all off, just about every state budget is in dire straits, higher education is losing financing from every angle, and library financial support appears to be the main target to cut. In the midst of this maelstrom, we're attempting to find our way through these dark and dangerous woods.

Internally, most libraries are reviewing title lists, pruning low-use material, balancing budgets, and trying to maintain footings in the ever-shifting paths of electronic access. We're trying to cull the deadwood of policy, procedure, and business as usual. Our colleagues in other parts of the library are attempting to simultaneously create library portals and instruct across the curriculum through various mechanisms such as virtual reference. Serials and electronic resources librarians are asked in one rapid breath to customize and standardize as the rules change and the interfaces upgrade.

Here lies a major quandary. The tension between customization and standardization is extremely hard to reconcile in today's serials world. Our various library, vendor, and publisher systems are designed to be customized, but in a specific manner and at times in ways that run counter to either the current or local standards. We are therefore unable to take full advantage of the customization. If we take full advantage of the customization, we are unable to follow the standards currently in use. A balance between the two is not always readily apparent. As more and more systems are developed and interlinked, we find this tension grows. The development of standards with the advent of new technology is always a step behind, and many of us now face the task of racing to keep up with the speed of use. The one truth we all know is that our end users want both customization and standardization and, at this juncture, we cannot provide both satisfactorily.

So what is a serialist to do? We do what we are known for doing. We attempt to understand the issues better and to solve the problems we face. We join together to develop new ways to handle the situations that develop daily; an example of this would be the work being performed by the Digital Library Federation Electronic Resource Management Initiative steering group. We also jettison practices and procedures that no longer seem practical to us; we develop internal tools for our organizations to use to help bring a better balance between standardization and customization; we develop new modules to be used by integrated library systems; we advise on publisher and vendor focus groups; we learn to take our knowledge down new paths; and we find different ways of providing for information exchange through serials literature that helps foster a more collaborative and open exchange of scholarly communication. We also learn that how we do things individually may not work for each and every one of us.

In the end, we learn to take from the harried, crazed woods what is needed to survive on an individual basis and bring to our own organizations the fruits of these ideas that make our own domain that much more tolerable. We must remain open to change, to taking risks, to attempting ways of processing and acquiring material that may fail–in order to push ourselves forward. In the end, we learn, there is no clear-cut solution, but a forest to choose from.

PROBLEM-SOLVERS, RULE-FOLLOWERS AND THE FUTURE OF SERIALS MANAGEMENT

Rick Anderson

I've worked in libraries for fifteen years, ten of which I've spent as a professional librarian. I've worked on both sides of the library/vendor divide and in several different regions of the continental U.S., and have hired, supervised, and managed student employees, classified staff, and faculty librarians.

Now, ten years is not really that long and I don't claim for a second that my experience is sufficient to make me any kind of real expert on the culture of librarianship. But there are a few things I've noticed in my time knocking around this profession, and one of those things has a direct bearing on the theme of our presentation, so I'd like to reflect briefly on that topic here today.

I've felt for some time that the mindsets of librarians in general can be divided into two broad categories: that of the *procedure follower*, and that of the *problem solver*. Procedure followers can be found in all areas of the profession; they may be reference librarians, serialists, catalogers, or acquisitions clerks. They tend to see their work as primarily a matter of applying established principles to different situations, and of defending the integrity of time-honored standards. As far as these librarians are concerned, we do things in certain ways because a century of library practice has demonstrated that those ways work and because consistency is important. These librarians are not necessarily inflexible; they recognize that the rules will be applied differently from time to time, but they adhere to a fixed set of underlying standards that have stood the test of time. Those standards may be either *procedural* or *normative*.

Procedural standards make it possible for a library patron from Schenectady to find her way around a library in Dallas using more or less the same kinds of research strategies as those she would use at home. Procedural standards also permit consistency over time, making it possible for patrons to use the same general strategies to find resources that were published fifty years ago as they would to find resources published one year ago. Normative standards define the level of thoroughness, the quality of service, and the ethical behavior that we expect from each other as professionals (and that our patrons should expect from us). For procedure followers, both kinds of standards are sacrosanct. Talk to a procedure follower about patron service, and you'll likely end up on the topic of how we need to be careful not to spoon-feed patrons, because patrons need to learn how to do research. Ask them what their ultimate goal is, and they'll probably say that it is to build a great library.

Librarians from the problem solver camp tend to see things very differently. To them, the world presents a basic problem, which is that of getting the best and most relevant possible information to patrons and giving them access to that information in the simplest and most efficient way possible. Indeed, to the problem solver the first job of serials management *is* efficiency–in other words, to provide the most and best service to library patrons with the least investment of work and expense. Rules and standards are of interest to problem solvers only to the degree that they contribute to that kind of efficiency. Problem solvers don't usually wonder whether, for instance, a particular LC subject heading is formulated correctly; instead, they tend to wonder first about whether library patrons are using LC subject headings in their research and, if they aren't, the problem solver is liable to ask what we're doing formulating LC subject headings at all. They're not very respectful of all the hard work that has been put into the establishment of either procedural or normative standards over the last century; instead they tend to want to clear the ground and ask what we would do now if all of those standards suddenly disappeared and we were forced to start all over. Problem solvers don't generally want to change patrons so that they will better know how to use the library; they see trying to change the behavior of thousands of people as an inefficient approach, and would rather change the *library* to make it easier for patrons to use. Ask a problem solver what her ultimate goal is and, regardless of her place in the library's organization, she'll probably say that it is to serve patrons. Building a great library is a means to that goal but maybe not the only means, and it is certainly not the goal itself.

There are downsides to both of these mindsets. Procedure followers tend to have perspective problems. The most egregious example I can think of comes from a rather well-known music librarian who once argued, in a public forum, that his job is to serve the collection, not to understand or cater to the needs of patrons. The idea that our goal is to serve the collection itself is an example of the procedure follower mindset taken to an absurd extreme. On the other hand, procedure followers often have a much longer and deeper perspective on library work than problem solvers do, and their understanding of the larger history and context of the profession can be extremely valuable.

The problem with problem solvers is that they're impatient, and often a bit too quick on the draw. Their willingness to turn their backs on time-honored standards and start again from scratch can lead them to throw out very useful babies with the bathwater of established practice. On the other hand, their lack of investment in the practices and policies of the past makes them much more likely than procedure followers to bring up innovative ideas that will improve library processes and services.

The good news, luckily, is that it isn't really necessary to choose between the two mindsets. If the profession were made up entirely of wild-eyed innovators, it would be a tremendous mess. On the other hand, if the profession were made up entirely of people who want to stick to the rules and fix our patrons so that they're better library users, then the library would become an even more marginal player in our patrons' information lives than it already is. But here's the real question: What does this have to do with e-journals and forests and trees?

Actually, quite a bit. If the forest is the collection and individual trees are the journals that comprise the collection, then the overarching goal of the procedure follower is to provide a forest that is designed and managed according to the best professional principles and standards and to provide patrons with an accurate roadmap through that forest. Procedure followers will tolerate different approaches to the care and feeding of individual trees as long as those approaches ultimately contribute to a forest that is up to established professional standards. Faced with new growth that is drastically different from the trees that have filled the forest and around which the forest was originally designed, procedure followers will look for commonalities between the old trees and the new growth, and will look for ways to integrate the new growth into the existing forest as seamlessly as possible. They will tend to want to make the new growth look and feel as much like the old trees as possible so as to preserve consistency, and will set up guided tours and courses of instruction to help those who want to walk around in it.

The problem solving serialist is likely to believe that the forest is patron service, and they're willing to call anything a tree as long as it deepens and improves that service. In other words, problem solvers see the nurturing and organization of trees as tools to be used in developing the forest of patron service, not as an end in itself–and they may not even see trees as an essential component of the forest. Problem solvers will tend to regard cutting–even large-scale cutting, even clear-cutting–as one possible tool in the larger project of providing the type of forest that patrons need. And when problem solvers are faced with a completely new type of tree, maybe even one that is made out of something other than wood, the first thing they wonder is not how to integrate it into the existing forest but whether the forest itself needs to change in order to accommodate it. When planning paths through the forest, they will look to see where people have walked through the underbrush already and will create and groom new paths accordingly rather than putting paths where they think people *ought* to walk, and then trying to make them go there.

By now, each of you is probably thinking one of three things: either "Those dumb procedure followers are going to be the death of this profession," or "Those dumb problem solvers are going to be the death of this profession," or "Who does he think he is, reducing an entire profession to two philosophical categories? Doesn't he realize that we're more complex than that, and that many of us combine the characteristics of both procedure followers and problem solvers in our professional personalities?" Those who are entertaining the latter thought are absolutely right, of course. I doubt that there are many pure procedure followers or problem solvers in the real world. But most of us are fooling ourselves if we say that we don't lean more in one direction than the other, and the way we lean in this regard is going to have a significant effect on the way we think about the work we do, and ultimately on the experiences our patrons have in our libraries. My advice–actually, my plea–is that, in general, we look at problems first and at rules second, and that we put our patrons' needs ahead of our own idea of what our profession should be. To put this in forestry terms: the forest that it is our job to manage no longer consists only, or even primarily, of trees that we recognize as such, but has rapidly become a much more diverse and confusing ecosystem–one which the established traditions and standards of librarianship have not prepared us to manage.

Changing our procedures will not be sufficient. We must take a radical look at our most basic principles and standards, and, where necessary, we must change them. Now. This is not a revolution that is going to happen, or that is happening. It is a revolution that has happened. It's our responsibility to build *new* traditions and establish *new* standards for future generations of librarians to reject and rebuild as the information forest continues to mutate.

Which of our traditions and standards need to change? Let me suggest three:

Doing only the jobs we were hired to do. There was a time, in the not-too-distant past, when a librarian could reasonably expect to be hired as a collection development officer or a cataloger or a serials manager and stay in that position indefinitely, or for at least a year or two. Let's be completely clear about this: those days are over. It can still happen that one of us might be hired into a job and remain there, performing the same tasks, until retirement, but we cannot reasonably expect things to go that way. Anyone who insists on doing the job he was hired to do will likely end up not only being sidelined (which he may actually find desirable, so that he can be left alone to continue in his comfortable niche), but also acting as a drain on the library's time and resources and an impediment to the library's patrons. This is not to say that traditional duties don't still need to be performed. Of course they do. What I am saying is that all of us need to be willing to adapt to the library's changing needs, even if that means accepting radical changes in our job description. The information world has changed too drastically for us to believe that we can all continue doing the same things we've been doing for the last twenty years and still be of service to our patrons.

The fetishization of completeness and accuracy. This is a difficult one. We are librarians; completeness and accuracy are articles of faith for us. I don't wish to belittle that kind of dedication. But I propose a thought experiment, using cataloging as an example: Which helps our patrons more, one perfect catalog record or ten slightly imperfect catalog records that could be created in the same amount of time? You can quibble with the numbers or the details of what constitutes imperfect, but the principle remains: To what degree are we pursuing perfection at the expense of access? And this is by no means only a cataloging issue. The same question applies to check-in, claiming, and myriad other traditional serials duties. If all of us honestly asked ourselves questions like this one, we would doubtless end up with a variety of answers, and some of us might decide that we should continue doing the things we always have. But are we even asking the question?

The "teach a man to fish" mindset. Frankly, I'm not convinced it should be our job to teach students how to do research. It seems to me that that is the job of their teachers. In a perfect educational world, students would learn how to find sources and how to discriminate between good ones and bad in the classroom and in consultation with their instructors (who actually have the necessary knowledge of their subject areas to train students in those skills), instead of from librarians, most of whom are generalists. In that perfect world, there would be rigorous and highly demanding training in the classroom and the library would be an oasis where intuitive search mechanisms and a friendly, flexible and knowledgeable staff make access to highly relevant, high-quality information almost completely friction-free. We would freely and happily give our patrons fish and we wouldn't worry much about whether getting the fish was a character-building experience for them. How much better it would be to offer them a library that they don't have to be taught how to use rather than trying (almost always in vain) to teach them how to use the library. Would this prepare them to find information in the real world? Of course it would. Most of the real world is actively trying to make information retrieval easier and more intuitive, *and it's succeeding*. Learning how to use subject headings or Wilson databases will not prepare most students for anything they're going to have to do after they graduate, nor, in and of itself, does it contribute substantially to their intellectual growth.

One last comment in conclusion. We are now living in a time when, paradoxically, it is much more risky to follow the rules than it is to take risks. By pretending that the forest around us is still the same one it was thirty, twenty, even ten years ago, we hurt our patrons' ability to do their research and we encourage them to turn their backs on us and look for needed information and services elsewhere. Those who do so will, for the most part, succeed in finding the information they need, and we'll be left standing in the cool shadows of our beloved trees, offering tours and handing out forest guides to people who are not there.

THE VIEW FROM THE PUBLISHER'S SIDE OF THE HOUSE

Adam Chesler

I'm not going to give an exhaustive review of the issues facing publishers. Rather, let's look at some of the questions that are emerging as technology changes the way information is conceived, created, distributed, and used. These days even the definition of "publisher" can no longer be taken for granted, as the very notion of what it means to publish is being revisited. Is it when a paper article appears in a bound journal? Is it when a version is posted on the journal's Website, or the author's? Is it when a copy is sent to a preprint server, or stored in an institutional repository? Which version takes precedence? Is it when a collection of content is consolidated in some form, and released with a formal title? Does it have to have some kind of standard or persistent identifier (e.g., ISSN, Digital Object Identifiers)? And if something is "published" but not cataloged (whether in a traditional library OPAC or so it can be found by a search engine), will it ever be found (borrowing from the NASIG 2003 theme, and analogous to the old puzzle "if a tree falls in the forest and no one is listening, does it make a sound?")

Workflow is changing. Whole departments are springing up to manage electronic content and its commercial impact. Marketing departments have to think about how graphics will look on a screen as well as on a printed page, understand the rules of new contact media (e.g., electronic discussion lists), and develop new contact media (e.g., alerting services). Publishers are grappling with the new kinds of information required by their content (metadata, Digital Object Identifiers, URLs) and who is responsible for maintaining them. Customer service has a new language to learn and new tools to use such as access control mechanisms; and, with negotiating now a factor in publisher-subscriber relationships, customer service needs to be aware of multiple pricing models and different fees for different customers. The interplay between previously distant departments is now daily and sometimes profound: Is a missing issue due to problems with IT (e.g., server problems), production (e.g., wrong URL keyed in), or editorial (e.g., manuscript delays)? Or, was the issue properly posted but something is amiss in customer service (e.g., access control), order processing (e.g., acknowledgement of payment), or sales (e.g., incorrect information in a license)? There are more places where things can go wrong, so effective communication and management tools become even more essential.

Pricing models are themselves in flux. While some basic guidelines seem to have been established, nothing is fixed in stone (after all, hieroglyphics are so BCE).[1] Package deals, pay-per-view, tiered pricing; single-site purchases vs. consortia/group buying options; subscriptions vs. page charges: every publisher is assessing these ideas, and that's just for journals. What about reference works, or e-books? What about databases, be they of links or abstracts, or full-text? What about portals/information communities? Much time is devoted to these questions, as the wrong decisions can put a publisher out of business. A large publisher can survive a mistake or two, but a smaller one might not.

Licenses are now part of our daily discourse. We all learn each day of new, subtle ways to phrase requirements or preferences; the insertion, or deletion, of a single word can hold up access to dozens, or hundreds, of files and documents. Sales people who previously concerned themselves only with ensuring that bookstores were stocking copies of new titles are now negotiating terms and conditions with libraries; in other words, just as much training and change is taking place at publishing houses as at libraries.

Whole new systems are being built and implemented internally by vendors. The cost is staggering; a new information system to handle marketing, sales, customer, and accounting data can cost a large publisher over $10 million, never mind the time/cost of training. Publishers are hiring IT help they never dreamed of in years past, and all these new people cost the company more than copy editors ever did. These experiences are familiar to librarians, who also need sophisticated staff and tools to manage electronic content.

Working with contributors is also moving in new directions. Camera-ready copy (manuscripts submitted in a format allowing for easier, faster inclusion in an issue, be it print or electronic) takes on new dimensions when metadata must be included. Brand new submission, tracking, and peer-review management software is necessary to streamline and automate more of the process, something that is time-consuming and difficult to implement. It's one thing to train a department of full-time staff, another to work with thousands of editors and authors. Without these tools, publishers will lose contributors who seek rapid publication of their work. Publishers must also take a new look at copyright as it affects the digital versions of content, and in many cases come to new understandings with their authors about what permissions are to be granted to whom (this works bi-laterally).

Partnerships are being re-evaluated. Subscription agents once handled all billings and renewals with the library; now both publishers and agents are scrambling to invent systems that effectively and accurately communicate the needs of each subscriber. Some customers prefer to bypass the agent altogether and order electronic access directly from the publisher. Sometimes publishers insist on handling the electronic access, giving no choice to the subscriber. The complicated ordering process is often even more complex under consortial agreements. IP ranges and access privileges (to name two items) must often be incorporated into orders. The agent's role as intermediary is always a fluid one and, in the wake of the Faxon/RowrCom/divine collapse, it is under greater scrutiny from all sides. New partnerships develop as publishers test relationships with full-text aggregators and others abandon them in favor of a single-channel approach. Publishers work with other publishers (CrossRef) and libraries (COUNTER, various archiving initiatives) in ways never considered before. Expectations are changing, and this is a daily source of concern at the publisher. For so long, each publisher knew almost exactly what to anticipate from its partners and subscribers; now it seems that something new crops up every month and publishers must have well-informed staff and management that is prescient enough to anticipate, or at least swiftly and correctly react to, these vicissitudes.

Roles are changing, too. Who is a publisher? Is it the institution/library (SPARC, BioOne, HighWire, institutional repositories)? Is it the author (preprint servers, open access/Public Library of Science initiatives)? Are there new players with re-engineered business models (e.g., BioMedCentral)? Who is an archivist? What about national libraries or library cooperatives? Publishers? Agents? Something new? Addressing these questions takes time, effort, and brainpower; brainpower that also must be used on the day-to-day issues that every organization faces as a matter of course.

What about looking ahead, though? What are some publisher goals?

- *Accelerate review process.* Submissions posted within weeks, not years
- *Single manufacturing process.* Content published in multiple formats

- *Information systems implemented.* Customer and product information managed properly
- *Customized products.* Buy packages or pieces
- *Subscribers notified about content availability instantly.* Metadata automatically loaded into ILS, and patrons alerted
- *Content conveniently purchased easily, directly or through channels.* Ordering process streamlined (with machine-readable invoices, for example)
- *Content is available persistently.*

There are numerous open questions to answer over time. Will publishers survive, or will self-publishing, institutional repositories, and open access take their place as successful, adequate means of delivering content and information to students and researchers? Will vendors survive, or will the possible elimination or dramatic adaptation of publishers to the new environment (which, of course, will include improved customer service, order processing tools, and the like) ruin them? Or will they find a niche that may very well include the content manufacturing process (EBSCO with Metapress, Swets with Extenza)? Will libraries survive or will the "googlization" of content suffice, and will the elimination of their traditional role of mediating and organizing content render them superfluous?

Publishers, libraries, vendors, authors, and readers will be pondering questions such as these for many years to come. And, of course, they will come up with new questions and answers along the way–for this is all part of the evolution of publishing.

QUANTUM ADMINISTRATION: HOW TO ACCOMPLISH MORE WITH LESS WORK

Joan Conger

Change is the new constant for libraries, especially when it comes to electronic resources. I'm sure I haven't surprised anyone with that statement. Yet here is a less-often repeated observation: Change is work. Going from tried-and-true to new-and-different takes work. Trusting that the new ways (necessary to deal with the new realities) will work out takes work. I have a secret for making this work less onerous, less consuming, less risky.

To handle this change, or work, decision-making needs to be saturated with information. The more decision-making is concentrated in a few hands, the less informed the decisions will be. To gather the right quality, breadth, and depth of information, decisions need to be not only pushed down as close to the person doing the work as possible, but also pushed out to as many people as possible. Line authority is interested in control, safety, stability. Responsibility (known in some circles as blame) is the watchword. These managers say, "You do your job, and I'll do mine, which is making sure you do yours to my specifications." Electronic resources are governed by adaptability, nimbleness, comfort with chaos. And chaos (known in some circles as learning) is the watchword. These managers know, "The world is run by those who show up, and I trust you to show up at the right place with the right ideas because I can't be there to do it all."

Line authority excludes all but those scripted (usually long ago) to be involved. In electronic resource management, "long ago" means anything more than 18 months ago. Because electronic resources require information saturation and instant involvement from all-important participants, and the definition of importance changes at a moment's notice, adherents to line authority will be overwhelmed by change. Changing line authority to "quantum" administration will therefore be a dramatic shift for some while patently obvious for others. The shift must occur, or our libraries will continue to lose net value (what our budgets purchase for our customers) and perceived value (the willingness of our customers and stakeholders to consider us relevant to their lives).

Allow me to illustrate the concept of quantum administration by comparing Newtonian and quantum physics. I apologize to all physicists in advance for indulging in a gross oversimplification of a beautiful but, to me, impenetrable field. I also cannot claim this as an original idea. Margaret Wheatley articulates this analogy much better than I will here.[2]

In Newtonian physics objects exert force on other objects (a common illustration is the balls on a billiard table). Observe: I am the Boss. "Jill, you and your co-workers will have to increase your output next quarter by 25 percent. All who can't will have to defend why at the next staff meeting." Jill nods. I walk away satisfied that Jill is a good employee and will do as I say.

Jill turns to Ted and they both snort. They know that half the campus is away on vacation next quarter and making even half of their current productivity would be difficult, much less making more than that. Jill resigns herself to working very hard at an impossible project that is only piled on top of all the others she is juggling. The only force I, as boss, have exerted on Jill (who is not an inanimate object) is possible defeat and a certain worry wrinkle on her brow.

In quantum physics, particles come into existence under certain circumstances and are waves of potentiality in others. Some illustrate this with the idea of relationships: relationships of particles/waves to each other and to their environment. Observe: I am again the Boss floating along in my wave potentiality. I pop into particulate existence: "Jill, by the end of next quarter we will have to show how the library has shown 25 percent more value over the past decade in order to get a budget increase from the administration. I think we need to show a 25 percent increase in productivity, but I will leave it to you to decide how best to increase our value to our Provost." (Notice how much information I give Jill, because I treat her as a decision-maker, not a member of the "troops.")

Pop. I turn back into wave potentiality: "Let me know if there is any information I can gather, any relationships I can facilitate, any problem-solving to which I can contribute to help you and your co-workers find a solution."

Jill is given agency, or, shall we say, particulate mass, and turns to Ted to ask for his help. The first relationship is formed. They plan a strategy. They know where secret stashes of existing value are. For example, no one has been reporting the skyrocketing usage of the Web-based subject guides just released by the reference department.

Pop. Jill and Ted turn into waves and go out into their environment to find other librarians who may themselves be waves of potential.

Pop. All the librarian-particles touched learn about the need for 25 percent more value. These librarian-particles turn into waves and find pockets of value already in existence (for example: letters of thanks and commendation that everyone has gathered over the past years), or pockets of potential value that require minimal effort to be released (for example: asking favorite faculty still on campus to write a letter of thanks or commendation about the library).

Pop. As waves, everyone finds extra value, learns from environment, collects information, gathers up value, becomes committed to seeing success happen. Jill and her fellow particles begin to interact with the environment as it exists, gathering data, drawing conclusions based not on assumption but on real life.

Pop. The remaining amount (around 2 percent) is created by an extra project that everyone pitches in to complete weeks before the budget is due. The relationships formed between these wave/particles have some magic energy that is passed to everyone and increases their effectiveness far beyond the "other duties as assigned" requirement. Please also note that during this entire process Jill herself has been energized by those willing to help, excited about the new things the organization is learning, and has a smile on her face.

In line authority, all the action relies on the people that form links in the chain of command. As boss, I focused on the individual, forcing her to toe the line, to be a team player, to grab hold of that chain and pull her weight, and to take responsibility (blame). Unfortunately, these players cannot, as individuals, know as much as an entire organization galvanized to pitch in. The project is "theirs," by command, important to them, but not necessarily to anyone else.

Quantum management is about trust. Quantum management is about risk. As boss, I trusted the project to those closest to the information. I stepped outside of my line authority role and sent out potentialities that I couldn't control to gather information of which I was not aware. But the risk is always rewarded even if only by learning for next time. These potentialities that I sent out brought back much more success than I could have reasonably asked for otherwise.

Quantum management is not new, nor is it different from any similar idea that has surfaced since Mary Follett wrote *The New State* in 1917. A quantum, or *learning* or *flat* or *quality* or *TQM* or *team-based* or *integrated* or *7 habits* or *customer-centered* or *enlightened leadership* or *six sigma* or *fifth discipline* or *loose tight* organization treats everyone as bundles of potential that will step up when the conditions create a need. The quantum organization recognizes the potential of everyone up and down the paycheck scale. The quantum organization uses the power not of force exerted but of the potential that already exists and needs only to be released. We are not born with these skills, and we are usually not given these skills in our developing years. We must now bend to the task of acquiring quantum management as a second nature. We can look first within ourselves at the potential that is already there and use that as the power to reduce the work permanent change will mean for us. Then we can look at our relationships with other people and the power inherent in them. Find their strengths, however elusive some may be, and put those strengths to work for both of you toward a common goal. Because electronic resource management will one day soon be (if it isn't yet) synonymous with library management, we can't afford to learn to be anything but quantum managers.

INTEGRATED LIBRARY SYSTEMS

Ted Fons

Ted Fons focused on the innovating and integrating roles of the integrated library system in the vast changes taking place in libraries. The roles are innovating in that new processes are available, new services are available to patrons, and new ways of working more efficiently are provided. The roles are integrating in that different information tools are brought together for the benefit of staff and patrons.

Integrated library systems provide a means for rigorous control of the library collections and for the accountability of suppliers including such functions as acquisition, serials control, and batch claiming. Communication tools are important as well, providing the status of print items such as "on shelf" or "at bindery." The Web world provides off-site searching of the library catalog. In addition, the integrated library system can provide online links, link checks, and authentication for remote access.

Historically, integrated library systems have played a large role in integrating collections with that role now encompassing the management of electronic resources. This step is a huge leap forward, allowing electronic resources to be accessed through the same familiar interface as print resources. In addition, integrated library systems can now store licensing information and help with management tasks such as report generation. Other new tools include federated searching, link resolvers, and the ability to bring patrons from citation to full text, even when the full text is in a different database.

Fons concluded by expressing the need for collaborative development between libraries and vendors. Libraries can bring problems to developers and describe the issues to be solved. Collaboration will enable integrated library system developers to put standards into place right from the beginning.

QUESTION AND ANSWER SESSION

A brief but enthusiastic question and answer session ensued after the presentations, centering largely on the issues of consistency and accuracy at the expense of efficiency. These concerns were in relation to Rick Anderson's comments regarding rule followers and problem solvers in the library profession. A participant from the Library of Congress gave a resounding "yes" to Anderson's concern that librarians must avoid the obsession with consistency and accuracy. In response, some participants stressed that it is necessary to be consistent and accurate because we are creating the databases to assist library users in accessing resources. The Library of Congress participant agreed to a point, stressing that while information must be accurate, librarians do not have to take the desire for perfect records to an extreme.

Another participant raised the point that too much money is spent on reference services if we are to de-emphasize consistency and accuracy and no longer teach patrons "to fish" as advocated by Rick Anderson. The money might be better spent on collection development and technical services since it would benefit more users.

Several other participants commented on the value of reference services, and questioned whether or not we are putting resources where they benefit patrons most. Joan Conger agreed that one-on-one reference service is a waste. She stated that librarians must go out of the library building, learn not to be so introverted, and get into faculty offices. By touching one faculty member, we reach thousands of students. There is value in reference work but no longer on a one-to-one basis. There is value in finding interfaces and using mass communication vs. one on one.

Another participant had a problem with the dichotomies of forests vs. trees and problem solvers vs. rule followers. The forest is more than just trees, and managers need to nurture all components. There was agreement with another person stating that data must be good. We have to figure out what we need and avoid the dichotomy of quantity or quality. Others responded that staff is limited and that we cannot avoid making some quantity vs. quality decisions.

Further clarification was offered, stating that the presenter was obviously discussing mini-details. We certainly want accuracy, but are talking about what does not affect access. Rick Anderson explained that he was not targeting catalogers. The attitude of "that's the way we've always done it" can get in the way of any job.

Joan Conger asked on the quantity side of the picture why we are looking at individual records rather than a central record to which we can add holdings. A response was made that the tools are in place, and we need to focus more on centralized work.

A final question was raised about how to go back and communicate to people that they could no longer "do the job they were hired for." The answer was given that we must use serious management techniques, communicating, and empowering people rather then delegating.

NOTES

1. Editor's note: before the common era; formerly known as BC.
2. Margaret Wheatley, *Leadership and the New Science* (San Francisco: Berrett-Koehler, 2001).

RESOURCES FOR JOAN CONGER'S PRESENTATION

For the Individual

Block, Peter. 1993. *Stewardship*. San Francisco: Berrett-Koehler.
Covey, Stephen. 1990. *Seven Habits of Highly Effective People*. New York: Simon & Schuster.
Maslow, Abraham. 1970. *Motivation and Personality*. New York: Harper & Row.
Follett, Mary Parker. 1995. *Mary Parker Follet–Prophet of Management: A Celebration of Writings from the 1920's*. Boston: Harvard Business School Press.
Patterson, Kerry et al. 2002. *Crucial Conversations: Tools for Talking When Stakes Are High*. New York: McGraw-Hill.

For the Group

Pande, Peter. 2001. *Six Sigma Way: Team Fieldbook*. New York: McGraw-Hill.
Scholtes, Peter. 1997. *The Leader's Handbook*. New York: McGraw-Hill.
Senge, Peter. 1994. *The Fifth Discipline Fieldbook*. New York: Currency/Doubleday.

For the Organization

Argyris, Chris. 1999. *On Organizational Learning*. Oxford: Blackwell Business.
Collins, James. 1994. *Built to Last: Successful Habits of Visionary Companies*. New York: Harper-Collins.
Deming, W. Edwards. 2000. *Out of the Crisis*. Cambridge, MA: MIT.
Drucker, Peter F. 1954. *The Practice of Management*. NY: Harper Brothers.
Wheatley, Margaret. 2001. *Leadership and the New Science*. San Francisco: Berrett-Koehler

If You Read Only One Book

Peck, M. Scott. 1978, 2003. *The Road Less Traveled*. CA: Touchstone.

CONTRIBUTORS' NOTES

Jill Emery is Director of Electronic Resources at the University of Houston Libraries. Rick Anderson is Director of Resource Acquisitions at the University of Nevada-Reno. Adam Chesler was until recently Vice President for New Business for Ingenta; previously he was Director of Library Relations for Kluwer Academic Publishers. Joan Conger is Database Performance and Assessment Librarian at the University of Georgia Libraries. Ted Fons is Product Manager at Innovative Interfaces. Debra Skinner is Serials Catalog Librarian at Georgia Southern University.

CONCURRENT SESSIONS

The Information Resource Matrix: A Revolutionary Method to Present Relationships Among Online Serial Objects

Carol Casey
Mark Jacobs
Lihong Zhu

Presenters

EDITORS' NOTE: This paper was inadvertently omitted from the 2002 NASIG volume, *Transforming Serials: The Revolution Continues*. The editors of that volume greatly regret the error and are grateful to the editors of this volume for presenting it here.

SUMMARY. Librarians are often hampered by the limitations of online catalog systems because of a lack of flexibility in how they present relationships among serial information objects and their bibliographic surrogates. Therefore librarians have to look outside the box and consider other methods for enhancing bibliographic clarity and access. They also have to be forward thinking and develop an information environment that is less encumbered by machine-imposed strictures such as linearity, polarization of viewpoint and visual constraint. *[Article copies available for a fee from The Haworth Document Delivery Service: 1-800-HAWORTH. E-mail address: <docdelivery@haworthpress.com> Website: <http://www.HaworthPress.com>]*

[Haworth co-indexing entry note]: "The Information Resource Matrix: A Revolutionary Method to Present Relationships Among Online Serial Objects." Casey, Carol, Mark Jacobs, and Lihong Zhu. Co-published simultaneously in *The Serials Librarian* (The Haworth Information Press, an imprint of The Haworth Press, Inc.) Vol. 46, No. 1/2, 2004, pp. 59-67; and: *Serials in the Park* (ed: Patricia S. French, and Richard Worthing) The Haworth Information Press, an imprint of The Haworth Press, Inc., 2004, pp. 59-67. Single or multiple copies of this article are available for a fee from The Haworth Document Delivery Service [1-800-HAWORTH, 9:00 a.m. - 5:00 p.m. (EST). E-mail address: getinfo@haworthpress.com].

http://www.haworthpress.com/web/SER
Digital Object Identifier: 10.1300/J123v46n01_08

In 1979 Michael Gorman wrote, "the best use of mechanization will be founded on a complete reconsideration of all our systems, an examination of what we are doing and why we are doing it."[1] Gorman made this statement at a time when librarians were just realizing the potential of automated catalog systems. The feeling at the time was that librarians would be able to keep up with and adopt the latest technology for library use. Less than a quarter century later, librarians feel lucky if they hear about a new technology before it has been replaced, let alone have time to work it into their digital outreach plans for patrons.

Librarians who are not directly involved in the development of library-related technologies can do little more than react, often too late, to technological innovations rather than be proactive in establishing the technological paths they want the world of information resource access to follow. They are forced to work with online catalog systems that are cobbled together out of generations of computer code that go back to the original versions of these automated catalogs. The need for bibliographic growth is severely hampered because a desired innovation in bibliographic access requires rewriting the code upon which a catalog system is based. Because vendors are reluctant to perform periodic overhauls of their online systems, librarians have to look outside their online catalogs for methods of enhancing bibliographic clarity and access.

Librarians often feel they are pushing boulders uphill when it comes to the application of new technologies in the workplace. Taking the initiative is one way to alleviate this feeling of never being able to keep up. To do this, librarians need to create specific goals and directions for library-related technological advancements rather than depend on short-term fixes and solutions. They must think out of the box, reach for the ideal, and take control of what they want technology to do for information resource access.

REACHING FOR THE IDEAL

The nice thing about hypothesizing an ideal is that the imagination is allowed to run free. While an ideal may be technically possible, it can also be impossible to implement when factors such as the access to proper technologies, knowledge, staffing, budget, time, and other constraints are considered. If the basis of an ideal is dependent upon what is currently within reach of a library, it becomes obsolete very rapidly and results in developmental dead ends. To truly establish an ideal model, one must present a goal and the path to reach that goal. Each step in the path can become a reality as technology catches up to the ideal. Another important factor in establishing an ideal is to create the culture that will be able to support it.

With this in mind, the goals for an ideal model for presenting the relationships between serial bibliographic and information objects in the online environment, called the Information Resource Matrix (IRM) model, encompass several aspects of that ideal. These aspects include the philosophy and the structure of the model itself, the working culture of the environment surrounding the model, and the impact of the model on those who utilize it.

These primary goals can be achieved by two further goals: reconsidering and reconstituting the concept of bibliographic control and bringing it in line with modes of information access in networked online environments; and promoting and engendering the innovative and industrious use of information technology tools to reach the ideal model.

The resulting library culture supporting the IRM model will alter the traditional division of duties in librarianship because of the meshing of these duties in the continual maintenance and enhancement of the model. The impact on patrons will go beyond making it easier to locate information. The IRM model will help create a more aggressive and more literate user of library information resources.

BIBLIOGRAPHIC CONTROL AND TECHNOLOGICAL INNOVATIONS

A singular and remarkable achievement of the library and information science profession has been the creation, development, maintenance, and use of catalogs composed of bibliographic representations of information objects. In the twentieth century, the resulting bibliographic surrogates have paralleled the increasing ease in the exchange of information over distance, allowing them to be shared among libraries and institutions–first in various print manifestations and then through automated databases. In developing an ideal model for accessing information, these past accomplishments should not be overlooked or forgotten, but must be used as the foundation upon which to build that ideal.

Although the development of bibliographic surrogates and the mechanism for information access in the print environment have always been limited by physical barriers such as catalog cards, filing cabinets, and floor space, for example, what is good and essential about the traditional methods of information access must not be limited by technology. When card catalogs were first automated, the technology for displaying bibliographic surrogates was in many ways more primitive than the card catalog. At the time, the computer's ability to automatically index and display records was considered more important than how searchers found information in catalogs, because the indexing and display enabled libraries to reduce the number of staff dedicated to filing cards.

At the beginning of the twenty-first century, the automated card catalogs may be more user-friendly, but they still haven't improved enough in their basic access and display of bibliographic information to match the searching flexibility of the physical card catalog. Technology still imposes linearity, polarization, and a constrained viewpoint through which information is accessed. Because of this, it is necessary to go back to the traditional print concepts of information resource access to develop a revolutionary method of presenting, displaying, and aiding information seekers to visualize information objects in the online environment.

Unless the vendors of the current online catalog systems drastically rethink their products, these catalogs will be developmental dead ends in library technology. This is already becoming evident in the recent proliferation of new tools that allow greater flexibility in front-end portals of access to bibliographic and information objects from multiple sources. The online catalog is suddenly no longer the single most important portal of access in the library world but simply one of many paths researchers can follow to find relevant information objects.

But the online catalogs have one advantage over most of the other portals vying for equal access to information objects: bibliographic control. In the online environment, it doesn't matter if the bibliographic surrogates or the actual information objects are accessed–the same methods of access and control must apply to both. Until the concept of bibliographic control is universally applied across all online methods of access, the online environment will be an imperfect resource for seekers of information.

INNOVATIVE USE OF INFORMATION TECHNOLOGY

The first rule of technological innovation should be to know what lies in the realm of machines and what must remain the job of humans. For the IRM model to work optimally, the information objects brought into it must be organized in a way that is meaningful to information seekers. This means that the organization scheme for the information objects has to be imposed before the search key is initiated, rather than afterwards, as is common with machine controlled search engines. Another important factor of the IRM model is that organization isn't just a linear hierarchy, but a method of showing information objects in context to each other and allowing the information seeker to see the relationships between these objects.

Any aspect of organization that requires more than simple matching of words without consideration of intellectual context requires human intervention. If the intellectual context of information objects is not properly analyzed and indexed and the relationships between these objects are not manually established, librarians risk participating in a process of information filtering–accepting the limitations of access from programs that sort data according to factors other than the intellectual context of the information objects. This filtering results in ever more limited spheres of information than can be used to create new knowledge, further fragmenting knowledge instead of bringing it all together within a holistic organic environment. It doesn't matter that all the knowledge in the world may reside in the online environment if it isn't organized so that information seekers can find it and control it during the search process.

In the world of libraries, technology is not being designed to think like people–people are being trained to think like the technology. The way information objects are displayed in the online environment promotes linear thinking, not a holistic or even a random approach that is important to seeking information. The presentation of information objects in the online environment also promotes polarized, rather than collaborative or inclusive, thinking. These limitations imposed on how information seekers must think when accessing the online environment can be corrected by increasing visualization of the information universe through the development of innovative ways in which information objects are displayed and manipulated by information seekers.

The purpose of the IRM model is to allow a holistic view of the section of the information universe in which an information seeker is working. The information objects can be organized by the information seeker in a way that is meaningful to him or her–in a sense, creating a personal information environment that can be kept for future reference and continually updated. This personal information environment can be a place to store newly created information and knowledge and act as a portal through which this new knowledge can be shared.

USER CONTROL IN THE INFORMATION ENVIRONMENT

Information seekers create their own interfaces–personal information environments–with information objects by combining the limitations imposed on how these objects are accessible with creatively overcoming some of these limitations.

In non-automated libraries, the search for information objects often involves two separate activities–looking through card catalogs and browsing through materials in the stacks. The process may be more labor-intensive, but it has some advantages that are lost in the online environment.

While some strides have been made to extend the concept of bibliographic control to take advantage of the expanding online environment, this concept is limited by a two dimensional, linear presentation that in many ways makes the online environment a less desirable bibliographic vehicle than card catalogs. Card catalogs have the advantage of a third dimension that allows information seekers to simultaneously view several cards from the same or different drawers. This ability to impose a user-controlled layer upon the basic structure of a card catalog enables information seekers to create impromptu maps of the relationships among bibliographic surrogates and the objects they represent.

More layers of user-controlled organization of resources can be implemented once the physical information objects themselves, such as in the stacks of a library, surround researchers. Several opened books can be spread out at one time and different parts of the stacks can be browsed for information objects to add to the on-the-spot personal information environment. This ability to see all of the relevant information at one time and to add more information objects while the other objects remain visible and accessible is an important parameter to research that is all but lost in the online environment.

The idea of the IRM model is to take advantage of the good points of both the print and digital environments. In the online environment, the efforts to implement interfaces that allow a certain amount of user control have been slow to develop because of the complexities involved when technology is called upon to do anything beyond what can be reduced to mathematical terms. But breakthroughs are happening and librarians must ensure that they have the strongest input into these technological developments. Otherwise, they'll follow the same technological dead-ends that most innovations for the online environment come up against.

At the beginning of the twenty-first century, the most severe problem with accessing information objects in an online environment is the loss of any sort of depth of knowledge, which greatly hampers user control of the information objects once they're found. As long as access is weighted in mathematical terms, online environments will not be the best resource for serious in-depth research.

SUPPORTING CULTURES FOR INFORMATION ENVIRONMENTS

According to Ronald Hagler, "to describe an item in terms of expressing its relationships is essential to the most efficient use of bibliographic data."[2] Whether those data are in the form of MARC records or some other type of metadata container, the description of information objects must encompass all the elements needed for access and accommodate the almost organic relationships that exist in the world of knowledge. As long as researchers have a holistic view of knowledge, the method in which the information objects in the online environment are organized, accessed, and displayed must reflect researchers' expectations and provide the necessary control for them to create personal information environments.

Because of a lack of true understanding of how information is organized in the online environment, patrons expect their informational needs to be easily accessible in a neat, complete package at the end of a simple search key. It is the librarian's job to understand the online environment enough to properly educate patrons and to dispel these myths of access. More importantly, librarians must never lose sight of the concepts of intellectual context and relationship among information objects in whatever information environment in which they are working.

Historically, librarians have followed the traditional mission to support patrons in their educational and research needs. This support has always gone beyond the superficial level of simply locating objects on a shelf or in a database. Librarians are subject specialists who can show patrons the intellectual context among information objects within a subject and how these objects relate to each other. To do this, librarians must have an in-depth knowledge of the information environments in which they are working. The physical library environment meets librarians halfway because it is organized to allow librarians to see the intellectual context and relationships among information objects. Librarians, after all, have a hand in forming the physical library environment. How can librarians expect to have the same understanding of the online environment, which flourishes and grows without any attention to organization and which does not always adhere to a hierarchical system of knowledge? Until they engage in an aggressive plan to organize information objects in the online environment in a manner that is meaningful to researchers, librarians are about as useful in the online environment as they are in a warehouse full of torn-up books.

The new information environments, digital and beyond, must not only support the structures that have been built into our knowledge systems but must reflect how this knowledge is approached by information seekers. It doesn't do any good to have all the organization and visualization in place if the culture supporting and using the information environment is not developed. Librarians must adapt libraries and library culture not only to support the outward manifestations of information environments, but also to sustain the organization, maintenance, and presentation of, as well as access to, these environments.

BUILDING THE IDEAL

As traditional caretakers of the world's knowledge, librarians have the responsibility to ensure that the knowledge record remains unbroken and survives to the next generation. Establishing a project such as the Information Resource Matrix model as a long-term goal is an opportunity for librarians to take control of the destinies of their professions and the institutions in which they work.

Building an actual front-end user interface based on the ideal concepts for information access requires librarians to dictate these ideals to the creators of new technologies instead of the other way around. Librarians must take a more holistic view of libraries and the methods in which they offer access to information objects, stop thinking in terms of division according to tasks and skills, and start focusing on unity according to information access and patron needs.

A multi-media version of the presentation is available for viewing at http://www.mindancer.net.

NOTES

1. Gorman, Michael, "Cataloging and the New Technologies," in *The Nature and Future of the Catalog: Proceedings of the ALA's Information Science and Automation Division's 1975 and 1977 Institutes on the Catalog*, ed. Maurice J. Freedman and S. Michael Malinconico (Phoenix, AZ: Oryx, 1979): 127.

2. Ronald Hagler, *The Bibliographic Record and Information Technology*, 3rd ed. (Chicago: American Library Association, 1997): 69.

CONTRIBUTORS' NOTES

Carol Casey is Bibliographic and Technical Services MARC Specialist at Blackwell North America Book Services. Mark Jacobs is Electronic Resources/Serials Cataloging Librarian at Washington State University. Lihong Zhu is Monographic Cataloging Librarian at Washington State University.

Serial Aggregations, Multiple Versions, and the Virtual Union Catalog: The California Digital Library Catalog, SUNY, and Ex Libris Experiences

Michael Kaplan
Presenter

SUMMARY. Librarians have long agonized over the challenge of the so-called multiple version problem: how to catalog, associate, and present related titles or related manifestations of a given work. The appearance of increasingly large aggregations of electronic serials that defy easy control has raised the level of interest in newer approaches. At the LC Bicentennial Conference on Bibliographic Control, Confronting the Challenge of Networked Resources and the Web, I argued that vendor supply of metadata for serial aggregations was essential if the library community was to achieve title-level control of these important and expensive titles. It was argued that keeping MARC records for the aggregations separate in the technical services view of the catalog but merging them on the fly for the public view of the catalog would allow a sophisticated ILS to achieve the best of both worlds by having individual records and supporting a multiple versions approach to the public display. Since that talk was delivered in November 2000, the California Digital Library and the State University of New York's Office of Library Information

[Haworth co-indexing entry note]: "Serial Aggregations, Multiple Versions, and the Virtual Union Catalog: The California Digital Library Catalog, SUNY, and Ex Libris Experiences." Kaplan, Michael. Co-published simultaneously in *The Serials Librarian* (The Haworth Information Press, an imprint of The Haworth Press, Inc.) Vol. 46, No. 1/2, 2004, pp. 69-81; and: *Serials in the Park* (ed: Patricia S. French, and Richard Worthing) The Haworth Information Press, an imprint of The Haworth Press, Inc., 2004, pp. 69-81. Single or multiple copies of this article are available for a fee from The Haworth Document Delivery Service [1-800-HAWORTH, 9:00 a.m. - 5:00 p.m. (EST). E-mail address: getinfo@haworthpress.com].

http://www.haworthpress.com/web/SER
Digital Object Identifier: 10.1300/J123v46n01_09

Services have worked with Ex Libris to implement a multiple versions approach to their virtual union catalogs. *[Article copies available for a fee from The Haworth Document Delivery Service: 1-800-HAWORTH. E-mail address: <docdelivery@haworthpress.com> Website: <http://www.HaworthPress.com>]*

I want to talk to you today about a new and evolving concept of the catalog which is particularly well suited for consortia, but also has implications for the further development and refinement of IFLA's Functional Requirements for the Bibliographic Record (fondly known to its aficionados as FRBR). It also has significant implications on how individual libraries and library catalogs can relate to loads of vendor-supplied data, particularly for aggregations, and to that data's regular ongoing maintenance.

The paper I delivered at the Library of Congress Bicentennial Conference on Bibliographic Control for the New Millennium in November 2000 was largely theoretical.[1] At that time, I was concerned primarily with metadata from different schemata, their resolution and presentation. Today I want to talk primarily about contextual, on-the-fly presentation of catalog data in a record structure that is both virtual and dynamic. In fact, it is the virtuality that makes for the dynamic record that I have under consideration today.

Libraries have long made use of union catalogs. For the most part, those union catalogs were physical union catalogs. The National Union Catalog is one example of a printed, cumulated, union catalog. In the electronic era it works differently; namely, a pool of candidate records is assembled electronically and the records themselves are examined programmatically to determine whether or not they are identical. The theoretical basis behind such a determination of like-identity or non-like-identity in batch loading processes for bibliographic data is well known and has been in use for well over a decade. OCLC, the University of California Melvyl® Union Catalog, and Harvard University's HOLLIS catalog all use flavors of a similar algorithm that relies on a threshold of positive and negative weights, where positive weight is added to matching fields and negative weight is subtracted for non-matching fields. More recently, the German KOBV consortium, an ALEPH500 implementation, has published a variation based on more recent studies of matching algorithms.

At the 2000 LC Conference, I spoke of the dynamic record as embodying a record concept that can be constructed on-the-fly from different data elements, both traditional bibliographic and non-traditional, including enhancements such as enriched table of contents information, abstracts, reviews, and cover jacket illustrations. Today I have something slightly different in mind, something that is more tightly tied to traditional bibliographic content and is particularly well suited to a consortial environment. I am pleased to be able to show you real examples of such a catalog construct because, while it was my personal fantasy at the time of the 2000 LC Conference, today it is reality at the California Digital Library in the Melvyl® Union Catalog (melvyl.cdlib.org), which contains 24 million titles contributed from a heterogenous set of ALEPH and non-ALEPH sites. This construct will soon also be operational in the State University of New York SUNYConnect Union Catalog. During late May and early June 2003, SUNY and Ex Libris were in the process of loading data and indexing an initial set of 7 SUNY libraries; once that is completed, data from a larger set of converted SUNY libraries will be loaded. Unlike CDL, SUNY intends to load only ALEPH sites into its union catalog. Because the SUNY data is only now being loaded, I have chosen examples to illustrate my talk from CDL but the principles are the same for both catalogs.

Librarians, or perhaps I should say catalogers, have long agonized over the challenge of the so-called multiple version problem (often referred to as *mulver*). Succinctly put, the problem is how to catalog, associate, and present related titles or related manifestations of a given work. For example, in the days of card catalogs, microform reproductions were frequently cataloged on the same card set with the paper original by use of the "dashed-on" method. For the cataloger, this method of cataloging a subsequent reproduction (or a later edition, or a supplement or index) was a quick and dirty means of providing access. For the patrons, the method produced an intuitive collocation of equivalent works in different formats or works related to one another in a logical sequence.

The famous Airlie House meeting on multiple versions was held in 1989.[2] While it led to a period of intense discussion on the advantages and disadvantages of such an arrangement in an era of electronic access, and, while various bibliographic tiers were proposed, nothing official resulted from it. The topic came to life once again during my tenure as Chair of the Program for Cooperative Cataloging with intense debate on the treatment of electronic serials and serial aggregations. Should libraries standardize on separate, discrete records for the printed version of serials and their electronic counterparts, or encourage a single record for both?

Let's take a look at a serial record with mulver characteristics from Harvard University's new ALEPH500 catalog.

It is possible to see in this record how Harvard University brought together records of all formats into a single record based on a long-standing tradition that existed even in the first-generation of their HOLLIS system (see Figures 1a and 1b).

Libraries have a pressing need to develop a cradle-to-grave approach to handling electronic sets. That means obtaining the corresponding electronic records from the aggregator and receiving regular maintenance and updates. Maintenance would ideally include additions, deletions, and changes in coverage. But what should libraries do with the records they receive from the creators of these aggregations? Should they standardize on separate, discrete records for the printed versions of serials and their electronic counterparts, or encourage a single record for both? Expediency has been the name of the game to date, and that

FIGURE 1a. Illustration from the Harvard University HOLLIS Catalog: Multiple-Version Style Record

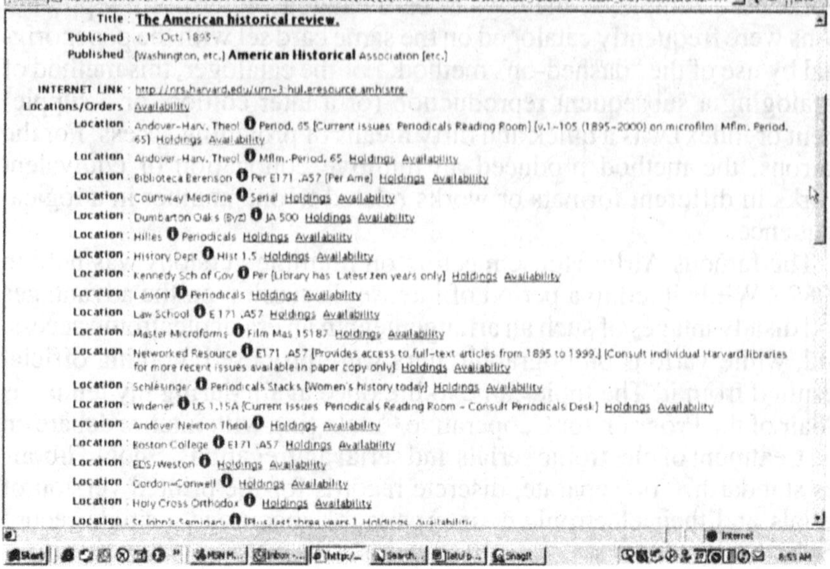

FIGURE 1b. Illustration from the Harvard University HOLLIS Catalog: Multiple-Version Style Record

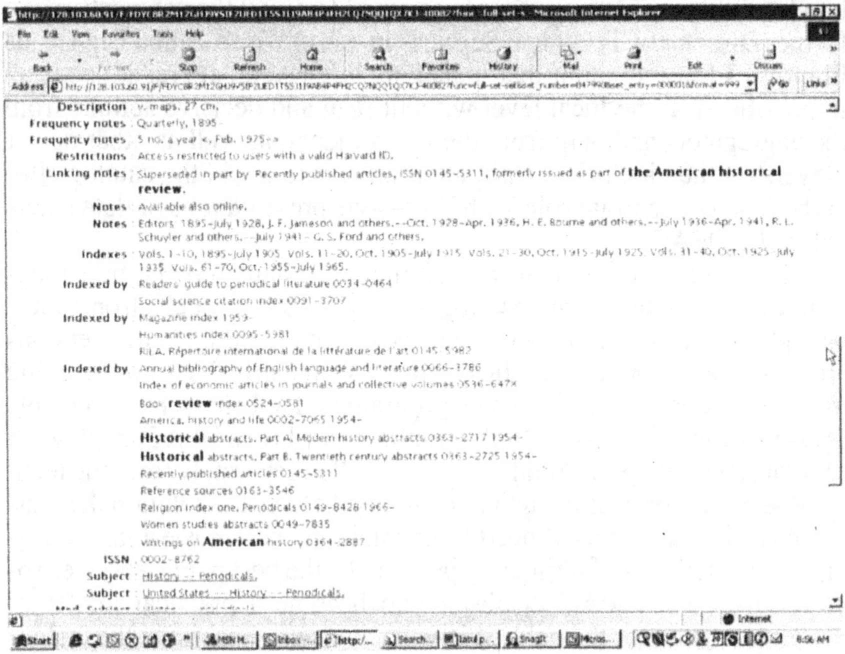

has largely meant that libraries add a holding location for the electronic manifestation of the serial to the record for the paper original. Interest in new approaches is greater now due to the appearance of large and increasingly costly aggregations of electronic serials that defy easy control. The Program for Cooperative Cataloging has released guidelines for aggregators to create distinct subsets of records for their electronic journals, and those subsets may or may not be based on the record for the paper journal.[3] And there are new players and new approaches to this conundrum, from vendors such as Serials Solutions and Ex Libris's own SFX product.

I have to admit that I am troubled about enabling the aggregator's data file to reach deep down into our integrated library systems and to touch data on this level if the data is buried within a mulver-style record, even though I am fond of the mulver concept for electronic journals. Mixing data for different versions in a single record is simply fraught with too many difficulties and has huge implications for maintenance over time. I have concluded that if we want to create a hands-off, computer-to-computer data interchange, we need to keep the basic building blocks of that exchange as simple as possible. From the perspective of a former Director of Technical Services in one of the so-called Big Heads libraries, I have to admit that managing large serial aggregations is an impossibility at the local level without firm and decisive actions from the aggregators and help from the ILS vendors, as well as other newer players on the block. The stark alternative is to avoid the catalog altogether and concentrate solely on Web-style presentations of data external to the OPAC.

I therefore conclude that the solution that maintains the best long-term viability of the library catalog is to keep records for electronic journals physically separate from their paper counterparts. If the versions are cataloged separately, an incoming record–particularly an incoming maintenance-level record–can be programmed to behave in predictable ways vis-à-vis the existing bibliographic record. The OPAC display is a separate issue altogether and can be controlled separately from the technical services application in this scenario. I believe the solution that best serves technical services' need to maintain the best, easiest, and most-up-to-date access will ultimately prove to be the best public services solution also. The OPAC display could become a practical matter of merging records for the public view that are kept separate in the technical services components of our catalogs.

There is one further aspect to consider–user preference and user understanding. In general, I have believed that a mulver record best serves users–provided that the display can be made clear and sensible. Users do not want to see a multiplicity of records for essentially the same title. The fact that the paper and the electronic may not technically be 100 percent the same or that the electronic record might suffer from the type of "moving wall" that JSTOR maintains may need to be overlooked. The simple fact is that users want to see one record and one record only. This also means that all the information pertinent to only one version needs to be clearly associated with the relevant description, whether for the reproduction, paper, or electronic version. Long ago, in my graduate-student lifetime, I would have been most satisfied to find all the relevant records, regardless of format, in a single, intelligible bibliographic construct. And this construct is just as applicable at the local, unitary, institutional level as it is in the context of the consortial union catalog.

Now what of the consortial arrangements? Consortia want to present not just a single institution's holdings but also those of a group of affiliated libraries. They need means to match, deduplicate, and merge holdings from a variety of libraries. As stated earlier, the algorithmic means to detect duplication are well known and have been refined in recent years. The matching algorithm looks first at key numbers. When these numbers cannot be guaranteed to be unique, secondary checks (on authors, titles, imprints, etc.) are employed. The matching algorithms are capable of being manipulated and fine-tuned to account for differences in different bibliographic formats–such as monographs vs. serials–and the threshold associated with them can vary and be adjusted based on experience. The California Digital Library uses this type of algorithm in the construction of the new Melvyl® Union Catalog.

Once different records are brought together, there is the question of selecting a preferred record for display or creating a composite record from the pool of duplicate records. Let's examine a sample record from CDL for the *SIAM Journal on Matrix* (see Appendix, Views 1-5).

In View 1 we can see the result of a keyword search for "Siam Journal Matrix." It brings up a single hit. View 2 shows a view of the global record that is an amalgam of several records, with underlined holdings representing the holdings and individual records for each of the owning campuses.

In these views of the record we can see the composite record for the paper and the electronic journal and we can also see that it is held at multiple campuses throughout the University of California. The record shows holdings for both paper and electronic versions, with partial holdings information (see View 3). In both the CDL and SUNY catalogs it is further possible to view the holding for any individual campus or any individual record because the original records are preserved intact and the merging is done on-the-fly based on pre-built tables of equivalencies that were part of the Ex Libris-CDL development for the new Melvyl®.

In Views 4 and 5, one can see the native records from UC Berkeley and UC Davis; these records are subsumed under the consortial view of the Melvyl Union Catalog's global record. For the library, this construct creates the best of both worlds. Records that are not intended to represent the same title are kept apart. They do not compromise one another's bibliographic integrity or existence. It is always possible to get back to first principles or to the original description. Yet, titles that a library or a consortium wants to treat as equivalents can be made to behave in that fashion. And the library has several options for handling incoming files of aggregated data, thus relieving its staff of much tedious, time-consuming, repetitive work involved with regular upkeep of large sets of aggregated data.

What does it mean for the end user? For the end user, it means a more sensible collocation of data. It presents a single record that has more meaning. It allows them to see variations in the presentation format of the data that in many cases are of significance only to technical services librarians. While it is true that some users will want to see the paper original, in many cases users would at least rather start with the electronic version that is readily available and revert to the original only if in need of the material in its Ur-format. Except for die-hard bibliophiles or antiquarians, it is the data that are important much more than the object itself. That is why the mulver-aspect of FRBR promises to be so important for our clientele. Why not offer them easy, collocated access from the inception of their search? As CDL has envisioned it, they not only have access to a combined, consortial record, but individual records are also only a click away.

Or, to quote another English phrase, this is like "having your cake and eating it too."

NOTES

1. Michael Kaplan, "Exploring Partnerships: What Can Producers and Vendors Provide?" (presentation at the Conference on Bibliographic Control in the New Millennium, Washington, DC, Nov. 15-17, 2000), http://lcweb.loc.gov/catdir/bibcontrol/kaplan.html (10 Oct. 2003).
2. *Multiple Versions Forum Report: Report from a Meeting Held December 6-8, 1989, Airlie, Virginia* (Washington: Network Development and MARC Standards Office, Library of Congress, 1990).
3. Program for Cooperative Cataloging, Standing Committee on Automation, Second Task Group on Journals in Aggregator Databases, *Final report*, http://lcweb.loc.gov/catdir/pcc/aggtg2final.html (10 Oct. 2003).

CONTRIBUTOR'S NOTE

Michael Kaplan is Director of Product Management at Ex Libris (USA) Inc.

APPENDIX

CDL Online Record for the SIAM Journal on Matrix Analysis and Applications

View 1. Melvyl® Search Result for "Siam Journal Matrix"

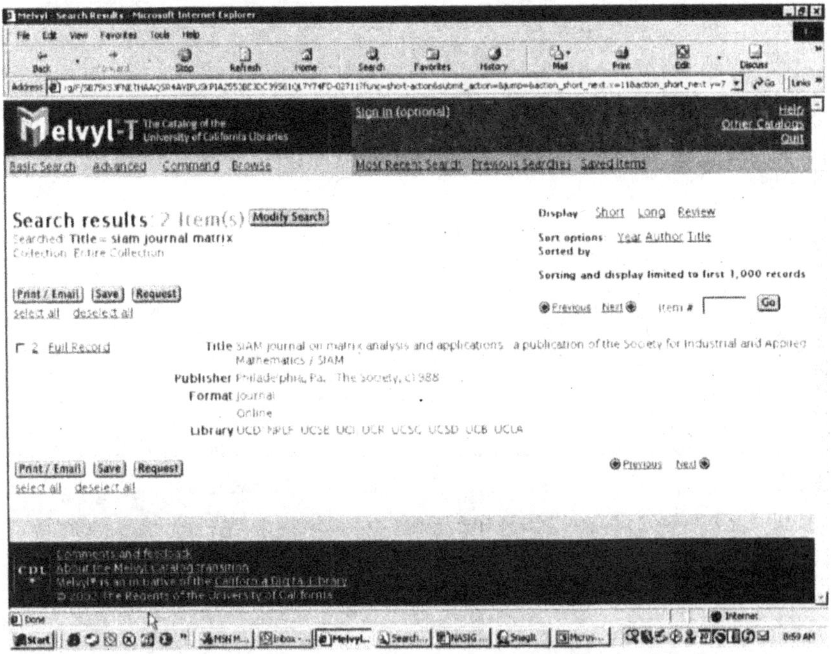

View 2. Global Record for Melvyl® and the Owning Campuses

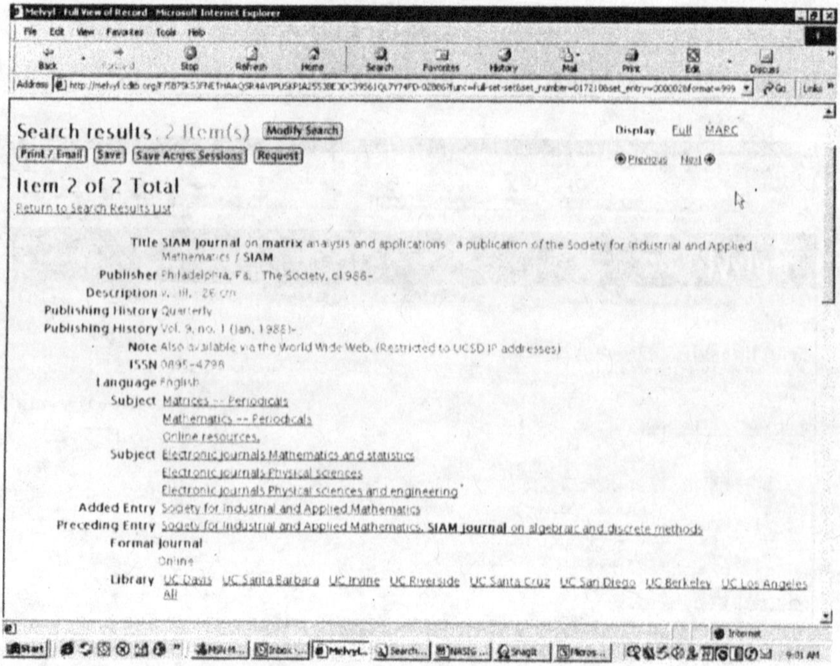

View 3. Partial View of the Holdings for the UC Libraries

UC Berkeley			
		Available online	v.28(1997)-
Math	QA1 .S732a	Circ status	Unbound issues on Display Shelves – Alphabetically 9(1988)-
UC Davis			
		Available online	Full text v.18 (1997)-, Abstracts v.15 (1994)- Access restricted to UCD IP addresses.
Shields	QA1 .S732	Circ status	Recent issues in SHIELDS Bio/Ag Current Per, older issues bound in book stacks. Bio/Ag Current Periodicals Status Active
	internet	Circ status	v.18, 1997- Electronic Resources
Shields	QA1 .S732	Circ status	v.11,1990- Status Active commitment. Recent issues in SHIELDS Bio/Ag Current Per, older issues bound in book stacks.
UC Irvine			
Sci Lib	QA 263 S45	Circ status	89-22(1988-2000/01) Drum Latest in Curr Per Rm
UC Los Angeles			
		Available online	v.18(1997)- Restricted to UCLA
SEL/EMS	QA1 .S56	Circ status	SEMSTAX-STAX 89-23(1988-2002) Stacks
SEL/EMS	QA1 .S56	Circ status	SEMSTAX-UJNL U24N1-2(2002) Stacks
UC Riverside			
		Available online	Connect to Abstracts only v.15 (1994)-v.17 (1996), Full text v.18 (1997)- UCR access only
Internet	Electronic journal	Circ status	Abstracts only v.15(1994)-17(1996), Full text v.18(1997)-
Science	QA1 S6252	Circ status	v.9(1988)-23:2(2002)- Latest in Math Dept., older in stacks
UC San Diego			
		Available online	v.18(1997)- Restricted to UCSD IP addresses
S & E	QA 1 S53	Circ status	9- (1988-) Current Journals Bound in Stacks

View 4. UC Berkeley's Individual Campus View of a Title

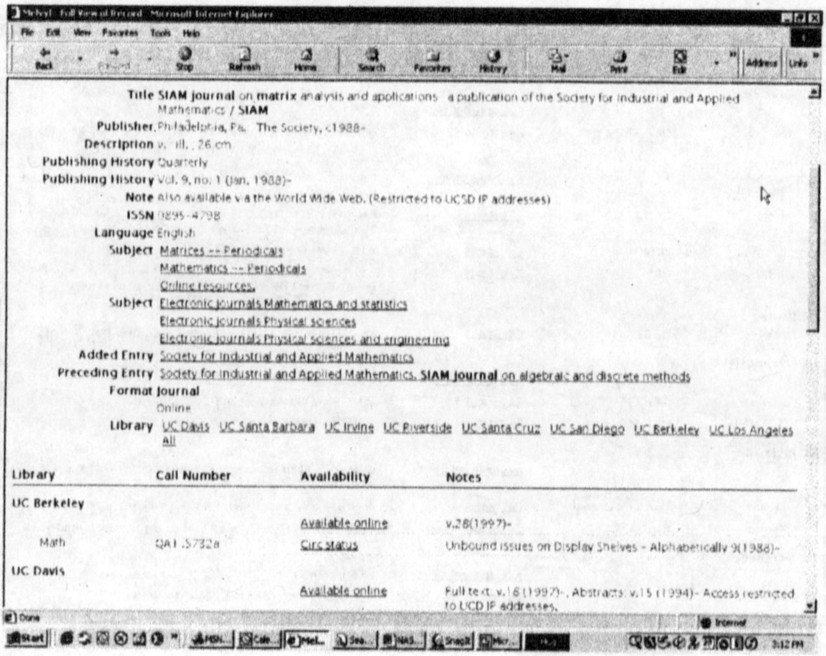

View 5. UC Davis's Individual Campus View of the Same Title

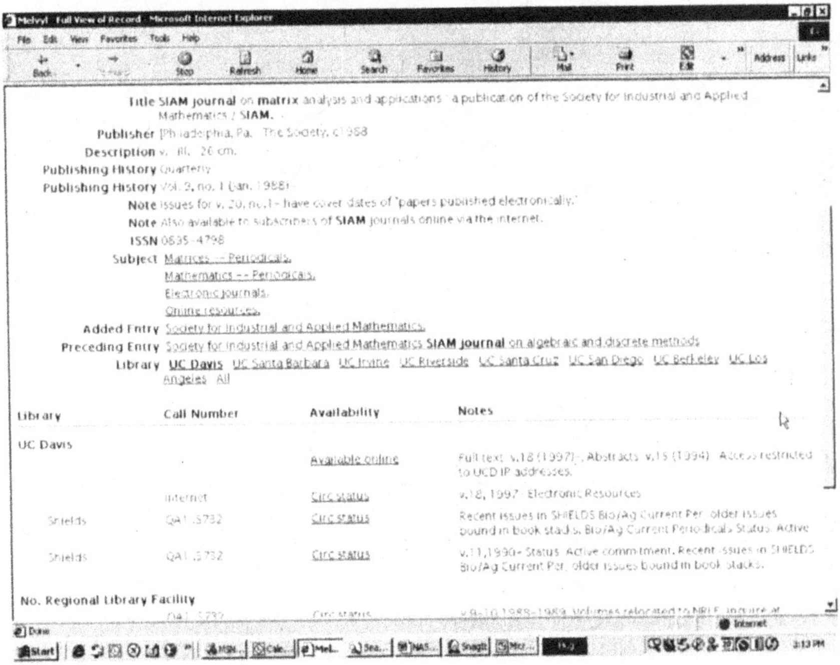

Finding a Better Trail Through the Journals Forest

Timothy Gatti
Heather S. Miller

Presenters

SUMMARY. SUNY Albany began to find its Web-based list of electronic journals (accompanied by an independent Serials Solutions list and OPAC records for some titles) increasingly unworkable, confusing to the library user and costly to maintain. Discussions during the winter and spring of 2001/2002 led to the decision to complete cataloging of all e-journals prior to the start of the fall 2002 semester (using a single record per title with multiple holdings for all formats and locations), including those in the Serials Solutions list, and to replace the e-journals and Serials Solutions lists with a link to the OPAC periodicals search box. This permits finding information on the library's holdings of all formats for a given periodical title in one place, as well as hot links to any available electronic form. *[Article copies available for a fee from The Haworth Document Delivery Service: 1-800-HAWORTH. E-mail address: <docdelivery@haworthpress.com> Website: <http://www.HaworthPress.com>]*

[Haworth co-indexing entry note]: "Finding a Better Trail Through the Journals Forest." Gatti, Timothy and Heather S. Miller. Co-published simultaneously in *The Serials Librarian* (The Haworth Information Press, an imprint of The Haworth Press, Inc.) Vol. 46, No. 1/2, 2004, pp. 83-98; and: *Serials in the Park* (ed: Patricia S. French, and Richard Worthing) The Haworth Information Press, an imprint of The Haworth Press, Inc., 2004, pp. 83-98. Single or multiple copies of this article are available for a fee from The Haworth Document Delivery Service [1-800-HAWORTH, 9:00 a.m. - 5:00 p.m. (EST). E-mail address: getinfo@haworthpress.com].

http://www.haworthpress.com/web/SER
Digital Object Identifier: 10.1300/J123v46n01_10

BACKGROUND

During the "serials crisis" of the 1980s, many librarians expressed a desire for electronic delivery of content, especially for journals. It would be easy, it wouldn't get lost in the mail, it would be fast, and–most importantly–it would be cheap, even free. Having to a large extent received what was wished for, librarians have found that the reality of electronic journals has been quite different; they are neither easy to handle nor cheap to purchase; they can get lost, and embargoes and technical problems make them not always fast. Nevertheless, electronic journals are here to stay, and librarians have been struggling to provide access to them for the many library users who like electronic information and have little patience in the pursuit of it.

A glance at history shows that the rise of the electronic periodical has been breathtakingly swift. In 1987, the University at Albany Libraries ordered the first CD-ROM for its collection. Over the next few years, CD-ROM periodical backfiles trickled into the collection, mostly unwanted and little used. By the mid-1990s, the first Web-based electronic journals had appeared. It was the start of a deluge. During this period, libraries commonly accepted the fact that the World Wide Web had to be incorporated into library services. The first library Webmasters were hired. Catalogers often looked on electronic journals as a kind of "other" and tried to ignore them. Some libraries cataloged electronic resources but did not classify them. The Webmasters, on the other hand, knew that these journals were in demand and made them available, along with other Web-based information resources on libraries' Web sites. It was reasonably easy to do. This period of time also saw the rise of the license agreement, another new thing that could not be ignored. At first, license agreements were often signed or clicked by whoever happened upon them. It took a few years for librarians to understand indemnification and the fact that they did not have it. With increased experience on the part of both librarians and publishers, the process of signing a license came to involve lawyers and a great deal of time. Few librarians today would respond positively to a publisher's demand that a faxed agreement be "signed and sent right back."

Thus, at the start of the new millennium many libraries found themselves awash in electronic information over which they had little control. They were also faced with library users who demanded easy access to everything over the Internet, unwilling or unable to distinguish between Internet junk and truly reliable information resources. Most libraries offered Web-based lists of electronic journals and other electronic resources. This worked well enough for a short list, but as the lists grew larger they became increasingly unwieldy. Meanwhile, aggregators began compiling databases of e-journals, permitting searching across the entire collection. Entrepreneurs created products intended to provide access to the thousands of e-journal titles in aggregator databases, but these were incomplete and often riddled with inaccuracies.

This is precisely the morass in which the University at Albany Libraries found themselves in 2001. Few e-journals had been cataloged, the Web-based list had grown unwieldy (even though it was generated from an SQL database and offered title searching), a separate Serials Solutions list was mounted on the Web site, and all other formats of journal titles were cataloged in the OPAC. Duplicative work was required to maintain the two modes of access to electronic information resources. Something had to be done.

By this time, it was becoming increasingly obvious that Web-based lists lacked search functionality such as fuzzy matching, variant titles and sophisticated subject searching, which was inherent in the OPAC. Libraries had begun to come to grips with cataloging e-journals, yielding to the obvious fact that the value of cataloging applies to all formats. Catalog records for e-journals rapidly began to be available in the OCLC database.

The purpose of this paper is to illustrate how one library concluded that OPAC access is the best route between library user and e-journal. It will focus on e-journals, a special subset of electronic resources fraught with all the usual problems inherent in periodicals plus others unique to the online environment. Numerous articles have been published on the topic of providing access to e-journals. It is not our purpose here to exhaustively examine this literature, but to indicate the development of some of the thinking that has led to a renewed focus on the OPAC as a means of connecting the library user to e-journals. In 1999, Hamaker declared that "if we do not craft a tool that is the one-stop pointer for our user's need to find relevant information, owned, leased or selected and included EVEN when it is free, our OPACs are headed towards irrelevance."[1] He goes on to say that "having only the paper version cataloged of ANY title easily available electronically is a disservice to library users."[2] Bevis and Graham noted that "user access and collection management can be greatly enhanced by integrating electronic journals into an OPAC."[3] Calhoun and Kara clearly delineated the problems associated with various methods of providing access to e-journals. They stated that "the challenge of optimizing end user access to aggregations of full-text electronic journals is turning librarians' assumptions about the catalog's scope and function upside down."[4] They noted three methods of providing that access–title lists, single catalog records, and multiple catalog records–and found them all wanting.[5] Li and Leung described an approach to integrating catalog records for aggregator databases into the OPAC using a computer program developed in-house. In the end, access to e-journals was provided by the OPAC and by a Web-based list generated from the OPAC.[6] Herrera and Aldana also described a project to catalog e-journals, the end result of which was to provide access to e-journals only through the OPAC. They note that "limited resources and a commitment to the library catalog as a master database of library holdings creates a very reasonable argument for using the library catalog to provide access to electronic resources."[7] At the 2002 NASIG conference, the University of Tennessee described its process of cataloging e-journals and its use of the OPAC as the definitive source of information about them and as the source of data for a Web-based list.[8] Briscoe et al. correctly note that best practices for providing access to online resources have not yet been established.[9]

In general, there seems to be an increasing awareness of the value of cataloging e-journals along with a continued, perhaps uncritical, commitment to providing Web lists of e-journal titles. Recent literature and exploration of library Websites show that some libraries have cataloged e-journals and some use the OPAC database to generate a Web-based list of e-journals, but few direct the library user solely to the OPAC for information on e-journals. The University at Albany chose to use just the OPAC to provide the best trail through the forest of journals in all formats. The decision to do so was the result of a difficult collaborative process.

In late 2001, the Director of Libraries established a small group consisting of the Assistant Directors for Technical Services and Systems and Collections and User Services, the Webmaster, and the Head of the Library Systems Department to begin conversations about how best to provide access to electronic journals. In addition to the need to provide library users with reliable and easily managed information access, she was concerned about the costs of duplicative effort. Proponents of the Web site devalued the OPAC, while OPAC adherents pointed to the weaknesses of the Web list approach.

The clearest advantage of the Web-based list of e-journals is ease of access. Users like to point and click, readily finding something they can use. They had developed the habit of using the Web-based list of e-journals because the Libraries had led them in that direction. Cataloging personnel did not immediately embrace e-journals, so the Libraries'

Webmaster stepped in to provide a list of those e-journals to which the Libraries subscribed. Gradually, e-journals began to creep into the cataloging workflow. As of July 1, 2001, 533 electronic journal titles were in the OPAC. By November 2001, there were 975 titles and/or URLs in the OPAC. By February 1, 2002 the number had grown to 2,150. Meanwhile, as of June 30 of that year, the Libraries actually provided access to over 11,000 electronic journals, through direct subscription and aggregator databases. The number was growing monthly.

The Web-based list was attractive, but it was a fragmented approach to journals because it lacked information about and access to other formats of the same titles. While users might say they only wanted e-journals, coverage in that format might be limited and might not provide needed information at all, while earlier issues of the title might be available in print or microform for many years back. The searching capability of the Web-based list was extremely limited. A single character difference between the user's search term and the entry in the list would result in a message reading "Sorry, there are 0 titles with that name." The Web-based list approach was also fragmented because the list did not include aggregator titles. These were found in a separate list created by loading files from Serials Solutions. Thus information about e-journals was found in three places: the OPAC, the Web list, and the Serials Solutions list. None was complete or fully accurate. The Web list was increasingly unwieldy to maintain.

THE PROCESS

When discussions began, library users connected to e-journals through a link on the Libraries' Webpage entitled "Databases & Online Journals." The group began discussion by contrasting the functional characteristics of the SQL database which generated the Web list and the OPAC. Some points were debated; but, in general, the OPAC was superior in terms of standardization, subject searching, combining all formats, offering multiple access points, and in dealing with initial articles and title variations. The Web list was seen as offering greater flexibility in terms of display options, ease of use (point and click) and collection of use data (later determined to be of little interest because statistics from aggregators are preferred). One of the most telling differences was in the level of staff skills, interest and leadership; staff who produced the Web list had these qualities in abundance, but they were lacking among the cataloging staff except for the department head. The group identified considerable duplicative effort; the Webmaster and her staff manually input the title and other information into the SQL database, maintained the descriptive data, and kept the URL current. The entire process of cataloging a title took place separately and by different personnel; the only interconnection was communication about a title's URL from the Webmaster to the cataloger.

The quality of information provided to the user was also a major focus of the discussion. The group discussed what users want, what the Libraries provide, and how far the Libraries could go in response to user desires. Opinion was divided, with the Web proponents arguing that a point and click list was what users wanted; this list (actually lists because of the separate Serials Solutions list) seemed fine to them. Proponents of the OPAC stressed that the OPAC was systematic, standards-based, format-inclusive, accessible via the Web or telnet, can specify formats and locations, can handle initial articles, provides multiple access points of all kinds and offers keyword searching in its Web version. The group considered generating the SQL database from the OPAC. Various complex scenarios between selectors, catalogers and the Webmaster were envisioned and discarded. Some discussions began to lead toward almost total replication of the OPAC in the SQL database. At this point the whole enterprise took on an air of the ridiculous.

In April 2002, the group received a memo from the Chair of the Libraries' Online Public Interface Committee requesting that e-journals be removed from the Webpage and that access to them be provided through the OPAC. In the memo, public service personnel (including user education librarians)–not catalogers–expressed a preference for the OPAC! The memo stated: "These suggestions come from our committee members' extensive contact with patrons and their searching behaviors. We have observed the many misconceptions that they have in their mental models of our systems, and the difficulties that they have distinguishing a database from a journal while searching for information." Users didn't understand the e-journals database. They had a tendency to search article titles rather than journal titles and were confused by the three different sources of information. Searching the SQL database was fraught with difficulties. For example, if one wished to locate the journal *L'Evolution française*, doing a keyword search on "l'evolution" or "evolution" produced nothing, whereas searching "l [space] evolution" would retrieve the title. Who would think of searching this way? An option to deal with this situation for French titles was tried and dropped because it caused other problems.

With the weight of public service opinion added to the view that the OPAC was best suited to provide access to e-journals, the path became much clearer. We were able to move quite quickly to the decision to refer users to the OPAC for e-journals.

MAKING IT WORK

The SUNY Albany University Libraries currently use the Geac ADVANCE library management system (version 6.8) and plan to migrate to the Ex Libris ALEPH system July 1, 2004. The process described here is system independent. The SUNY Albany University Libraries had decided not to catalog electronic resources. That had changed by the late 1990s. Nevertheless, few e-journals had actually been cataloged despite the fact that a policy had been in place since Dec. 1998 stating that electronic resources would be cataloged (see Appendix for current policy). In the fall of 2001, a project was begun to catalog all electronic resources then available through the Libraries' Website, including those provided by aggregators. At the time, the Cataloging Services Department consisted of three and a half librarians (the department head, a serials cataloger, a monograph cataloger, and a half time person devoted to Special Collections) and four paraprofessionals (three monograph copy catalogers and one serials copy cataloger). None had time for additional duties cataloging the e-journals. It was clearly not a one-person job.

It became an "all hands on board" situation. Staff members who had previously never seen a serials record–or, at best, knew enough to send it to the serials cataloger or serials copy cataloger–were now enlisted to catalog the e-journals backlog. The serials cataloger trained the four copy catalogers in Cataloging Services, as well as a librarian in Acquisitions Services (the Electronic Resources Coordinator) to catalog e-journals. She also trained clerical staff and student assistants to add URLs and holdings for e-journals to existing records of the same titles in other formats.

The one-record approach was used for a number of reasons: (1) past practice had been to do this in cases in which the Libraries held both print and microform; (2) ease and timeliness in cataloging–rather than downloading an electronic resources record from OCLC (or having to perform original cataloging), the existing print record could be modified to reflect the online access; and (3) there was a general consensus that multiple records would lead to confusion on the part of the user.

While there was some concern that this might cause difficulties if it became necessary to delete records for a particular aggregator, Cataloging Services and Library Systems were confident that this could be dealt with either by using scripts and/or manual modifications. For journals that had one or more title change, all records for successive titles are updated to show electronic holdings, regardless of whether the Libraries held the previous or later titles in print.

The serials cataloger first identified which of the aggregator databases needed to be cataloged and the titles that were included. The aggregators included Project Muse, JSTOR, and ScienceDirect. Workforms and macros were developed for each of the aggregator databases. Staff and students were each given a list of the titles in an aggregator (or a portion) and instructed to add fields to the existing print bibliographic record to reflect the online access (including adding an 856 with the URL and holdings) or to download the electronic resources record from OCLC and alter the record to conform to local practices. After these aggregators were cataloged, other titles were cataloged including titles accessed directly from the publisher and/or journal Website. By February 2002, when most of the titles in the SQL database had been cataloged, over 2,150 titles were available via the OPAC with full bibliographic records.

As new titles were activated, they were cataloged on a rush basis. This was to emphasize the need to provide rapid access to these intangible titles and to avoid the temptation to concentrate solely on new print resources which continued to enter the department at a steady rate and take up physical space. By the end of July 2002, all titles included in BioOne, Catchword, IDEAL, Ingenta, JSTOR, Project Muse, and ScienceDirect were cataloged, along with a significant number of independent titles. Over the five months, 363 new titles had been cataloged, bringing the total number on the OPAC to just over 2,500 titles.

In mid-August, the Serials Solutions report was converted into a combination of brief bibliographic records or online holdings attached to existing print records. The list was converted into a set of MARC records using the Library of Congress's MARCMaker program (available at http://www.loc.gov/marc/makrbrkr.html). These brief records were loaded into the OPAC database using a script that matched them against existing records based on ISSN; the information from each aggregator was put in its own location record. Brief records were created for those that did not match and were enhanced with a workform that included some extra descriptive data (tags such as a 516, 530 and a 655 for electronic journals). Once the first brief record was created, any additional instances of that title from other aggregators loaded onto these brief records unless ISSN were not present, in which case duplicate brief records were created.

In total, over 19,000 URL links for e-journals were added to the OPAC. Suddenly it became possible to locate all formats of any journal title on one OPAC record. In late August, 2002, e-journals were removed from the Libraries' Website and users were given a link to the OPAC instead. The Serials Solutions list was removed from the Website as well.

The project to catalog the e-journals was the result of tremendous effort on the part of staff of all levels. We have not found serials cataloging, even cataloging of e-journals, to be so difficult that clerical staff, paraprofessionals, and student assistants cannot do the work if it is defined carefully, training and documentation are provided, and truly complex problems are filtered out for experienced serials catalogers.

In August 2002, an Electronic Resources Librarian joined the department and was quickly incorporated into the process. One of his first responsibilities was to begin cleaning up duplicate records (either brief records that failed to match against an existing full record or multiple brief records). Over 500 were cleaned up in September and October.

On an ongoing basis the Electronic Resources Librarian runs a Perl script against the bimonthly Serials Solutions file to determine added and deleted titles. The ISSNs for new titles are given to a Lead Programmer Analyst in Library Systems who runs the list against the OPAC. This determines if the title is already in the database. Those that match simply have the new aggregator URL added to the existing record. For new titles, records are downloaded from OCLC and the URLs are added to these records. Records for titles that have been removed from the Serials Solutions list are adjusted by deleting either the URL (if other formats remain) or the entire record (if no other formats remain). The adds and deletes are primarily handled by the Electronic Resources Librarian and three clerical staff. On the average, a bimonthly update is completed within one week.

E-journals records have undergone a number of subsequent cleanup projects since the initial Serials Solutions load. The primary project standardized where the holdings information was located. During the initial cataloging, holdings notes were placed in a static 866 field, along with some additional information. The brief records created from the Serials Solutions load had their holdings in the 856 $3, thus displaying in a separate place. The brief records also had a static 866 field, but this only referred the patron to check the holdings in the 856 $3. Library

Systems was able to create a script that moved the 866 holdings note to the 856 $3 for manually cataloged records and a global change was run to convert the old 866 with holdings to the new generic 866 fields. The new holdings note reads "ONLINE Check availability." In a further enhancement, a note reading "Available from [aggregator name]" was added for each aggregator URL. These were also scripted by Library Systems based upon the 856 $u and were placed in the 856 $z (see Figures 1-3 for examples of brief and full OPAC displays and the associated MARC coding for the brief e-journal records).

Search qualifiers were added for "Journals–Print & Online" and "Online Resources (Databases, E-Texts, Online Journals). Hotlinks to the full-text were placed on the brief display screen in order to speed access to the full-text. At the present time, user authentication occurs when a person links to a given electronic resource using EZProxy software. We expect to discuss the pros and cons of proxying the entire OPAC in the near future.

FIGURE 1. Brief E-Journals Record (Brief Display)

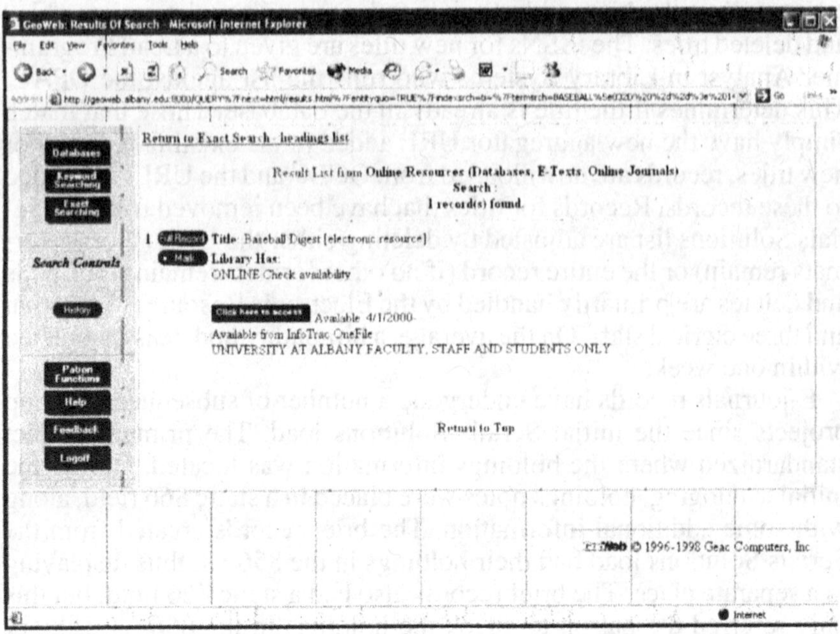

FIGURE 2. Brief E-Journals Record (Full Display)

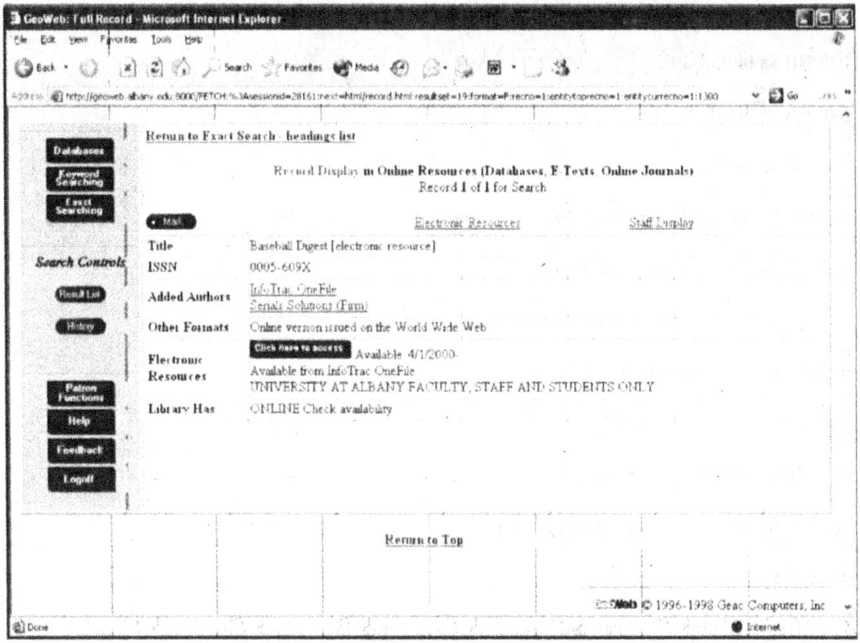

In July 2003, the Libraries will implement Ex Libris's SFX software. This is currently seen as a supplement to, rather than a replacement of, e-journal records in the OPAC. An SFX button will appear in the OPAC and its presence will cause the "blue box" links to be suppressed for those that are available in the SFX KnowledgeBase. The hope is that between title access via the OPAC and the coverage and embargo information in the SFX KnowledgeBase, our users will have an up-to-date and useful source for their information needs.

Directing users to the OPAC for access to e-journals has worked well, even though proponents of the Web-based list remain somewhat unconvinced. Is it perfect? Of course not. Oddities and glitches remain, but that is life with OPACs and the constant change involved with e-journals.

Fallout? There has been little. User education librarians are enthusiastic about the new method of accessing e-journals. A brief survey was conducted in winter 2003 to gather input regarding the design of the Li-

FIGURE 3. MARC Record (Bibliographic and 856)

008 020812uuuuuuuuuxx p u|| uundud

022 BB $a 0005-609X

040 BB $a NAIU $c NAIU

099 BB $a WWW

245 00 $a Baseball Digest $h [electronic resource].

516 BB $a Text (electronic journal)

530 BB $a Online version issued on the World Wide Web.

655 B7 $a Electronic journals $2 lsch

710 2B $a InfoTrac OneFile

710 2B $a Serials Solutions (Firm)

866 BB $a ONLINE $i Check availability

908 BB $p *PER*

856 41 $3 4/1/2000- $z Available from InfoTrac OneFile $z UNIVERSITY AT ALBANY

FACULTY, STAFF AND STUDENTS ONLY $u

http://silver.ulib.albany.edu:2048/login?url=http://infotrac.galegroup.com/itweb/albanyu?db=IT

OF

braries' main page. Anecdotal evidence was presented by proponents of the Web-based journals list among the Libraries' faculty saying that "some" respondents wished for the return of the list. No numbers were presented. It was decided that some people may like the ease of such a list without understanding its shortcomings. The Library Policy Group, consisting of the Libraries assistant directors, responded vigorously, stating that we had taken the list down for good reason and saw no reason to reinstate something that was long, unwieldy, cumbersome, unnecessary, and misrepresentative. The group briefly considered feeding such a list from the OPAC database, but it quickly became clear that doing so would simply replicate the OPAC records and would add nothing of value.

There are those who argue that users are best served by offering differing modes of access to satisfy different information seeking styles. Providing a Web list of e-journals is not equivalent to the OPAC. Briscoe et al. state that providing access to online resources via an OPAC *and* a Website "actually benefits users by increasing the number of paths leading to information."[10] We disagree because the two paths are not equally reliable and accurate. Some functional differences between OPAC and Web lists for accessing e-journals have been described above. A Web list is greatly limited and misleading and does a disservice to those who use it. Users who like such a list may not know what is missing from it. Giving them what they want, in this case, is certainly a disservice. Secondly, a Web list generated from the OPAC that offers only selective OPAC functionality is, likewise, misleading and incomplete. A Web list generated from the OPAC, if it offers all the functionality of the OPAC, will simply *be* the OPAC in another place. There is no advantage in this.

Now that all e-journals are cataloged, the OPAC has become the master database for them. Extracts from it feed the master URL database, which is still used as a single source for linking by bibliographers and others. This is one bridge we have not been able to cross even though, as Herrera and Aldana point out, using the OPAC as the central repository for URLs is more efficient than creating divergent databases.[11]

Discussions about the value of that database and its relationship to the OPAC continue and are complex, but the primacy of the OPAC as the master database for all information provided by the Libraries is secure. The policy is to catalog *all* resources selected for the Libraries collections. We have not yet cataloged all free Web sites to which the Libraries provide access. Given the success of the massive e-journals cataloging program, these too will be done soon.

NOTES

1. Chuck Hamaker, "The Rules Have Changed: Library Catalogs and Internet Resources," *The Charleston Advisor* 1, no. 1 (1999): 38.
2. Ibid.
3. Mary D. Bevis and John-Bauer Graham, "The Evolution of an Integrated Electronic Journals Collection," *The Journal of Academic Librarianship* 24, no. 2 (2003): 118.
4. Karen S. Calhoun and William J. Kara, "Aggregation or Aggravation? Optimizing Access to Full-Text Journals," *ALCTS-Newsletter (Online)* 11, no. 1 (2000).
5. Ibid.

6. Yiu-On Li and Shirley W. Leung, "Computer Cataloging of Electronic Journals in Unstable Aggregator Databases: The Hong Kong Baptist University Library Experience," *LRTS* 45, no. 4 (2001).

7. Gail Herrera and Lynda Aldana, "Integrating Electronic Resources into the Library Catalog: A Collaborative Approach," *portal: Libraries and the Academy* 1, no. 3 (2001): 245.

8. Kay Johnson and Maribeth Manoff, "The Report of the Death of the Catalog is Greatly Exaggerated" (workshop presented at the annual meeting of the North American Serials Interest Group, College of William and Mary, Williamsburg, VA, June 2002), http://www.nasig.org/proceedings/2002/workshop21.html

9. Georgia Briscoe, Karen Selden and Cheryl Rae Nyberg, "The Catalog vs. the Home Page? Best Practices in Connecting to Online Resources," *Law Library Journal* 95, no. 2 (2003): 159.

10. Ibid., 173.

11 Herrera and Aldana, 245.

APPENDIX

Policy and Procedures for Cataloging Electronic Resources

Cataloging Services Department
Policy for Electronic Resources
Last revised: April 15, 2003

Electronic Resources Routinely Cataloged:

1. Electronic resources that have paid subscriptions, whether it is a direct purchase or available through a consortium.
2. Electronic resources that are available free as part of a paid print subscription.
3. Free Internet resources selected by bibliographers or other staff members with collection development responsibilities.
4. When possible, if the University Libraries has a resource in print format and gains electronic access, the electronic access will be added to the print bibliographic record.

URL Maintenance

On a monthly basis, Library Systems will run a link-checking program against the OPAC. Broken links that are not federal government documents (resources classified J 85 . . .) will be sent to the Cataloging Services Department for problem solving. Federal government document links needing problem solving will be sent to the Government Documents Department.

Priority of Electronic Resources Cataloging

Electronic resources shall be considered "rush" cataloging and of the highest priority, second only to "rush" print materials.

Extraneous Electronic Resources

URLs to such resources as table of contents, personal Webpages, etc., will be removed from the bibliographic record. Catalogers will first examine the resource to make sure that the resource is extraneous.

Use of Vendor-Supplied Records and/or Brief Records

As appropriate, the Cataloging Services Department will either load vendor-supplied bibliographic records or create brief records for electronic resources.

PROCEDURES FOR CATALOGING ELECTRONIC RESOURCES

General

Cataloging Online Electronic Resources: General policies; single record approach; original and copy cataloging; brief cataloging; cloning a print record.

MARC 856 Guidelines: Description of subfields; failed links; multiple URLs on one copy set.

Constructing MARC 856 for URLs: How to construct an 856 for proxied, unproxied, free, and restricted titles, including specific monographic series.

MARC 5XX Order for Electronic Resources: Order of notes fields according to Olsen and CONSER.

Creating an ONLINE Loc Copy: How to create an ONLINE loc copy manually or with workforms.

ADVANCE Workforms for Online Electronic Resources: Chart of available bibliographic and holdings workforms.

E-Journals

Policy for URLs for Print Periodicals/Serials: When to retain, add, or remove a URL from a record for a print periodical or serial.

Processing Aggregators, Platforms . . .: How to augment print and download online periodical/serial records.

Copy Cataloging of Electronic Journals: Tag-by-tag instructions for editing downloaded online periodical/serial records.

Summary Holdings Statements (MARC 856$3): How to format an 856 $3.

Adding Another URL: How to add a second URL to a record.

Aggregators, Platforms Needing 710 . . .: List of platforms, etc. needing 710 and 856 $z.

Available from . . .: List of publishers for 856 $z Available from . . . note.

Title Change Diagram: Title change examples that show the relationship between the 130/245 and the 780/785.

Monographs

Policy for URLs for Monographs: A current list of titles and categories.

Procedures for Adding URLs to Monograph Records: How to augment a print record to include online access.

Constructing MARC 856 for URLs: How to construct an 856 for proxied, unproxied, free, and restricted titles, including specific monographic series.

Procedures for Deleting URLs from Monographic Records: How to delete the URL and augment the 530 field.

Workflow for Electronic Version of a Print Monograph: Workflow between Acquisitions/Cataloging/Webmaster for new electronic monographs

CONTRIBUTORS' NOTES

Timothy Gatti is Head, Cataloging Services Department, University Libraries ULB34, State University of New York at Albany, 1400 Washington Avenue, Albany NY 12222 (E-mail: tgatti@uamail.albany.edu). Heather S. Miller is Assistant Director for Technical Services and Systems, University Libraries ULB34, State University of New York at Albany, 1400 Washington Avenue, Albany NY 12222 (E-mail: hmiller@uamail. albany.edu).

Expose Yourself to Electronic Journals

Jill Emery
Claire Ginn
Dan Tonkery

Presenters

Kevin Petsche

Recorder

SUMMARY. Libraries have found that trying to force the print journal workflow model onto the electronic journal world is unsuccessful. In two sessions, the presenters attempted to reflect the point of view of end users, publishers, and librarians as they laid out their view of the current environment and offered suggestions for managing electronic journals in the future. After presentations, the sessions were opened for comments, questions, and discussion from the audience. *[Article copies available for a fee from The Haworth Document Delivery Service: 1-800-HAWORTH. E-mail address: <docdelivery@haworthpress.com> Website: <http://www.HaworthPress.com>]*

Each presenter opened with a short description of an aspect of the current electronic journals environment, after which the audience was given a chance to respond and pose questions about the presenters' ideas.

[Haworth co-indexing entry note]: "Expose Yourself to Electronic Journals." Petsche, Kevin. Co-published simultaneously in *The Serials Librarian* (The Haworth Information Press, an imprint of The Haworth Press, Inc.) Vol. 46, No. 1/2, 2004, pp. 99-105; and: *Serials in the Park* (ed: Patricia S. French, and Richard Worthing) The Haworth Information Press, an imprint of The Haworth Press, Inc., 2004, pp. 99-105. Single or multiple copies of this article are available for a fee from The Haworth Document Delivery Service [1-800-HAWORTH, 9:00 a.m. - 5:00 p.m. (EST). E-mail address: getinfo@haworthpress.com].

http://www.haworthpress.com/web/SER
Digital Object Identifier: 10.1300/J123v46n01_11

Jill Emery laid out a succinct overview of the perspectives that librarians and end users currently have for electronic journals. She said that end users want information in electronic form and they want access to be easy and fast. They also want to be able to manipulate full-text (e.g., copy and paste) and they want it in a version that looks like print. Further, users want more uniformity in the appearance and use of interfaces.

The librarian perspective is similarly multifaceted. They want to provide as much content in electronic form as possible. In a case of "be careful of what you hope for," many content types are moved to electronic form, but the content types are now "serialized," which complicates bibliographic control. Librarians want to pay for access through subscription agents as well as have agents set up access. Unfortunately, many publishers want only direct subscriptions and/or require that titles be completely registered by the library. Librarians want seamless and intuitive linking between resources. They find that communication with vendors is slow at best. And they find that customization is possible if they agree to do it the way the vendor thinks that it should be done.

Further, workflows have become a complex patchwork of processes which are just a reaction to each different puzzling resource. Librarians keep redundant files in paper and electronic format for different audiences. Further, with all of the work of setting up and maintaining access, librarians find it difficult to give needed information to our users such as restrictions on licenses.

Claire Ginn talked about trends for electronic journal access from the publisher perspective and the consortia perspectives. The majority of titles are still tied to print except for non-core titles or those with stable online archives. Some small publishers, having seen large publishers successfully bundle their titles, are starting to form consortia in the hope of selling to library consortia; other small publishers have decided to forego offering deals to consortia.

While library consortia do not seem to be pursuing a wider variety of vendors, they are looking to maintain and strengthen relationships with existing vendors. Library consortia seek "economic breathability" by opting for one to two year agreements rather than three, asking for ILL permission, ability to archive, and multiple format pricing options. So far, there seems to be no standard for pricing models and one respondent to her survey said that no matter the model, the price seemed to be the same. The impact of document delivery on electronic journal subscriptions has been insignificant other than for non-core titles and ones that are high priced. Smaller institutions find it difficult to subsidize document delivery and some consortia are not renewing their contracts. It would seem that as document delivery gets quicker, it could become more of a factor.

Dan Tonkery began his discussion by articulating ideas with which most serial professionals would agree. One point was that e-journals are having a major impact on all players in the field–libraries, publishers, subscription agents, and end users. The number of journal titles available electronically continues to swell with no letup in sight. Delivery of content to the desktop is now an accepted service standard for users, as is the ability to link to the original title using the OpenURL protocol. Further, non-full-text databases that lack the ability to use this protocol will continue to see usage statistics drop.

From a publisher perspective, the current science/technology/mathematics titles have all moved to electronic format; other subject communities have done so to a lesser extent. Publishers are still largely in experimental mode regarding delivery systems and acquisition models. License agreements are the preferred tool for obtaining access and publishers are not willing to fight over copyright control. Also, most publishers lack the technical expertise to offer content in an e-format and outsource this functionality. Finally, publishers are shifting away from a free electronic access with a print subscription to other pricing models. Tonkery suggests that this model may not even exist in another three years.

From the library perspective, managing electronic journals is a complex and costly process. Costs have increased as much as tenfold in comparison to maintaining a print collection. Aspects of growing costs are represented in the resources needed to set up and maintain access, the renewal process, and provision of bibliographic control of e-journals. Some major universities are developing dedicated software to support the growing task of managing e-resources. Also, many integrated library system (ILS) vendors are responding to this situation by attempting to create separate modules that manage electronic resources, but they have not brought these to market yet. In addition, subscription agents have built systems to support managing these resources. Libraries will need these e-resource management tools standardized as quickly as possible, and the Digital Library Foundation is working on such standards.

Tonkery encapsulated the process of managing e-resources into what he calls the "E-Resources Life Cycle" (see Figure 1).

This representation shows the separate tasks that libraries must perform to manage electronic resources. The diagram is cyclical rather than

FIGURE 1. E-Resources Life Cycle

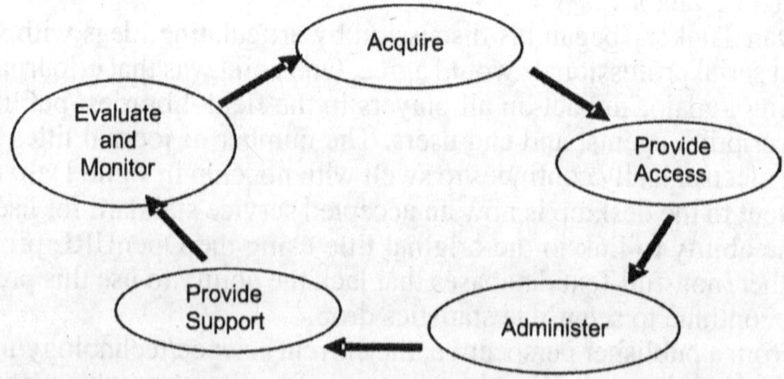

linear in nature to reflect that maintaining electronic resources often requires ongoing renewal and vigilance unlike their print counterparts. Further, Tonkery articulated a separate cycle that occurs within the life cycle at "Provide Access" stage (see Figure 2).

The tasks of license negotiation, license administration, e-resource registration, access support, maintenance and troubleshooting are inherent in the process of providing access. The management of e-resources is made more complex by the fact that each of these tasks is handled differently by each vendor.

Subscription agents have created *knowledgebases* to support these management tasks. A knowledgebase stores information regarding all e-resources. Such information includes how the resource is offered, where it is available, licensing information, registration procedures and technical support requirements.

Tonkery then gave a list of myths related to electronic resources that some librarians still believe. For example, some still believe that e-resources will solve serials budget crises or that supporting e-resources will require less technical service staff in the library than print materials do; they may think that Big Deal packages will save library costs and that shifting to e-journals will eliminate the need for monitoring of the collection (e.g., check-in). Library experience in the electronic environment has shown these notions to be untrue.

In fact, Tonkery argued, the reality of library experience is far different. He opined that never have so many worked so hard to make a ser-

FIGURE 2. Provide Access Stage

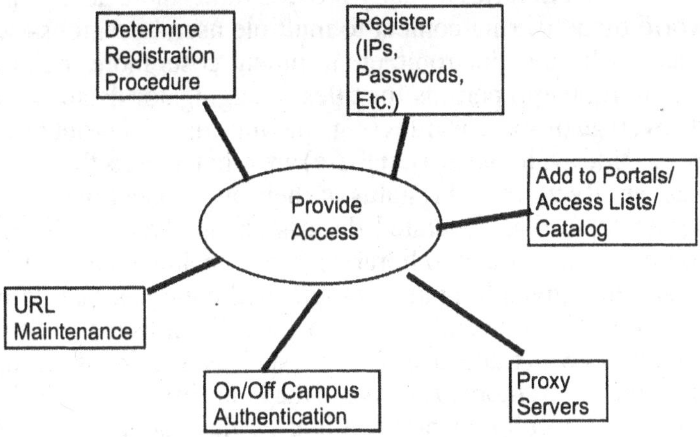

vice successful. Also, users now expect desktop delivery of content and usually want more than most libraries can afford or support. Further, most publishers are not set up to handle the volume of customer needs for acquisitions, renewals, and other service issues. And while publishers are not saving money by moving to electronic format, they do seem to be making money on licensing terms that require libraries to purchase content in multiple formats (print, electronic, archival, etc.) Tonkery concluded by saying that the benefits to libraries have been outstanding despite the expensive and time-consuming processes required to provide electronic content.

The presentation was then opened to the audience for comments and discussion. The topic that generated the most discussion revolved around the question of "How do we account for that for which we have paid?" There was a lot of interest in research and development being done to track the availability of online issues, which parallels the check-in process that is in place for print issues. It was noted that CONSER is investigating the level at which holdings should be created for e-resources. Another potential approach would be to develop a centralized registry that would list the availability of online content. It is interesting to ask exactly what we mean by access when we refer to the check-in procedure for print titles. It was argued that just because an issue was received does not necessarily mean that it is accessible, given the potential for thousands of patrons attempting to obtain the same, single issue. It was noted that libraries actually provide much more access in the online world by delivering content to multiple users' desktops– which is one reason why the electronic environment costs more than the print equivalent. Embargo periods for titles in aggregator databases and selected coverage of specific titles (e.g., having ten articles out of a total of 300 from a title available in a database) are other aspects that complicate libraries' ability to track the status of their own collections.

Another topic that generated discussion involved the licensing of electronic journal content to libraries. Many in attendance voiced frustration at being given long and complicated contracts that do more to protect publishers and vendors than to allow libraries the ability to provide their users with traditional services such as ILL. In response, libraries were urged to be more proactive in the licensing process. This would entail a change in culture whereby libraries view themselves as the customer, requiring publishers and vendors to meet their needs and not the other way around. Libraries were encouraged to add language to the licenses that would protect their interests and to delete language that would harm their interests. Also discussed were actions whereby vendors have tried pricing models that are unacceptable, and how libraries should refuse to sign such agreements. It was also mentioned that publishers should be held responsible for outages in access. But fear was expressed that tighter license control would be a two-way street, and that publishers would begin to shut down access to (and perhaps even seek damages from) libraries whose patrons violate the licenses. While acknowledging that it would be rare to find any institution that had not had access turned off for a violation of license (perceived or actual), all presenters agreed that publishers and vendors would probably not behave this way. The audience was reminded that libraries are viewed as being honest institutions and that vendors and publishers do not want to jeopardize relationships with customers, especially when the costs would be high and the potential financial benefit would be doubtful.

An overriding theme that came out of the discussion is that libraries now realize that electronic journals are beasts of a very different nature than their print counterparts–and the difference is only going to become greater as electronic journal content continues to evolve and become less like print. The introduction of the ability to link and to access to datasets associated with the research for an article is only the beginning of this new information resource. Libraries will need to continue to think differently about how they do things–discarding old practices that provide little or no benefit in an online environment and creating new practices that give end users access to the content that is needed.

RECORDER'S NOTE

I have quoted liberally from Mr. Tonkerey's PowerPoint presentation, from Ms. Emery's notes, and from Ms. Ginn's e-mails.

CONTRIBUTORS' NOTES

Jill Emery is Director of the Electronic Resources Program at the University of Houston. Claire Ginn is Vice-President of Content Sales at the Publishers Communication Group in Cambridge, Massachusetts. Dan Tonkery is Vice-President and Director of Business Development for EBSCO Information Services in Birmingham, AL. Kevin Petsche is the Electronic Journals Collection Manager at the Indiana University-Purdue University, Indianapolis (IUPUI) University Library.

The Digital Preservation Conundrum, Part 1

Abby Smith

Presenter

SUMMARY. Digital information is difficult to preserve for long-term access because of several factors: the dynamic nature of the content; the lack of libraries' clear rights and incentives to preserve content that is usually licensed; the effect of copyright extension on the roles and responsibilities for preservation; and the changing needs of the users. Several institutional responses to these challenges are discussed. *[Article copies available for a fee from The Haworth Document Delivery Service: 1-800-HAWORTH. E-mail address: <docdelivery@haworthpress.com> Website: <http://www.HaworthPress.com>]*

The topic Eileen Fenton and I have been asked to address is the digital preservation conundrum. Refreshing my memory of the precise meaning of the word by consulting with *The American Heritage Dictionary*, I find that a conundrum is "a paradoxical, insoluble, or difficult problem; a dilemma."[1]

Preserving digital information is, indeed, a dilemma and a paradox. It is by nature malleable, unfixed and unfixable, immaterial and without stable physical manifestation. The idea of preserving the virtually unpreservable forces us to make difficult choices between options that may seem equally inadequate at best.

[Haworth co-indexing entry note]: "The Digital Preservation Conundrum, Part 1." Smith, Abby. Co-published simultaneously in *The Serials Librarian* (The Haworth Information Press, an imprint of The Haworth Press, Inc.) Vol. 46, No. 1/2, 2004, pp. 107-113; and: *Serials in the Park* (ed: Patricia S. French, and Richard Worthing) The Haworth Information Press, an imprint of The Haworth Press, Inc., 2004, pp. 107-113. Single or multiple copies of this article are available for a fee from The Haworth Document Delivery Service [1-800-HAWORTH, 9:00 a.m. - 5:00 p.m. (EST). E-mail address: getinfo@haworthpress.com].

http://www.haworthpress.com/web/SER
Digital Object Identifier: 10.1300/J123v46n01_12

I would like to think, however, that the problem–going back to the dictionary definition–is difficult but not insoluble. And I would like to propose ways to define digital preservation as a problem that is difficult but not insoluble. (I will note in passing that the dictionary's first definition of conundrum is "a riddle in which a fanciful question is answered by a pun."[2] I only wish there were some humor and fancy in this subject. So far, I have found little.)

To be successful at preservation, one should have a clear idea of what to preserve, for whom, for what purpose, and for how long information is to be preserved. In the print world this has been hard enough, as we have learned so often that what seems of little research value to one generation may be highly prized by another. But I believe that getting any part of that equation right in the digital realm is particularly hard because of the paradoxes of digital content, organizational paradoxes, the legal and regulatory paradox, and the paradox of the user.

First, the *content paradox*: digital information is immaterial and it resists fixation. This sounds like quite a metaphysical statement, but the fact that digital information comes to us as 0's and l's, and has physical presence only when momentarily "instantiated," has serious implications for preservationists and archivists. The preservation model we know from print–to ensure access to information over time by preserving the medium on which that information is recorded–does not do here. Nor, for reasons that I will go into in a moment, does reformatting information fixed on a fragile medium–brittle paper, say, or wax cylinder–onto a more stable archival medium solve our problem.

That is because digital information is (usually) dynamic, easily changed, and designed to be updatable. What we think of as information or content is often produced on-the-fly by an interaction between a database and a query system–think of Weather.com, Amazon.com, or NewYorkTimes.com. How do you preserve or fix those information objects? The latter two examples at least would qualify as information resources that we would wish to include in one or more library or archival collections claiming to document important aspects of the early twenty-first century. We expect future users to want access to these kinds of dynamic sites. We can also expect that they will demand that information be archived in a way that makes it easily repurposable, a demand that flies in the face of traditional models of preservation.

What does this mean for serials librarians? To find out how complex that demand may be, let us look at a fairly banal and uncomplicated instance of current scholarly communication: a journal that is published electronically. It often comprises a series of different formats and digital objects, between the article text, the embedded executables or images within the articles, the table of contents, the list of editors, the advertisements that actually change from one distribution model to another, and so on. All of those are discrete elements that some researcher of the not-too-distant future will wish to see when they search the retrospective literature of the early twenty-first century, the era of digital incunables.

In academic journals there is also the crucial problem of fixing and preserving a chain of references that undergird an author's argument. Articles referred to by an author from another source may disappear over time, be taken down, migrate to a new site, or be absorbed by copyright-owning entities, such as a publisher, that allow linking only under certain conditions. Often, the underlying source for an author's assertion may reside in a database that itself changes over time, so that an article written in 2003 and consulted in 2013 may have embedded a reference to a database that has persisted for 10 years but is now substantively different from what it was in 2003. Lack of stable and authentic references undermines the deepest claims of scholarship for evidence-based proof. None of these current realities are amenable to the traditional solutions offered by the print-on-paper preservation paradigm.

There is one last problem that serials librarians are not called upon to solve, but which deeply affects the integrity of the work that they do: Whose job it is to preserve the underlying data for a scientific article? Libraries have traditionally declared secondary scientific literature to be their domain and responsibility. Now this preservation charge is threatened by the lack of corresponding responsible players in the information landscape who declare long-term stewardship of primary scientific sources of information to be their domain.

This takes us to the *organizational paradox*: libraries license electronic texts, by and large, and do not own them. I will not spend much time on this, as librarians are already more intimately knowledgeable about this than they wish to be. But to point out the obvious, it is hard to identify incentives for libraries to preserve electronic information that they do not own and do not have some future control over. Although some publishers and libraries have taken–in good faith–some measures to address that issue by giving licensed text to institutions on CD-ROMs, these are half-measures at best. CD-ROMs are not preservation formats. Their sole purpose is to ensure continuity of access in the short run to materials that were licensed at one time.

The library mission to preserve has worked in the past because it was legally, physically, and economically feasible for them to do so. Libraries bought stable physical objects–paper things–and with the acquisition of those imprints came the legal exemption from copyright monopolies, allowing libraries to copy information to preserve it. Furthermore, major up-front investments in preservation were rare. More shelving, better environments, disaster preparedness and recovery plans–all these things were costs that could be (and too often were) deferred. In the case of special collections, even creating bibliographic and inventory controls has been too easy to put off indefinitely without seriously jeopardizing the physical life of the collection items. This is not true of digital information. With digital information, the preservation mantra seems to be "use it or lose it." That is a serious problem for collecting institutions that are working to ensure the integrity of the historical, intellectual, and cultural record. Low-use materials by definition die a premature death.

Where does this leave us? How deep and true is our mission to preserve? Is it deep enough to find wholly new economic models to meet preservation demands up-front, even if this means close collaboration with each other and even with commercial producers? Like it or not, this is absolutely necessary if we are to resolve the *legal/regulatory paradox*: the only ones with unambiguous rights to preserve in the current digital copyright regime are the copyright owners, not the institutions that society normally relies upon to preserve the record.

The copyright owners–in many cases the creators themselves–are too often either oblivious of the need to preserve, or simply not in the business of preserving. Given the short life span of digital information, the preservation of digital media falls to creators, publishers, or distributors by default, and those whose mission is the long-term preservation of the historical record do not gain access to those materials, even for preservation purposes, until the material passes into the public domain. Since copyright has been extended to be several times longer than the life cycle of digital information, that content is likely to be dead on arrival or to have simply vanished. In this environment, then, preservation must be attended to by *both* sectors–the owning and the preserving. Libraries and publishers must work together to determine which parts of the digital object life cycle are best handled by which entity, in full cooperation and transparency, with respect both for rights of various owners and for the integrity of the historical record, for the private good and the public. This means that publishers actually have an incentive for developing a partnership with a preserving institution. It would even argue for developing business incentives, such as tax breaks or credits, to those entities that forge such partnerships for preservation on behalf of the greater public good.

There are several publishers who are now experiencing difficulties in preserving the integrity of their online files because of legal liability issues they may face. When a publisher is forced to change or take down information, how can they find a safe harbor for the material in order to keep the historical record intact? We should be working with publishers and legal experts to develop ways that libraries can offer a safe harbor for "purged material" that keeps both libraries and publishers free from legal liability. That is only one instance of the many reasons that libraries must work with publishers and other distributors to secure digital content now, even if it comes with uncomfortable restrictions on near-term access.

And finally, to the *user paradox*: our traditional academic users have changing expectations of information, making it very hard to meet those expectations. Some scholars, particularly in certain scientific disciplines, are doing a lot of self-publishing on the Web, managing their own pre-prints. Taking the scholars behind the Public Library of Science as an extreme example, there are many who are trying to cut out any middleman who may impose some fee for the services they provide, declaring scientific information to be a public good, and proposing shifting the financial burden of publishing to the author. That may be a fairly typical set of user expectations. Whether these costs will be borne by authors and will truly cover the costs of publishing and preserving over the long term remains to be seen. But clearly we have at least one set of important users who are prepared to completely overturn publishing models that we are used to. That has had and will have serious consequences for preservation, because it is unlikely that they have thought through and planned for the curation and long-term preservation of the record they are publishing.

There are other scholars–very many, in fact–who are simply posting their work on their Websites, thinking of its longevity only when they are not actively adding to or using the digital objects and want to pass them off to the library for preservation. This new-model scholarship is rapidly evolving, and it will take careful observation on the part of librarians to determine what is most valuable about these sites. Now more than ever, librarians need to stay close to the faculty and track their changing behavior. And that is harder than ever because fewer and fewer of them need to come physically into the library to use the library. The best preservation decisions now, at least those made in this early development phase of digital publishing, will be those most informed by the user.

What are the institutional responses to the digital preservation conundrum? There are some significant research institutions such as the University of California and MIT that are capturing a portion of the born-digital scholarship created on their campuses and developing institutional repositories to manage that material. The incentive for becoming campus-wide managers of faculty output is clear and unimpeachable: they are taking responsibility for what they view as institutional information assets, in much the same mode they take care of the journals and books and gray literature that they have invested in for decades. However, the world of scholarly publishing is not divided into physical and proprietary domains of universities, but rather into disciplines that transcend legal and geographical entities such as universities. So the continuity of MIT' s output, say, may be secured, but not that of any given discipline. This is a start, but even were the institutional repository model to be extended to all the universities that can afford such an infrastructure, that would not solve the problem of preserving digital scholarship, which happens in labs, colleges, independent research centers, and so forth.

Other emerging players in the digital preservation landscape are federal agencies, from the National Libraries of Medicine and Agriculture to the Library of Congress and the National Archives. The two former libraries have an explicit mandate to preserve a significant portion of the literature in their domains, and they are making rapid progress in defining the standards and best practices they need to follow, in addition to capturing and securing at-risk content. The Library of Congress has been authorized and funded by Congress to develop and build a networked infrastructure to support the preservation of digital content. They will focus on the usual flow of materials coming into the Library of Congress, that is, those that are often deposited for copyright, and build a network of committed preservation partners to shoulder the burden of collecting, curating, and preserving them. The partners will no doubt develop their own areas of specialty, leaving the Library of Congress to assume custody of those materials unlikely to come into, say, research libraries, such as the latest Hollywood feature films or electronic papers of the Supreme Court Justices. This means that the research library community should look to take primary responsibility for academically oriented publications, such as the secondary literatures of the disciplines.

A final player that is emerging on the digital horizon is the so-called trusted or trustworthy third-party archive. The premier example of this is JSTOR, an access and preservation service well known to serials librarians. As JSTOR moves from preserving print journals to converting them into digital files for distribution and preservation, they are also looking ahead to the day when those very journals will be born-digital only. Eileen Fenton will delve more deeply into the planning that JSTOR is undertaking to secure the future of its publishing partners' digital journals.

Looking ahead to the day when most preservation decisions will concern chiefly those materials born digital and born to change, so to speak, I think the only way to resolve the conundrum of digital preservation is to understand not only the dynamic nature of the information, but also the interaction between the user and that information, which is itself dynamic. The preservation paradigm will shift from being collection-centered and seeking fixity to becoming user-centered and seeking to preserve change and mutability.

NOTES

1. American Heritage Dictionary, s.v. "conundrum."
2. Ibid.

CONTRIBUTOR'S NOTE

Abby Smith is Director of Programs at the Council on Library and Information Resources.

The Digital Preservation Conundrum, Part 2: Preservation and Electronic-Archiving

Eileen Gifford Fenton

Presenter

INTRODUCTION

As those familiar with JSTOR know, JSTOR's mission is to help the scholarly community take advantage of advances in information technologies. Our initial focus is to create and maintain a trusted digital archive of the full back runs of academic journals. Through the development and enhancement of this searchable, interdisciplinary collection, our objective is to help all participants in the scholarly community–libraries and publishers, faculty and students–to be more productive, while simultaneously reducing systemwide costs and increasing convenience.

JSTOR is committed to maintaining journals–whether originally print or electronic–for the long term. The need to develop a way to ensure the longevity of electronic resources has become increasingly obvious and urgent as scholars, librarians and publishers have increasingly come to prefer the electronic format. JSTOR launched its Electronic-Archiving Initiative in January 2003 in response to this need and in recognition of the unique preservation challenges digital resources raise. The purpose of this initiative, known informally as *E-Archive*, is to develop the organizational elements necessary to ensure the long-term preservation and access of electronic scholarly resources. As we begin our work we are confronting some of the issues that Abby highlighted in her remarks.

[Haworth co-indexing entry note]: "The Digital Preservation Conundrum, Part 2: Preservation and Electronic-Archiving." Fenton, Eileen Gifford. Co-published simultaneously in *The Serials Librarian* (The Haworth Information Press, an imprint of The Haworth Press, Inc.) Vol. 46, No. 1/2, 2004, pp. 115-119; and: *Serials in the Park* (ed: Patricia S. French, and Richard Worthing) The Haworth Information Press, an imprint of The Haworth Press, Inc., 2004, pp. 115-119. Single or multiple copies of this article are available for a fee from The Haworth Document Delivery Service [1-800-HAWORTH, 9:00 a.m. - 5:00 p.m. (EST). E-mail address: getinfo@haworthpress.com].

http://www.haworthpress.com/web/SER
Digital Object Identifier: 10.1300/J123v46n01_13

The challenges and questions raised by the long-term preservation and access of electronic scholarly resources are many. What content should be preserved? How should this material be preserved? What are the technical requirements of a system preserving digital resources? What are the most efficient workflows? What are the appropriate data integrity controls? The list of practical questions is long. In this paper I would like to step away from the "how to" questions and focus instead on the less frequently examined but extremely important "why" questions. It is only through understanding the preservation motivations revealed by these "why" questions that we can hope to address the most challenging "how" question of all: How will preservation of digital resources be paid for?

Today I would like to discuss some of the basic assumptions regarding the preservation of print resources, to consider how these do or don't apply to electronic scholarly resources, and to weigh possible implications for sharing the costs of digital preservation. Because our time is limited, I will necessarily draw a simplified view of preservation, but I trust that even this brief look at the issues will be helpful. I am pleased to have the chance to share my thoughts with you, but Abby and I value the opportunity to hear from you even more. We welcome your comments and questions as we go, and we look forward to a good discussion at the end of our formal presentations.

PRESERVATION: THE PRINT REALM

The most basic assumption regarding the preservation of print resources is: *preservation is very important*. Well, yes, of course, it is, but it is worth asking, why? Why do libraries preserve print materials? Libraries engage in preservation not for its own sake or in a vacuum but rather because it supports the library's mission to meet the information needs of the local community. In the print realm, a library can meet the community's needs only by purchasing and locally holding a copy of the print resource. As long as this print resource persists, the information need of the community is met and it is, therefore, in the library's interest to extend the life of the print object as long as is practical. Local ownership and local access are all very tightly bound together in the context of preserving print resources. Without owning and preserving a local copy of a printed resource, a library cannot provide access to the information it carries.

The second assumption to examine today is: *preservation is more than what happens in the basement*. Virtually all of the preservation departments I have encountered have been rather modestly sized units housed in even more modest quarters, typically in the basement of the library. These modest settings suggest a rather limited range of activities, but I do not believe that preservation is truly limited in this way. Inspired by Abby, I also consulted a lexicon aid–dictionary.com to be precise–and I found five very helpful definitions of "preserve" that, taken together, are highly relevant to today's discussion.[1] These are:

1. To maintain in safety from injury, peril, or harm; protect
2. To keep in perfect or unaltered condition; maintain unchanged
3. To keep or maintain intact
4. To prepare for future use
5. To prevent from decaying or spoiling

As a whole, these definitions describe very nicely the effort that a library extends in order to care for its collection–all of its collection, not just the tiny percentage of the collection that might receive formal preservation attention (i.e., in the basement). Though the specialized preservation treatments that selected items receive are very important, a library expends great effort to extend the life of and care for the entire body of its collection. In this sense, the whole range of activities a library engages in order to care for its collections should be understood as preservation.

When preservation is understood in this broader way, it becomes clear that a significant infrastructure investment has been made by the library and also by the parent institution in order to support the longevity of the printed resources needed by the community. This infrastructure investment includes miles of shelving, multiple buildings, complex physical plant systems, and costly real estate. This investment is not made to support narrowly-defined preservation but rather to support the broad educational mission of the parent institution by making it possible for the library to play its role as information provider.

PRESERVATION: THE DIGITAL REALM

Now we have to ask whether these assumptions are valid in the world of digital resources. As in the world of print, the most basic assumption is: *preservation is very important*. When we again ask why, the answer parallels the world of print in many ways. Electronic resources must be preserved because scholars rely upon the information and knowledge developed by earlier generations. If we are to ensure that each generation can continue to build on the progress of those who have gone before, we must ensure that the scholarly record is preserved. As scholarly progress is increasingly recorded electronically, the need to preserve electronic resources in order to avoid a damaging gap in the record of scholarly achievement has become quite real and pressing.

This leads us to a second assumption worth examining: *for electronic materials, ownership and preservation and access are no longer linked as they are in the world of print resources.* As Abby and others have noted, a library does not typically purchase an electronic resource; these resources are "rented" or licensed instead. This shift from local ownership to licensing has important implications for the preservation of electronic resources. For print materials, a library could fulfill its mission to provide for the information needs of its community only through local ownership and local stewardship. This local stewardship required and led naturally to the development of a significant infrastructure. In the world of licensed resources, however, a library no longer must own and store locally electronic resources in order to meet the information needs of the community it supports. Because these materials are not held locally, neither the library nor the parent institution is compelled to make the same kind of infrastructure investment as with print materials. The link between local ownership and preservation and access is broken.

IMPLICATIONS FOR INFRASTRUCTURE

Though the motivation to develop a local, complex infrastructure may no longer be present in the world of licensed electronic resources, the *need* for this infrastructure is quite real and is becoming urgent. Just like their print counterparts, electronic resources cannot be maintained for the long term except within the safe confines of a supporting infrastructure. For electronic resources, this infrastructure includes sophisticated technical systems, staff to care for the necessary hardware and software, workflow processes and controls to safely add materials into a digital archive, and a business model that ensures sufficient revenues to support the work of the archive.

To date, this infrastructure does not exist, although the urgency of its development seems to be increasingly clear. Developing this infrastructure raises many challenges, but perhaps the most important of these is cost sharing. If we agree that electronic resources can be preserved only within the safe confines of an infrastructure designed to meet the needs of these materials, this may suggest something about how the costs of this preservation task might be shared. Infrastructure development is not funded from the library preservation budget, but is instead shared broadly within the parent institution or in some cases across a network of institutions with a shared mission or goal.

A dialogue about the best ways to develop the infrastructure needed to ensure the long-term preservation and access of electronic resources is necessary if we are to answer the most pressing practical question of all: how will the preservation of electronic resources be paid for? It is only by answering this most basic question that we can move with confidence toward the development of a long-term trusted archive of digital resources. If we can succeed in developing this archive we will, to draw from dictionary.com once again, have "a repository for stored memories or information," which is surely the happiest and best resolution possible to the digital conundrum.[2]

NOTES

1. http://dictionary.reference.com/search?q=preserve (16 Oct. 2003).
2. http://dictionary.reference.com/search?q=archive (16 Oct. 2003).

CONTRIBUTOR'S NOTE

Eileen Gifford Fenton is Executive Director of JSTOR's Electronic-Archiving Initiative. For more information about JSTOR's Electronic-Archiving Initiative, please see www.jstor.org/about/earchive.html or contact Eileen Gifford Fenton, egfenton@jstor.org.

How Electronic Journals Are Changing Patterns of Use

Peter Boyce
Donald W. King
Carol Montgomery
Carol Tenopir

Presenters

SUMMARY. Surveys of faculty, students, and scientists in non-university settings over time show that journals and journal articles continue to be a valued resource. Scientists today read from a variety of sources including print journals, electronic journals, e-print servers, and full-text databases; the amounts for each vary with subject discipline and library collection decisions. Scientists expect the library to provide resources and electronic journals that are designed to meet the needs of their specific discipline. *[Article copies available for a fee from The Haworth Document Delivery Service: 1-800-HAWORTH. E-mail address: <docdelivery@haworthpress.com> Website: <http://www.HaworthPress.com>]*

INTRODUCTION

Electronic journals have become increasingly commonplace within the past decade. According to the *Ulrich's Periodicals Directory*, over 80 percent of today's active, peer-reviewed journals are now available

---

[Haworth co-indexing entry note]: "How Electronic Journals Are Changing Patterns of Use." Boyce, Peter et al. Co-published simultaneously in *The Serials Librarian* (The Haworth Information Press, an imprint of The Haworth Press, Inc.) Vol. 46, No. 1/2, 2004, pp. 121-141; and: *Serials in the Park* (ed: Patricia S. French, and Richard Worthing) The Haworth Information Press, an imprint of The Haworth Press, Inc., 2004, pp. 121-141. Single or multiple copies of this article are available for a fee from The Haworth Document Delivery Service [1-800-HAWORTH, 9:00 a.m. - 5:00 p.m. (EST). E-mail address: getinfo@haworthpress.com].

http://www.haworthpress.com/web/SER
Digital Object Identifier: 10.1300/J123v46n01_14

in some digital form. A few of these are only electronic with no print equivalent, but more are electronic journals that replicate print versions or add additional information and features to what is available in a print version. Selected articles from journals are also available in full-text databases from aggregators such as ProQuest, Ovid, Factiva, InfoTrac, and from individual journals on a pay-per-view basis. Readers in some disciplines also obtain scholarly articles from e-print servers such as arXiv.org, institutional repositories based on the Open Archives Initiative, or directly from authors' Websites. Archives such as these are commonly called electronic journals but in reality are selective repositories of articles rather than complete journals.

Libraries vary in the rate with which they have adopted online sources although most member libraries of the Association of Research Libraries (www.arl.org) show a steady increase in their use. Some institutions, such as Drexel University in Philadelphia[1] and the Coalition of Australian University Libraries, have formulated collection development policies that favor the licensing of electronic journals or full-text databases over the continued purchase of print journals.

We can expect that the widespread availability of electronic journals and electronic separate articles will have some effect on the reading patterns of scholars. This paper reports on surveys of reading patterns to show how electronic journal collections are changing reading patterns over time; it also analyzes which patterns are more a function of a specific work field or work place rather than the availability of electronic journals or electronic articles.

SELECTED LITERATURE REVIEWS

Reading patterns of scientists and social scientists through the 1990s are summarized in Tenopir and King[2] and King and Tenopir.[3] These two sources provide extensive literature reviews of reading and authoring studies and serve as background to the data presented here. The ongoing massive bibliography by Bailey[4] and a review article by Kling and Callahan[5] also point to many articles that discuss the development of electronic journals and their use. A report from the Council on Library and Information Resources (CLIR) discusses lessons learned from many usage studies of digital library resources.[6]

Although the studies differ in methods and their conclusions, many common findings emerge. Faculty, students, and scientists in non-university work settings prefer journal versions that allow them to do their work most efficiently and that are most convenient. For many, that means desktop access to electronic versions with PDF for printing. Medical practitioners seem to be an exception, still preferring personal print subscriptions.[7] There are other variations as well in reading patterns among different disciplines.[8] This paper discusses the specific reading patterns and how these patterns have changed with the widespread adoption of electronic journals and articles.

READING PATTERNS OVER TIME

In a recent article in *D-Lib* magazine, we examined three evolutionary phases in journal use.[9] We compared results of surveys of scientists and social scientists in a variety of work settings conducted by the authors over the last fourteen years to see how (or if) reading changed. The first evolutionary phase (*early phase*, 1990-1993) was a pre-Web world, where full-text databases of journal articles existed online or on CD-ROM, but only a very small percent of the total article readings by scientists and social scientists came from anything other than print journals. The second phase (the *evolving phase*) began in the late 1990s and continues today. It is marked by the availability of both print and electronic journals, with readings from print journals, electronic journals, and journal alternatives. We call the third time period the *advanced phase*, an era existing today in some subject disciplines where electronic information systems are designed specifically to enhance the way scientists or social scientists do their work. In our comparison, these mature electronic journal systems are represented by the system developed by the American Astronomical Society (AAS) together with NASA's Astrophysics Data System for astronomers.

Results in the early phase are from surveys of scientists and social scientists in two universities and eight other organizations (over 860 respondents). Data on the evolving phase came from surveys of the University of Tennessee, Drexel University, and Oak Ridge National Laboratory (235 respondents). The advanced phase survey provides results from over 1,000 members of the AAS.[10] In all of the surveys, scholarly articles were defined to include "those found in journal issues, author Websites, or separate copies such as preprints, reprints and other electronic or paper copies." Reading was defined as "going beyond the table of contents, title, and abstract to the body of the article."

The total number of articles read per year varies considerably by work field but, overall, the number of articles read is increasing.[11] The number of articles read and total time spent reading increased in each of our three evolutionary phases: an average of 100 articles per year in just under 90 total hours in the early phase; nearly 160 article per year in about 130 hours in the evolving phase; and nearly 230 articles per year by astronomers in 144 total hours in the advanced phase.

How articles are identified and the source used to obtain them varies throughout these three phases as well. Reading from various electronic sources grew from under 1% of total readings (.3%) in the early phase, to 39% in the evolving phase, to nearly 80% in the advanced phase. Library collection development policies influence where readers obtain articles, as nearly half of all readings in both the evolving and advanced phases come from library subscriptions (either print or electronic).[12] Table 1 shows that the use of separates (mostly electronic) rose considerably in the advanced phase. The growth in separates from full-text databases,

TABLE 1. Source of Articles Read, in Three Phases

	Evolutionary Phase		
Source of Article Read	Early % 1990-1993	Evolving % 2000-2002	Advanced % 2001-2002
Personal Subscription	**46.3**	**36.0**	**15.2**
Print	[100.0]	[67.8]	[54.5]
Electronic	[0.0]	[32.2]	[45.5]
Library Subscription	**40.6**	**49.1**	**49.0**
Print	[99.1]	[80.0]	[12.7]
Electronic	[0.9]	[20.0]	[87.3]
Separate Copy	**13.1**	**14.9**	**35.8**
Preprint	0.2	1.5	18.5
Archive (ADS)	0.0	0.0	10.2
Colleague Provided	9.2	9.2	4.5
ILL/Document Delivery	3.6	3.8	0.6
Author Website	0.0	0.3	0.8
Other	0.1	0.1	1.2
Total	100	100	100

Sample Size: Early (n = 862), Evolving (n = 235), Advanced (n = 508)

e-print servers, and author Websites means that readers now read articles from a wider variety of journal titles–at least one article per year from 13 titles in the late 1970s, to 18 in the mid-1990s, to approximately 23 titles by the year 2001.

Another change observed in three phases occurs in how readers find out about the articles they choose to read. Table 2 shows that browsing in journal issues (print or electronic) has steadily gone down, while online searching by topic has increased and is likely to increase even more as linking services such as SFX become commonplace.[13] Scientists and social scientists continue to rely on their colleagues and following links from citations to locate additional readings.

This should not be interpreted to mean that browsing is no longer important. A relatively lower percentage of total readings come from browsing, but the overall total number of readings has increased. In addition, browsing remains important in journal titles considered to be core to an individual's work, and is especially important for current awareness reading of current issues. Searching is done more for new topics, older articles, and for primary research and writing.

One thing that does not appear to change over time or with the different evolutionary phases is the relative age of articles read. In all three

TABLE 2. How Scientists Learned About Articles, in Three Phases

Method of Learning About Article	**Evolutionary Phase**		
	Early % 1990-1993	Evolving % 2000-2002	Advanced % 2001-2002
Browsing	57.6	46.4	20.6
Print Journals	[100.0]	[65.3]	[45.2]
Electronic Journals	[0.0]	[34.7]	[54.8]
Online Search	8.5	14.4	39.0
Other			
Colleagues	15.5	22.0	21.1
Citations	5.6	12.8	16.0
Other	12.8	4.4	3.3
Total	100	100	100

Sample Size: Early (n = 862), Evolving (n = 235), Advanced (n = 508)

phases, approximately two-thirds of readings occur within one year of publication. The remaining third are distributed over time in about the same proportion. Older readings are often re-readings of something read in a cursory manner when it was new and are reported to be highly valuable to the purpose of the reading (Table 3).[14]

Tables 1-3 show overall averages of all of the surveys within each phase. A closer examination of some recent surveys provides a more in-depth look at reading patterns. Surveys done from 2000-2003 of AAS members, and faculty and students at Drexel University, the University of Tennessee, and the University of Pittsburgh reveal both differences among disciplines and sub-disciplines, as well as how publishers' design decisions and libraries' collection development decisions can affect reading patterns by users.

HOW COLLECTION DEVELOPMENT POLICIES INFLUENCE USE

Three of our readership surveys provide us with an opportunity to examine how the size of a library's electronic collection might influence readers' information seeking and reading patterns. In 1993, we conducted a survey of faculty at the University of Tennessee when the uni-

TABLE 3. Age of Articles Read, in Three Phases

Age of Articles Read	Evolutionary Phase			
	1960	Early % 1990-1993	Evolving % 2000-2002	Advanced % 2001-2002
1 yr.	61.5	65.2	68.8	63.8
2 yrs.	13.3	14.5	10.2	9.9
3 yrs.	2.6	2.6	5.2	5.5
4-5 yrs.	8.4	5.7	5.4	7.8
6-10 yrs.	10.2	4.2	5.2	5.7
11-15 yrs.	1.7	2.6	1.7	2.8
> 15 yrs.	2.3	5.1	3.5	4.5
Total	100.0	100.0	100.0	100.0

Source: Early (n = 862), Evolving (n = 235), Advanced (n = 508)

versity library had a negligible electronic collection, and another survey was conducted in 2000 for science faculty only (including engineers and social scientists). By 2000, the university library had installed a partial electronic journal collection and also had made cuts to the print serials collection. In 1998 Drexel University began migrating to an almost exclusive electronic collection, and by 2002 the print collection had declined from about 1,700 titles to 370 titles and the electronic collection had increased to 8,600 unique titles.[15] In 2002 a readership survey was performed with Drexel faculty and doctoral students using the same instrument as the two surveys above.

We felt that these three readership surveys could provide an indication of how three levels of university library electronic collections might influence information seeking and use patterns. Because the survey of faculty in 2002 involved only scientists, we extracted survey responses from scientists' responses in the other two surveys, yielding sample responses from scientists of 71 in 1993, 96 in 2000 and 71 in 2002 (i.e., negligible, partial, and nearly all electronic collections respectively). We emphasize that the three surveys merely provide an indication of the effects of electronic collection size; there have been clear trends over the years in use patterns, and there may also be natural differences in faculty journal use patterns at Drexel University and the University of Tennessee. Nevertheless, we provide this evidence for others to contemplate. This analysis will follow the format as given above for the three evolutionary phases and definitions of reading remain the same.

As shown in Figure 1, the average number of article readings per scientist increased from 188 in 1993 to 201 in 2000 to about 214 in 2002–a trend that has generally held since 1977.[16]

The amount of time spent per reading was estimated to be 49 minutes in the 1993 survey, 36 minutes in 2000 and 42 minutes in 2002. More is said about the observed differences later.

There was a substantial difference in the sources used by scientists when they had the three levels of electronic collections available to them. The sources are categorized by personal subscriptions, library collections (including through interlibrary loan), and separate copies obtained from other persons such as colleagues and authors. The amount of reading from print journals decreases substantially with the availability of electronic collections–from 188 articles in 1993 to 159 in 2000 and 115 in 2000 at Drexel (Figure 2). Also shown in Figure 2 is the corresponding increase in reading from electronic articles from zero in

FIGURE 1. The Annual Amount of Reading by Scientists in Universities with Libraries Having Different Levels of Electronic Collections

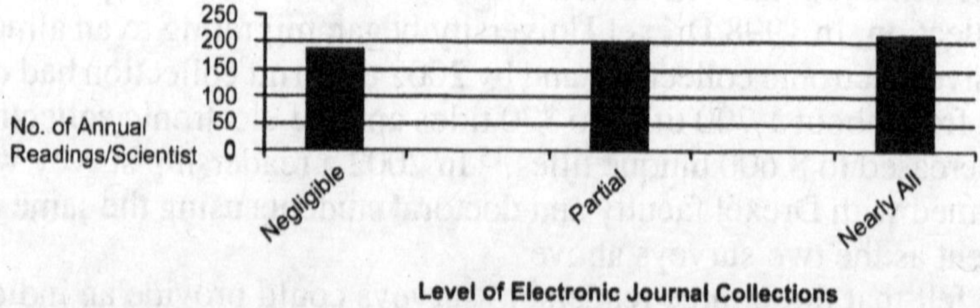

Source: University of Tennessee 1993 (n = 71), University of Tennessee 2000 (n = 96), Drexel University 2003 (n = 71)

FIGURE 2. Amount of Reading from Print and Electronic Articles by Scientists in Universities with Libraries Having Different Levels of Electronic Collections

1993 to 42 in 2000 to nearly 100 in 2002 at Drexel, where the collection is nearly all electronic.

Reading from the print format seems to vary somewhat. For example, reading from personal print subscriptions varied, as shown in Figure 3, from 72 in 1993 to 86 in 2000 and back to 72 in 2002. This shows that scientists continue to rely on print rather than electronic personal sub-

FIGURE 3. Amount of Reading from Personal Print Subscriptions by Scientists in Universities with Libraries Having Different Levels of Electronic Collections

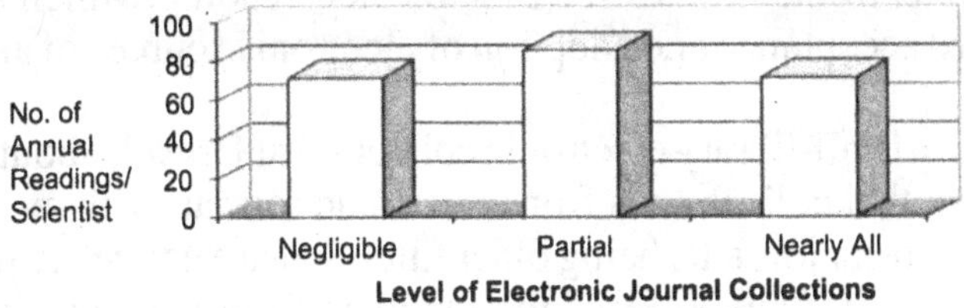

scriptions. Also, the amount of reading from the print personal subscriptions increased some from 1993 to 2000 (with a partial electronic collection) even though the average number of personal subscriptions decreased from 3.86 in 1993 to 3.64 subscriptions per scientist in 2000.

The reading from print library collections was 103 in 1993 (negligible electronic collection), 52 in 2000 (partial electronic collection) and down to 18 readings from print articles in 2002 (nearly all electronic collection). Thus, this pattern appears to be related inversely to availability of the library electronic collections. The same is true of reading from separate copies of articles in print that rose from 13 in 1992 to 21 in 2000 and 24 in 2002.

Examination of reading from electronic sources is more complex, since there is some evidence that the survey respondents in 2000 reported that they obtained electronic versions of articles from personal subscriptions (e.g., the pre-coded responses "free Web journals") when, in fact, the journals were from the library electronic journal collection. There appears to have been a library "branding" problem at that time at the University of Tennessee (and observed elsewhere as well). At Drexel, the conversion to the electronic collection was particularly well publicized to the relatively small faculty and, therefore, this appears not to have been a problem.

After the University of Tennessee adopted a partial library electronic collection, the scientists began using it to the point that, in 2000, about 17 articles per scientist per year were reported as read from this source. However, this amount could be as high as 25, if our sense of the branding issue is correct. The respondents reported an average of 15 readings from their personal electronic collections. This seems high, although it may be that scientists subscribed to electronic collections because the library had only a partial electronic collection. Altogether the scientists in 2000 used electronic articles for 21% of their reading, which shows a trend toward acceptance and adoption of electronic sources of articles at that time.

With a nearly all-library electronic collection at Drexel, about 82% of reading from that collection is from electronic format, with most of the reading from print journals being older titles that are not yet available in electronic format. Only 14% of the readings from personal subscriptions are in electronic format, and about 20% of separate copy reading is from electronic format. That is, of 100 total readings from electronic articles, 82 are from the Drexel electronic collection. Collectively, about 46% of all reading is from the library collection, which is a typical proportion observed in other universities.

In Table 4 we show how scientists learned about the articles they read. The amount of reading found while browsing remained about the same with the three levels of library electronic collections (i.e., 114, 106

TABLE 4. How Scientists Learned About Articles Read in Universities with Libraries Having Different Levels of Electronic Collections

Method of Learning About Article	Level of Electronic Journal Collections					
	Negligible		Partial		Nearly All	
	%	Reading	%	Reading	%	Reading
Browsing	**60.5**	**113.7**	**52.9**	**106.3**	**52.9**	**111.7**
Print Journals	[100.0]	[113.7]	[79.5]	[84.5]	[68.6]	[76.6]
Electronic Journals	[0]	[0]	[20.5]	[21.8]	[31.4]	[35.1]
Online Search	**14.6**	**27.4**	**22.9**	**46.0**	**26.6**	**56.9**
Other Persons	**14.1**	**25.6**	**13.3**	**26.7**	**10.6**	**22.7**
Citations	**6.5**	**12.2**	**10.8**	**21.7**	**9.1**	**19.5**
Other	**4.3**	**8.1**	**-**	**-**	**1.5**	**3.2**
Total	**100.0**	**188**	**99.9**	**201**	**100.0**	**214**

Source: University of Tennesse 1993 (n = 71), University of Tennessee 2000 (n = 96), Drexel University 2003 (n = 71)

and 112 readings per scientist in 1993, 2000 and 2002 respectively), although the amount read from print personal subscriptions dropped from 114 to 77. The most dramatic change has been in the use of online searching as a method of identifying articles (an increase from 27 to 57 articles identified and read). This increase reflects a general trend, observed elsewhere, and may simply be due to increased use of electronic resources.

The age of articles read is shown in Table 5. The pattern of age of articles is similar for 1993, when there was negligible availability, and for 2002, when Drexel had a nearly all-electronic collection. Thus, it appears that the latter availability with a relatively new electronic collection did not affect the use of older and more valuable articles. However, the pattern of use is different when the partial library collection is available. Here, a much higher proportion of readings is from recently published articles (i.e., 71% in the first year following publication). All of this evidence suggests that the new, partial electronic collection in 2000 may have altered use patterns, at least for a time. The University of Tennessee library collection was used far less in 2000 (69 articles) than in 1993 (103 articles), including for older articles. Greater use of current materials in 2000 (71%) vs. 1993 (61%) and the reduced time spent reading articles (49 minutes in 1993 to 36 minutes in 2000) support this finding, since older articles that are read tend to be more useful and

TABLE 5. Age of Articles Read by Scientists in Universities with Libraries Having Different Levels of Electronic Collections

	Level of Electronic Journal Collection		
	Negligible	Partial	Nearly All
1	58.5	71.6	61.2
2	12.3	9.1	12.9
3	6.2	4.5	7.2
4-5	7.7	4.6	5.9
6-10	9.2	5.7	4.7
11-15	1.5	2.2	4.7
> 15	4.6	2.2	3.5
Total	100.0	99.9	100.1

Note: Totals do not add to 100% due to rounding.

Source: University of Tennessee 1993 (n = 71), University of Tennessee 2000 (n = 96), Drexel University 2003 (n = 71)

readers spend more time reading them. A combination of adapting a new partial electronic collection and cuts to the library's print journal collection may have caused a shift from the library use to personal collections and other sources of articles.

DIFFERENCES IN ASTRONOMERS' READING PATTERNS BY AGE AND PRODUCTIVITY

The American Astronomical Society (AAS) spearheaded the development of the advanced information system in 1992 when it initiated a plan for publishing their journals in electronic form. By 1995, their first journal appeared on the Web. The full-featured system for electronic journals was developed in conjunction with the University of Chicago Press based on partial support of the National Science Foundation and NASA.[17] A sophisticated set of links and protocols was constructed in collaboration with the NASA-supported Astrophysics Data System (ADS), which simultaneously developed a searchable abstract database and complete, full-text backfiles of the core literature, dating back to the mid-1800s.[18] The complete system includes extensive interlinking features (backward and forward citations, a searchable abstract database, published and original numeric data sets, moving graphics, etc.). In addition, the system includes deep links to the numeric data sets maintained in international astronomical databases which in turn refer to the literature.

All of these advanced features reside in a single system of standards and protocols that facilitates the interlinking and the delivery of the information directly to the reader's desktop. Since the system is well established, astronomers and astrophysicists are well aware of its capabilities and have had ample experience in its use. Even though astronomy and astrophysics are different from other scientific disciplines in some ways, examination of their journal use provides a glimpse of what might occur in reading patterns of other disciplines as they progress towards advanced e-journal systems designed specifically to meet their research needs.

Our surveys of the AAS members reveal that within a relatively short period of time nearly all users adopted the electronic information system for some of their readings. Five years after launch, the critical elements of an electronic information system–that is, the journals and the abstract database–are used by more than 90% of all astronomers, and the system is the most frequent source of their readings. The widespread adoption of the ADS by astronomers indicates an important aspect of the scholarly information system. It needs to be a unified total information system. Too frequently we tend to think in terms of the individual links in the information chain. As producers and servers of information, we separate the information (the journals) from the tools we use to locate the relevant articles (the ADS) and from the system used to store and make the information (the library) available. But the working scientists need all the units in the information system, and all the units must work together effectively.

The tasks a scholarly researcher performs in order to use (and produce) information can be represented in five categories listed in Table 6. The corresponding components of the information system are listed in the right-hand column.

An effective electronic information system must encompass each of these components, providing tools with which to accomplish all the tasks. In most information systems, these components are developed independently by different groups of people with little thought given to how each unit will interoperate with the other units. Consequently, the various tasks do not operate smoothly with one another. In contrast, the astronomical information system was built with all the tasks in mind. Each component is tightly linked to all the other components, and the level of interoperation is excellent. This makes for a system that is easy and efficient for the user.

The rapid adoption of ADS by the astronomical community illustrates the importance of having a comprehensive and effective mechanism for locating information. We believe that our surveys show that having a system such as the ADS, from which the full-text can be accessed seamlessly, is just as important as the availability of the informa-

TABLE 6. Tasks and Components for an Electronic Information System

Tasks	**System Component**
Find	Searchable Abstract Database
Access	Linked Accessible Collection
Read	Journal Article
Use	Tabular and Auxiliary Data
Publish	Journal
Store	Accessible (Archival Quality) Collection

tion itself. The sharp increase in online searching shown in Table 3 results from the widespread use of the ADS as shown in Table 7.

One surprising result of our usage surveys of astronomers is the small effect that age plays in the adoption of electronic resources. Astronomers of all ages use the ADS electronic system for locating articles. Table 7 shows that nearly all (97%) of PhD astronomers under age 35 use the ADS, and this percentage drops off only slightly with age. Having an effective electronic search mechanism available on the users' desktop must account in part for the sharp rise in the use of online searches to locate articles.

The small correlation between usage of electronic information and age is mirrored in nearly all the survey data we obtained. Astronomers of all ages will move to electronic information resources for much of their reading if they serve their needs; age is no barrier. Presumably, this would be true for other academic disciplines as well.

Astronomy has a long tradition of using preprints, first in paper form and now in electronic form. The purpose of the preprints is to disseminate research results quickly. Astronomers have been active users of the Los Alamos e-print service (now moved to Cornell at http://arxiv.org/), which includes preprints of articles accepted for publication in journals, some reprints of published articles, and some e-prints that will never be printed in traditional journals. Table 7 shows that, while a smaller percentage of astronomers use the ArXiv e-print service than the ADS, a significant portion of astronomers are aware of the service and use it. Again there is only a small drop in numbers with the age of the user.

Given this relatively high usage, some vocal supporters of the e-print servers have even questioned whether or not the traditional journals are

TABLE 7. Awareness and Usage of the Searchable Abstract Database (ADS) and the E-print Service (ArXiv) by Astronomers

Awareness and Usage	Young (Under 36)	Middle Aged (36 - 49)	Old (Over 50)
Aware of ADS	98%	98%	94%
Use ADS	97	92	88
Aware of ArXiv	91%	87%	79%
Use ArXiv	80	77	69

still needed. One of the great attractions of the arXiv.org preprint server in physics was that it was available long before the traditional journals were available online. The popularity of the e-print servers in physics represents a vote for the online literature, and should not be construed as a statement about the worth of the unrefereed (some would say self-published) literature. In our view, any online source is more convenient than the same information in paper form. A majority of articles posted to arXiv.org are also submitted to peer-reviewed journals.

Electronic versions of astronomy journals became available beginning in 1995. At about the same time, the e-print services were becoming well known in the astronomical community. By 1997 there were competing electronic services available to astronomers, and the choices should represent the importance of e-prints as compared to the journals as well as online vs. paper. One of our surveys' goals was to determine the impact of the freely available, but unrefereed e-prints upon user habits and preferences. To this end, we asked astronomers to rank their preferences and usage of journals and e-prints both for keeping up with recent developments in the field and for providing definitive information (defined as information more than 2 years old).

Our results showed that PhD astronomers slightly preferred the refereed journals for keeping up with the field, although the e-prints were also judged to be an important source of information. Astronomers preferred the journals by a large margin for definitive information, however. Among our respondents, 97% of PhD astronomers found the journals to be either important or absolutely essential to their work, versus 26% for the e-prints. Some astronomers like the e-prints for the rapid access to new developments, but virtually all astronomers preferred to go to the journals for their definitive information.

We analyzed the survey data further based on the productivity of the responder in terms of the number of journal articles they submitted per year. Table 8 shows the percentage of PhD astronomers who rate the information source as either "very useful" or "absolutely critical" to them.

We found that the more productive astronomers (those submitting 2 or more journal articles per year) were substantially more likely to rank both the journals and the e-print servers as critical to their needs in keeping up with recent developments in the field than were those who submitted less than one article per year. Journals were the top choice as a source of definitive information. It is important to note that the more productive, and hence more active, astronomers were more likely to also value the e-prints highly. Those of us in the business of providing information are thus reminded that the productive users value our work

TABLE 8. Usefulness of Journals and E-prints

Percent rating resource as very useful or critical	Less Productive (< 1 per yr)	Average (1 - 2 per yr)	Productive (>2 per yr)
Journals (for recent developments)	70%	72%	74%
E-prints (for recent developments)	41	58	67
Journals (for definitive information)	93%	98%	96%
E-prints (for definitive information)	13	21	23

more than do our less active colleagues. Perhaps in planning for the future by analyzing what the usage patterns tell us, we should count more highly the responses from the more productive users.

WHAT FACTORS AFFECT JOURNAL USE PATTERNS?

We have shown that journal use patterns are influenced by the evolutionary stages of the journal systems, the level of library electronic journal collections, and some personal factors such as age and productivity. In other studies we have found that additional personal factors affect journal use patterns as well, such as a person's profession or discipline, place of employment, gender, and so on.[19] We will discuss next some recent studies of the use patterns of engineers and scientists, and the factors which emerge that have been shown to affect journal use patterns. Such factors affect readers' choices for using a particular journal, specific articles or their information content, the means used to identify articles, and the sources used to obtain them. The results in this section come from general faculty and all disciplines, and will be representative of the university environment as a whole. The results in some cases contrast with the advanced, discipline-specific, well-integrated information system which has been developed for astronomy. The results are more representative of the emerging phase referred to earlier.

A few of the factors that affect readers' choices are:

- Ease of use, including physical and intellectual effort required
- Importance of attributes of journals and related services

- Awareness of journals and related services
- The usefulness and value of the information content

Examples of how these factors influence use patterns follow. The physical and intellectual effort required to use a journal or service is one of the most important factors in its use. Meadows clearly articulated this fact when he observed that "One of the firmest conclusions of information usage surveys seems to be, indeed, that the intrinsic value of an information channel has little, or no, bearing on the frequency with which it is used. The ultimate factor is always its accessibility."[20]

While it is true that the ease of locating and accessing information is the primary factor, we see from the case of astronomy that when two sources are equally accessible, the users overwhelmingly prefer the "trusted" source, the refereed journal, over the unrefereed source.

Some examples of the importance of ease of use are:

- Readers tend to choose to use a library electronic collection because they don't have to go to the library. Our surveys show that this saves them about 15 minutes per reading on average.
- On the other hand, they tend to prefer a print format for their personal subscriptions. We believe that they find it easier to browse print.
- Readers tend to print out electronic articles when they read them in depth, because it is easier to do so.
- Scientists in non-university environments tend to use reference librarians to perform difficult online searches because they can do them faster and better.

Attributes of journals and services also have a strong bearing on use. For example:

- *Journal attributes*: their price, quality (due to review and editing), available format, added features, size, and so on.
- *Library collection attributes*: comprehensiveness, available format, hours that the library is open or electronic access is available, age of the collection, existence of a periodicals room, collection-related services (e.g., reference support, workstation capabilities, photocopying and printer availability), and so on.
- *Search services*: price, search quality (recall and precision), special search features, display features, and so on.

All of these attributes have a bearing on use patterns. Our studies have shown that each use is unique, even to a particular reader; however, the astronomy data show that when the information system is interlinked effectively and operates as one system, the adoption of the electronic resources is rapid and complete.

Availability and attributes of alternatives are also important in choosing a journal or service. For example:

- Information content is often available from alternative sources (e.g., large e-print services, reports, conference presentations and proceedings, the author, colleagues) or a combination of other research and articles.
- Readers often know about the information reported or discussed in an article before they first read the article, yet they read it anyway (often in great depth).
- There are many alternative search engines available to readers, and readers search for themselves or use intermediaries. This is in contrast to the astronomy system, where the ADS is overwhelmingly the search system of choice.
- Readers can obtain articles from a range of sources (in alternative formats), such as personal subscriptions, library collections, author Websites, e-print archives, and colleagues.

Readers have many options and they make their choice based on ease of use and how the attributes meet their needs. But when a system is designed to meet the needs of a specific set of readers, such as the astronomy system, it becomes the overwhelming choice.

Another important factor that determines choice of system is awareness of the existence of a journal or alternative services. Examples of awareness issues are:

- The range of journals read by scientists has increased significantly due to emergence of electronic journal and online searching, suggesting that previously they may not have been aware of some of the journals.
- Author Websites are used as a source by readers, but lack of awareness and their long-term availability can be a barrier to use. The data from astronomy indicates that when a large e-print server is available, the use of author Websites becomes negligible.
- Our studies show that users are often unaware of many important library services, but many would use the services if aware of them.

Recently we asked faculty at the University of Pittsburgh about their awareness of special electronic journal features, with the following results:

- All science respondents indicated they were aware of electronic journals, but 15% had not used them in the past 30 days.
- 89% were aware of journals published exclusively in electronic format but only 4% have published in them.
- 70% were aware of backward and forward citation linking; 41% have used one or the other.
- Over half (52%) were aware of links to numeric databases and images; only 15% have used such features.
- 63% were aware of "large preprint archives"; 26% have used them.
- 44% are aware of author Websites and have used them; 19% reported they have their own author Website. As in astronomy, only a small percentage of the readings come from author Websites.

Scientists appear to be aware of advanced features of electronic journals, but less than half of the respondents in our recent survey used any one advanced feature.

CONCLUSION

All of the readership surveys discussed earlier show that scientists spend a great deal of time reading scholarly journals. Reading is their most important resource, but they would not spend as much time on it if the information was not worthwhile. Our studies since 1977 have repeatedly shown the use and value of scientific journals as follows:

- The amount of reading time and the time spent on it are both indicators of the value of article information.
- Primary research is by far the principle purpose for reading.
- The information content is very important in doing primary research; other purposes for reading (such as teaching, writing, continuing education, etc.) are also important.
- There are essential ways in which primary research (and other purposes) is affected by reading; these include inspiring new thinking, improving results, and so on.
- Amount of reading is correlated with reader productivity.
- Many articles save readers' time and other valuable resources.

- Reading is shown to help achieve the readers' organization's goals.
- Award recipients tend to read more than non-award recipients.

We have found that these indicators continue to hold since the emergence of electronic journals. There appears to be little difference between reading from electronic or print articles, however. Perhaps this is because the information content is essentially the same in peer-reviewed journals or articles from peer-reviewed journals regardless of format. We believe that as new features are used more, as, for example, the astronomers have used them, electronic journals will become even more useful and valuable.

A finding that has held throughout our studies is that indicators of usefulness and value tend to be higher for articles obtained from library collections than from elsewhere. One possible reason is that nearly all older articles are obtained from library print or electronic collections and older articles are rated by our respondents as more useful and valuable on average than newly-published articles. Also, librarians contribute to the intellectual aspect of identifying, locating, and acquiring relevant information.

NOTES

1. Donald W. King. and Carol Hansen Montgomery, "After Migration to an Electronic Journal Collection: Impact on Faculty and Doctoral Students," *D-Lib Magazine*, 8, no. 12. (Dec. 2002), http://dx.doi.org/doi:10.1045/december2002-king.

2. Carol Tenopir and Donald W. King, *Towards Electronic Journals: Realities for Scientists, Librarians, and Publisher* (Washington, D.C.: Special Libraries Association, 2000).

3. Donald W. King and Carol Tenopir, "Using and Reading Scholarly Literature," in *Annual Review of Information Science and Technology* 34, ed. M. Williams, 423-477 (Medford, NJ.: Information Today, Inc., 2001).

4. Charles W. Bailey, Jr., *Scholarly Electronic Publishing Bibliography* (12 May 2003).

5. Rob Kling and Ewa Callahan, "Electronic Journals, the Internet, and Scholarly Communication," in *Annual Review of Information Science and Technology* 37, ed. B. Cronin, 127-177 (Medford, NJ. Information Today, Inc., 2003).

6. Carol Tenopir, *Use and Users of Electronic Library Resources: An Overview and Analysis of Recent Research Studies* (Washington, D.C.: Council on Library and Information Resources, 2003), http://www.clir.org/pubs/reports/pub120/pub120.pdf.

7. Carol Tenopir, Donald W. King, and Amy Bush, "How Medical Faculty Use Print and Electronic Journals," *Journal of the Medical Library Association* 92 (April 2004).

8. Rob Kling and Geoffrey McKim, "Not Just a Matter of Time: Field Differences and the Shaping of Electronic Media in Supporting Scientific Communication," *Journal of the American Society for Information Science* 51, no. 14 (Dec. 2000): 1306-1320.

9. Carol Tenopir and others, "Patterns of Journal Use by Scientists through Three Evolutionary Phases," *D-Lib* 9, no. 5 (May 2003), http://www.dlib.org/dlib/may03/05contents.html (25 Oct. 2003).

10. Carol Tenopir and others, "Relying on Electronic Journals: Reading Patterns of Astronomers," *Journal of the American Society for Information Science and Technology* 55 (forthcoming).

11. Carol Tenopir and Donald W. King, *Towards Electronic Journals: Realities for Scientists, Librarians, and Publisher* (Washington, D.C.: Special Libraries Association, 2000).

12. Carol Tenopir and others, "Patterns of Journal Use by Scientists through Three Evolutionary Phases," *D-Lib* 9, no. 5 (May 2003), http://www.dlib.org/dlib/may03/05contents.html (25 Oct. 2003).

13. Ibid.

14. Ibid.

15. Carol Montgomery and Donald W. King, "Comparing Library and User Related Costs of Print and Electronic Journal Collections: A First Step Towards a Comprehensive Analysis," *D-Lib Magazine* 8, no. 10 (October 2002), http://www.dlib.org/dlib/october02/montgomery/10montgomery.html

16. Carol Tenopir and Donald W. King, *Towards Electronic Journals: Realities for Scientists, Librarians, and Publisher* (Washington, D.C.: Special Libraries Association, 2000).

17. Peter B. Boyce, "The AAS Program of Electronic Publication," in *Electronic Publishing for Physics and Astronomy*, ed. André Heck, Astrophysics and Space Science Library 224 (Dordrecht, Netherlands: Kluwer Academic Publishers, 1997); Peter B. Boyce and Heather Dalterio, "Electronic Publishing of Scientific Journals," *Physics Today* 49, http://www.aas.org/~pboyce/epubs/pt-art.htm.

18. Michael J. Kurtz and others, "The NASA Astrophysics Data System: Overview," *Astronomy and Astrophysics Supplement* 143 (2000): 41-59.

19. Donald W. King and Carol Tenopir, "Using and Reading Scholarly Literature," in *Annual Review of Information Science and Technology* 34, ed. M. Williams, 423-477 (Medford, NJ.: Information Today, Inc., 2001); Carol Tenopir and Donald W. King, *Communication Patterns of Engineers* (New York: Wiley, 2003); Carol Tenopir and Donald W. King, *Towards Electronic Journals: Realities for Scientists, Librarians, and Publisher* (Washington, D.C.: Special Libraries Association, 2000).

20. A. J. Meadows, *Communicating Research* (San Diego, CA: Academic Press, 1998), 124.

CONTRIBUTORS' NOTES

Peter Boyce is a research associate at the Maria Mitchell Association. Donald W. King is a research professor at the University of Pittsburgh. Carol Montgomery is Dean of Libraries at Drexel University. Carol Tenopir is a professor at the University of Tennessee.

Usage Statistics: Taking E-Metrics to the Next Level

Oliver Pesch

Presenter

SUMMARY. "You can't manage what you can't measure" is the popular quote attributed to Peter Drucker. E-metrics is all about measuring for the purpose of managing the many aspects of e-content and e-collections. The notion of what to measure and how to manage depends on your perspective, however. There are a number of players in the online information business. For this talk we will focus on three of them: libraries, publishers, and aggregators. Each of these participants has somewhat different requirements for e-metrics.

The subtitle of this presentation is "Taking E-Metrics to the Next Level." We will start with the prerequisite look at why we need usage statistics. This will be followed by a discussion and examples of reports available today and a look at some of the challenges faced when e-metrics are provided from several sources. Next will be an overview of some of the standard efforts in process that could reduce or eliminate these challenges. Finally, we will look ahead to expanding uses of e-metrics and some additional challenges to be faced as well. *[Article copies available for a fee from The Haworth Document Delivery Service: 1-800-HAWORTH. E-mail address: <docdelivery@haworthpress.com> Website: <http://www.HaworthPress.com>]*

[Haworth co-indexing entry note]: "Usage Statistics: Taking E-Metrics to the Next Level." Pesch, Oliver. Co-published simultaneously in *The Serials Librarian* (The Haworth Information Press, an imprint of The Haworth Press, Inc.) Vol. 46, No. 1/2, 2004, pp. 143-154; and: *Serials in the Park* (ed: Patricia S. French, and Richard Worthing) The Haworth Information Press, an imprint of The Haworth Press, Inc., 2004, pp. 143-154. Single or multiple copies of this article are available for a fee from The Haworth Document Delivery Service [1-800-HAWORTH, 9:00 a.m. - 5:00 p.m. (EST). E-mail address: getinfo@haworthpress.com].

http://www.haworthpress.com/web/SER
Digital Object Identifier: 10.1300/J123v46n01_15

WHY USAGE STATISTICS?

Usage statistics and e-metrics are important not only to libraries but also to publishers and aggregators. For many libraries, e-metrics are a required element of their regular reporting to funding and accreditation agencies. Usage statistics can play a role in driving bibliographic instruction, internal marketing and the development of the library's own Website. For publishers, the number of full-text requests for a given journal is a strong indicator of its impact. Monitoring usage over time is a good way of determining the effectiveness of various content and marketing strategies that may be implemented. Aggregators, like publishers with larger services, want usage statistics not only to assist with collection management but also to help with the overall management of the service. Monitoring searches and full-text retrieval over time helps with capacity planning and allows these services to plan ahead for growth and peaks.

The following tables show the typical elements that are captured and how these are useful for the various players (see Tables 1a-1e).

CHALLENGES FACING LIBRARIES

Libraries must compile and consolidate statistical data obtained from a number of different sources. There are several challenges to this endeavor ranging from inconsistent naming of e-metric elements to differing definitions of what is counted to consistency and reliability issues to the varied level of detail that is available. Some e-metrics are collected

TABLE 1a. Basic E-Metrics: Numbers of E-Resources

Element captured	Use
Number of full text e-journals; Number of electronic reference sources; Number of electronic books	*Libraries* • Reporting nature of the collection on surveys. • Group by subject or topic area to assist in collection sharing. • Perform overlap analysis of various packages and individual journals to assist in appropriate budget allocation. *Aggregators and publishers* • Marketing lists to present offering to customer base.

TABLE 1b. Basic E-Metrics: Logins

Element captured	Use
Logins (sessions)	*Libraries* • Measurement of extent a given service is used. • For remote users these can be reported as virtual visits to the library. • A low number of sessions for a given resource or service may indicate that users are having a hard time finding the resource or don't understand its use. This information can be used to influence bibliographic instruction, internal promotion of services and/or design of library's Web site. *Aggregators and publishers* • Level of activity on the service. • Track use patterns by hour of day, day of week and month of year to plan hardware needs.

TABLE 1c. Basic E-Metrics: Turnaways

Element captured	Use
Turnaways (logins rejected due to exceeding simultaneous use)	*Libraries* • Indicates if a resource, licensed by simultaneous use, is at capacity of the license. • Number of Turnaways per hour can be used to indicate if a license should be increased. *Aggregators* • Simultaneous use is typically monitored on the service database level. • Report to library when number of Turnaways is consistently high and suggest increasing number of licensed users. *Publishers* • Most often tracked at the individual journal level, though some publisher sites sell ports to access the overall service. • May use to inform libraries when more copies of a journal may be needed.

directly by the library from their own Web logs (counting visits to the e-resources Web page, for example). E-metrics may also be obtained from multiple aggregators, e-journal gateways, and publishers.

The first challenge comes in retrieving the data from various sites. Some sites have administrative modules that allow the library to retrieve statistics directly. On these sites the statistics may be displayed on screen to be saved, downloaded directly, made available via FTP, or

TABLE 1d. Basic E-Metrics: Searches

Element captured	Use
Searches (queries)	*Libraries* • May be viewed similar to reference questions answered. • Indicates level of activity on a given online service or database. • Count of searches can be used to compare the relative importance of databases and/or resources licensed. • Monitoring trends in searches (most frequent terms being used) can help in discovering new or changing areas of interest and thus be an input to collection development. • Actual search terms can be analyzed to understand mistakes being made and used to influence bibliographic instruction or provide feedback to vendor. • Number of searches per session indicates how resources are being used. Use to influence bibliographic instruction, internal marketing or how library Website is designed (can users find the resources they are looking for). To be most effective, this analysis should be coupled with a view of actual search terms being used as the counts alone are not a good indicator–for example, a low search count per session could indicate a service is so confusing the users give up after one search, or so effective that it takes only one search to find what they are looking for. *Publishers and Aggregators* • Monitor level of activity on given databases. Use in capacity planning to ensure there are enough resources and/or replicas of popular databases to ensure good performance. • Analysis of search terms used to determine common mistakes and how features being used. Assist in enhancing search features, making existing features more prevalent if they are being under utilized (e.g. applying synonyms) or making changes to search syntax. • Tracking frequently used search terms can be helpful in seeing changing areas of interests and hot topics (depends on the nature of the service).

sent via e-mail. Other sites require that statistics be requested via e-mail or a phone call. Depending on the nature of the analysis being performed, multiple reports may be needed from each vendor. For example, activity by site, by database, and by journal title are likely three separate reports. If a finer breakdown is required (e.g., remote versus in library use) multiples of each report must be obtained.

Once the reports are obtained, the next challenge is to extract the right numbers from each report. Differences in file format and naming conventions must be accounted for. Perhaps the biggest challenge facing libraries is in understanding how transactions are being counted at

TABLE 1e. Basic E-Metrics: Items Examined

Element captured	Use
Items examined (full text requested)	*Libraries* • Provides usage information at the journal level. • Just one input to importance or impact of a given journal in the overall collection. • When a journal is available from multiple sources helps determine which sources are most popular. • Use the cumulative items examined to compare full text aggregations and help determine value of one over another. *Publishers* • Judge relative impact of a journal. • Track usage trends to evaluate marketing or content management strategies. • A measure of visibility of the publisher's site and of the journals on it. *Aggregators* • Track usage trends to help gauge network bandwidth needs. PDFs can have the largest impact on bandwidth and tracking or forecasting use can be an effective capacity planning tool. • Provide publishers with royalty reports. • Relative levels of use for particular journals can be an input for collection development decisions (e.g., replacing little-used journals with new more highly desired content can be a way to improve the product yet control the cost--and price to the customer).

the various sites and trying to accommodate the differences so that combining or comparing counts from different sites is reasonable. Tables 2a-2c have some examples of how things can be different.

STANDARDS OFFER HOPE

Table 3 shows just some of the challenges facing librarians trying to make sense out of their usage statistics. The good news is that several efforts are underway (and have been for some time) to introduce standardization and accountability into this area. Tables 3-6 review four standardization initiatives.

These initiatives have raised the awareness of the importance of usage statistics to libraries. With NISO Z39.7 providing a standard set of definitions and element names, and COUNTER developing a code of practice, it is reasonable to expect life to get easier for libraries in the

TABLE 2a. Challenges when Dealing with E-Metrics: Sessions

Element	Where things can go wrong
Sessions	• This could be considered a measure of virtual visits to the library. • Searching multiple resources in a single visit will increment session counts on each online service accessed. • Each click of a link to journals or articles in A-to-Z lists, e-reserves or reading lists may be counted as separate sessions on one site and not counted as a session at all on the next. • Time-out settings may differ from one site to the next, greatly affecting session lengths. (Time-out settings, which may range from a few minutes to a few hours, are used to control the "state" of a session. If a user is not active for more than the time-out period then the session is automatically terminated by the service.)

TABLE 2b. Challenges when Dealing with E-Metrics: Searches

Element	Where things can go wrong
Searches	• A search could be viewed as the equivalent to answering a reference question. • Some sites include zero-hit searches in the total, others do not. • Some sites remove duplicate searches conducted by the same user within a short period of time and thus eliminate counting double clicks. • If a single search is simultaneously conducted against several databases on a single site, the site may count this as one search or multiple searches (one for each database searched). • Direct links to articles, like those found on course reading lists, may be counted as a search (search by article identifier) on some sites and not on others.

TABLE 2c. Challenges when Dealing with E-Metrics: Full-Text Items Requested

Element	Where things can go wrong
Full-text items requested	• Some sites will remove duplicate requests for the same item by the same user (within a short period of time) and others do not. This is known as the double-click problem. • If Web logs are used and a PDF is presented one page at a time, the Web server may record a transaction to the log for each page retrieve resulting in some sites counting pages sent rather than articles sent. • Some sites (such as e-journal gateways) link the user to the article at another site. In cases like this there is the potential of both sites counting the same transaction as an item requested. • Some sites allow the library to configure the service to automatically show full-text when it is available. While this reduces clicks for the end-user, it will inflate the full-text requested number as the user will not always have intended to view the full-text. • Articles that are viewed then printed or e-mailed may be counted as two transactions on some sites and one on another.

TABLE 3. Summary of ICOLC Guidelines for Statistical Measures

ICOLC Guidelines	
Date initiated	First guidelines published November 1998 and revised December 2001.
Objectives	• Ensure consortia members receive usage stats for licensed resources • Assumes information providers want same to understand the market for their services • Define and create common set of basic use information requirements • Applies to vendor operated Websites and software provided to libraries for local operation
Elements defined	• Number of sessions (logins) • Number of queries (searches) • Menu selections (like searches) • Full content units examine (full-text) • Collect by journal or e-book • Turnaways
Report breakdowns required	• By database • By institution • By overall consortium • By time period
More information	*http://www.library.yale.edu/consortia/2001webstats.htm*

TABLE 4. Summary of ARL E-Metrics

ARL E-Metrics	
Date initiated	Initial project spanned May 2000 through December 2001
Objectives	• Serve ARL community • Provide measures for Electronic Resources • Explore feasibility of defining and collecting data on use and value or electronic resources
Elements defined	*Collections* • Number of full-text e-journals • Number of electronic reference sources • Number of electronic books *Usage* • Number of logins (sessions) • Number of searches • Number of items requested (full-text)
More information	*http://www.arl.org/stats/newmeas/emetrics*

coming years. COUNTER is also planning to implement an audit component to its COUNTER compliance program in 2004 and thus introduce a level of trust in the quality of statistics that are provided. Librarians can help by supporting these initiatives and providing feedback when asked.

TABLE 5. Summary of NISO Z39.7 Library Statistics Standard

NISO Z39.7 Library Statistics	
Date initiated	• First released in 1968 with revisions in 1983 and 1995. • Currently under revision.
Objectives	• Standardize definitions of elements. • Standardize terminology. • Includes e-metrics. • Cross reference surveys such as: ARL; Public Library; State Library Agency. • Provide guidelines for methods of measurement. • Provide linkable definitions to facilitate use in surveys.
Elements defined	• Definitions are provided for metrics found in most of the national and state surveys. Where possible, these different terms for the same metric have been cross-referenced.
More information	*http://www.niso.org/emetrics/*

LOOKING AHEAD

Meeting basic e-metrics needs will become easier as standards initiatives are adopted and vendors and librarians become better educated in this area. The future, however, is likely to bring more opportunities for usage analysis as well as more challenges.

Several librarians and publishers have requested an additional dimension to the reporting of full-text requests. One example of this is to provide a breakdown by year of publication. With this element stored as part of the transaction, it will be possible to determine the amount of use as data becomes older. When a library can determine how frequently various subsets of their user community are accessing full-text based on age of articles, they can make more informed decisions on the relevance of subscribing to backfile collections versus paying for on-demand access. Publishers and aggregators can use this information for capacity planning; if older data is not accessed as frequently, less expensive storage systems can be used and different caching mechanisms can be employed.

With OpenURL becoming a standard and the notion of linking to full-text becoming an expectation (demand?) of end users, tracking linking activity will be another important aspect of e-metrics. Knowing how many times full-text articles are retrieved for a certain journal is

TABLE 6. Summary of Project COUNTER Initiative

Project COUNTER	
Date initiated	• Launched in March 2002 • The first code of practice released in December 2002. • Resulted from work initiated by PALS (Publisher and Library Solutions) in 2000 and 2001
Objectives	• Count Online Usage of Networked Electronic Resources (COUNTER) • Focus on journals and databases • Facilitate recording and exchange of online usage statistics • Provide a code of practice • Formalize "COUNTER Compliance" • Include definition of elements (uses Z39.7) • Define required reports for Journals and Databases • Specify exact report column and row headings • Define file formats to deliver • Provide guidelines for processing data • Include an auditing requirement
Elements defined	• Sessions • Searches • Full-text article requests • Turnaways
Reports defined	• Journal Report 1: Number of successful Full-Text Article Requests by Month • Journal Report 2: Turnaways by month and journal • Database Report 1: Total searches and sessions by month and database • Database Report 2: Turnaways by month and database
Reports categories (level of detail)	• Consortium • Institution • Department within institution
Delivery requirements	• Deliver as CSV (comma separated values) file or Excel spreadsheet • Reports available on password controlled Website • Reports provided at least monthly • Data updated within 2 weeks of end of month • Provide data for all of previous calendar year and current year
More information	*http://www.projectcounter.org*

important for basic reporting and collection development; however, understanding how a user discovered the full-text can be critical for overall system planning and configuration. Tracking the number of link-outs to full-text from a secondary database (a database providing index and abstract entries only) is an indicator of how effectively the database works for discovering information and for actually delivering the full-text to the user. OpenURL resolvers provide further opportunities for libraries to track use patterns by being able to record which systems they linked to, as well as which service they came from.

Another hot topic of late is *metasearching* (also known as broadcast searching or federated searching). Many institutions are looking to metasearch engines to provide a single, uniform user interface to all of their e-resources. A user is able to conduct a single search across a multitude of systems without the need to know the syntax or idiosyncrasies of the systems in question. The metasearch engine "magically" conducts the search and retrieves the records and often consolidates them into a single list for the user. The metasearch approach, which has been around for years with products like WebFeat, ExLibris's Metalib and OCLC's Web-Z, brings with it some additional challenges and opportunities for usage statistics. Metasearch engines do their job by performing simultaneous searches on many databases from many services at one time. In order to do this work in a time-efficient manner, a metasearch engine may access the various services acting as many users, each searching one database. Figure 1 shows how a single user conducting one search in a single session may cause a total of twenty sessions and twenty searches to be recorded across the four sites involved.

One answer to the metasearch statistics problem is for online services to track the source of a session. Search and session counts can then be broken down by source of the session and the totals coming from metasearch engines can be ignored. The metasearch engine can provide its own search and session counts, which will map much more closely to

FIGURE 1. Metasearch Impact on Session and Search Counts

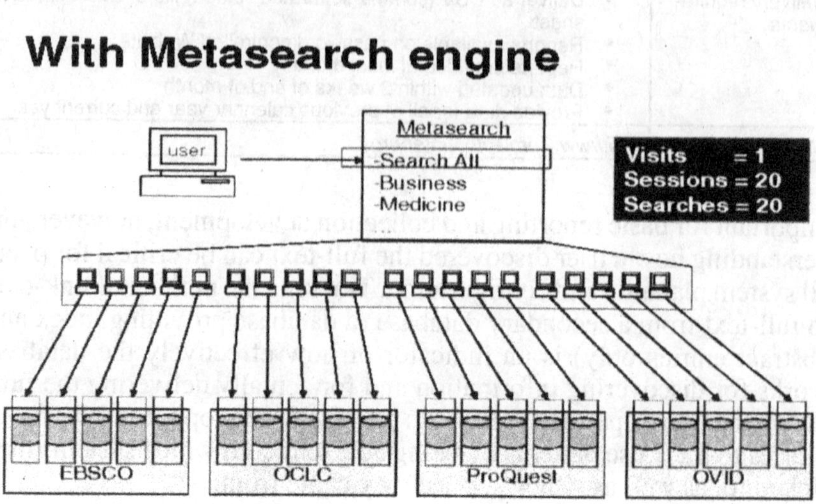

virtual visits of users. In this way, statistics from the metasearch engine can be safely combined with activity recorded by the other online services to ensure that all activity is accounted for–including the searches and sessions from users who access these services directly. The good news in this is that counts for full-text requests are typically not affected by the metasearch engine due to the fact that the end user is still making explicit requests to view full-text when desired.

Upcoming NISO guidelines on metasearching will present some options for a Metasearch engine to identify itself to the content provider. In the meantime, metasearch activity can be isolated by having the metasearch engine use a dedicated user account to access the services or using the IP address of the metasearch server.

Tracking the source of a session has benefits beyond solving the problems with metasearch engines. By tracking this information, it is also possible to segregate activity on online services resulting from following persistent or durable links from the regular search activity on the service. Link-ins to retrieve a single article or to browse the contents of a journal can skew averages for searches per session (a link-in will normally create a single-search session) as well as session length (sessions are often seconds in length as they only last long enough to retrieve the article). A library may want to use session length and the average count of searches per session as one measure for evaluating the performance of a bibliographic instruction program or to judge the effectiveness of an option change for a given online service. For the statistical information to be relevant, both metasearch and link-in activity should be ignored and the comparison done only on activity from normal logins.

NEXT STEPS

The world of e-metrics is still a big scary place, although standards initiatives are giving us hope that we soon will be able to have more faith in basic e-metrics. As access to information becomes more online-centric, librarians and vendors should be looking for new opportunities to capitalize on this electronic world.

Statistics are a measurement of users' actions that we try to correlate to their intentions. For example, we want to count the number of full-text articles a user retrieved and used; however, we can only measure the number of times an article was requested by the system and we do not know if the user really intended to fetch the article or if it was an accident or if the retrieval was automatic and beyond their control. Use statistics in a traditional library setting suffer the same flaw–reshelving counts, for example, are a general indicator of use for journals but are not particularly precise. As we move from the traditional methods of gathering statistics to the online world, there may be a tendency to try and relate the electronic actions with the traditional measures, such as relating a search to a reference question answered. A statistical correlation between traditional and e-metrics may not exist even though the intent of each measure may be similar. Further investigation into the area of e-metrics is needed. Perhaps some old and outdated measures can be retired and new, more meaningful ones embraced.

Standards remain the key to ongoing success and credibility of e-metrics, and Z39.7 should be promoted as the standard set of definitions. Various groups creating surveys and related initiatives should be encouraged to use these definitions in their instruments. Project COUNTER can be very effective if vendors of online services see value in being and remaining COUNTER-compliant. It is up to the library community to help provide this value by making COUNTER compliance a requirement. Finally, librarians and vendors alike should be active participants in the standards process to ensure that the objectives being set are reasonable and attainable.

CONTRIBUTOR'S NOTE

Oliver Pesch is Chief Architect at EBSCO Publishing in Ipswich, Massachusetts.

Seeing the Forest and the Trees When Developing a New Acquisitions System

Shelley Neville

Presenter

SUMMARY. A library's automated acquisitions system can be the workhorse of technical services. Developing a new acquisitions system for any automation vendor can be a challenge. How does an ILS vendor create an acquisitions system that meets the needs of libraries when workflows vary from library to library? Dynix has used a process called Contextual Inquiry as they develop a new acquisitions system. Contextual inquiry, or CI, is a process in which one or two members of a development team spend an amount time at libraries watching staff as they work while taking notes and asking questions. This happens before software coding even begins. This information is taken back to a development team where engineers are immersed in how libraries order, receive, and invoice serial titles. Only after the development team has a good understanding of the process does coding begin.

This presentation will discuss how an integrated library system (ILS) vendor develops software and describe the methods and processes we use. Although I think that ILS vendors probably use many of the same processes, my remarks will be based only on my own experience. *[Article copies available for a fee from The Haworth Document Delivery Service: 1-800-HAWORTH. E-mail address: <docdelivery@haworthpress.com> Website: <http://www.HaworthPress.com>]*

[Haworth co-indexing entry note]: "Seeing the Forest and the Trees When Developing a New Acquisitions System." Neville, Shelley. Co-published simultaneously in *The Serials Librarian* (The Haworth Information Press, an imprint of The Haworth Press, Inc.) Vol. 46, No. 1/2, 2004, pp. 155-159; and: *Serials in the Park* (ed: Patricia S. French, and Richard Worthing) The Haworth Information Press, an imprint of The Haworth Press, Inc., 2004, pp. 155-159. Single or multiple copies of this article are available for a fee from The Haworth Document Delivery Service [1-800-HAWORTH, 9:00 a.m. - 5:00 p.m. (EST). E-mail address: getinfo@haworthpress.com].

http://www.haworthpress.com/web/SER
Digital Object Identifier: 10.1300/J123v46n01_16

WHY DEVELOP A NEW ACQUISITIONS SYSTEM?

One year ago, Dynix made enhancing its acquisitions product a priority. Technologies and workflows had changed and our existing product needed improvements. As a company, we evaluate our software development priorities constantly. Acquisitions and "back room" applications are generally nearer the bottom of the enhancement list than the top. I believe that circulation and the public access catalog tend to get higher priority because they are the applications in front of the users, and get the most exposure. At this time, however, acquisitions made it to the top for three reasons:

1. *Market requirements.* An acquisitions system needs to be flexible enough to accommodate the various workflows incorporated by different libraries. Workflows have been changing over the past few years to accomplish more with fewer staff. Outsourcing, blurring lines between cataloging, acquisitions, and serials, and new technologies all contributed to Dynix's decision to develop a new acquisitions system. Dynix recognized that more and more libraries are using the Web as a source for selection and ordering of titles and posed the question, how do we build a tightly integrated interface with multiple vendors?
2. *Existing customer requirements.* Most ILS vendors work with a users' group which submits enhancements. These enhancements are prioritized initially by the users group and then by the ILS vendor. Our users were more than ready for acquisitions enhancements.
3. *Competition.* Because librarians talk amongst themselves, ILS vendors have a pretty good idea of where they may be strong or weak against a competitor. If the weaknesses are something which undermines sales, this ranks high on our list of priorities.

SOME BACKGROUND ON DYNIX AND ACQUISITIONS

Dynix had already redesigned its acquisitions system before. Several years ago, I was involved with the rewrite of the Dynix ILS acquisitions system. We put together a customer focus group made up of representatives from several different types and sizes of libraries. The group was invited to our corporate headquarters, and we spent a lot of time together discovering what we could do to improve our acquisitions system. I led this group and worked closely with the engineers who developed the software. One of the engineers had worked for a major book retailer and had developed their ordering system. He also had a great deal of accounting experience. He was surprised to learn that bookstores and libraries have unique order procedures that are sometimes indifferent to standard accounting principles. The new acquisitions software delivered robust functionality. We were still working with an older technology, however, and, while we handled firm orders very well, other types of orders such as serial renewals, standing orders, and multi-volume sets were less strong.

Last year Dynix staff were given the resources and time to develop a new acquisitions system. While our first focus group was successful to a point, we knew there were better or different ways to design a powerful acquisitions system. One of our engineers was an expert in a process called Contextual Inquiry (CI). This process is well known in the software industry and is a good idea for any software development. This engineer was able to get the buy-in from management to go ahead with the process.

THE PROCESS OF CONTEXTUAL INQUIRY

The Dynix Engineering Department has a position called Library Systems Analyst (LSA). This is usually filled by a librarian who works very closely with engineers, helping them understand workflow in the library, and also with customers to get a better understanding of requirements. The LSA acts as a translator between the engineers and the librarians, so that each group understands the others' vocabulary. The LSA worked with the engineer with CI experience and became familiar with the planning process. She began setting up site visits with eight libraries. It turned into a global endeavor as she visited with acquisitions librarians in Canada, the UK, and the United States. The engineer accompanied her on several visits, which gave him the opportunity to discover the unique things librarians deal with on a daily basis. I often hear engineers say "They would never do this," or "Why would they want this–it doesn't make sense?" After the first visit it started making sense. They watched how the librarians worked, asked lots of questions and took copious notes. They reported their findings back to the development team.

During one trip to a large library, the LSA watched how the serials librarian processed renewals and found that they were not done through the library's Dynix system. Vendors become concerned when customers need to use other software because it means something is lacking in the system. The advantage to tracking serials renewals through the ILS is that the system handles fund encumbering also. If the system is well designed, it correctly links the serials records with the acquisitions records so updates are made in just one place. This library considered the Horizon system's renewal process too cumbersome, so they relied on the serial agent's Website instead. The Dynix team recognized that this needed specific attention as we reevaluated serials renewals processing.

After eight site visits, hours and hours of information had been relayed back to the engineering team. They worked full time interpreting the information gathered at the libraries. They reviewed workflows such as the serials renewal process and mapped them out on large pieces of paper. Workflows from the different libraries were consolidated. There were similarities in the serials renewal processes from the eight libraries and also many differences. Storyboards were prepared to show the workflows. Storyboarding is a critical step in CI. It involves drawing out processes, diagramming a common workflow, inserting differences, and merging these differences into one workflow. The challenge for Dynix was to accommodate the differing workflows without causing additional work for those libraries that didn't use them.

Through the use of CI, our engineers gained a much better understanding of acquisitions. They were able to design a common workflow, and a large list of requirements was created. Unfortunately, company priorities shifted before coding began for the information we had gathered. Other key projects took development resources and there was personnel turnover. For several months new acquisitions development was placed on the back burner.

WHAT DID WE LEARN?

Where are we now? Interestingly enough, we're back on track for serials and acquisitions development. While the CI process was time consuming, all the information gathered was very valuable. While building our timelines and schedules for completing this project, we evaluated the strengths and weaknesses of CI and discovered a few things. To use the CI technique well, the process must be built into the development time schedule. Now we divide the CI process into smaller, more manageable pieces. We continue our site visits to watch how librarians work, and we ask questions in order to improve our software. We continue to help our engineers understand what goes on in serials and acquisitions departments. Probably the most important thing we learned is that we do not have the luxury of spending many months just in the CI process. It needs to be an iterative process where actual development goes on for one feature while CI begins on another.

CONCLUSION

Will ILS vendors ever create the perfect acquisitions system? I highly doubt it, as the definition of perfect varies from library to library. What most ILS vendors can and will do is to continue to ask librarians what is required, and perfect their juggling skills as they determine priorities and build software that makes librarians' lives easier, not more difficult.

CONTRIBUTOR'S NOTE

Shelley Neville is Library Systems' Analyst at Dynix.

From Tiny Acorns to Great Oaks: Taking a Nationwide Approach to Library Cooperation

Pauline La Rooy

Presenter

Ko te manu kai I te Miro nōna te ngāhere,
Ko te manu kai I te mātauranga nona te ao.
The bird who eats of the Miro tree owns the forest,
The bird who eats of the Tree of Knowledge owns the world.

This *Māori* proverb, which has been adopted by LIANZA–the Library and Information Association of New Zealand *Aotearoa*–is in keeping with the conference's theme of *Serials in the Park* and an apt way to start a presentation on nationwide library cooperation in New Zealand.

Interlibrary and inter-librarian cooperation is nothing new. Libraries share catalogue records, loan materials between libraries, build shared-stores, and enter consortia; librarians share information and network through listservs, associations, publications, and conferences. Serials librarians are very involved with collective purchasing and site licensing arrangements, cooperative archiving projects, and shared collection development strategies. Why come all this way to tell you about library cooperation in New Zealand? Because in New Zealand librarians have taken stock of their profession and noted the trend towards greater library cooperation; they have considered this in relation to the New Zealand context, and now they aspire to a nationwide approach to library cooperation to form a national information strategy.

[Haworth co-indexing entry note]: "From Tiny Acorns to Great Oaks: Taking a Nationwide Approach to Library Cooperation." La Rooy, Pauline. Co-published simultaneously in *The Serials Librarian* (The Haworth Information Press, an imprint of The Haworth Press, Inc.) Vol. 46, No. 1/2, 2004, pp. 161-171; and: *Serials in the Park* (ed: Patricia S. French, and Richard Worthing) The Haworth Information Press, an imprint of The Haworth Press, Inc., 2004, pp. 161-171. Single or multiple copies of this article are available for a fee from The Haworth Document Delivery Service [1-800-HAWORTH, 9:00 a.m. - 5:00 p.m. (EST). E-mail address: getinfo@haworthpress.com].

http://www.haworthpress.com/web/SER
Digital Object Identifier: 10.1300/J123v46n01_17

What is so unique about the New Zealand context? New Zealand is an island nation in the south of the Pacific Ocean. It is small. As of April 2003, it has a population of four million people. It has approximately five hundred libraries, eight of which are university libraries. It is English speaking, in a world where English is still the dominant language of publishing. It has a strong education sector from kindergarten through to higher education. It sports a healthy information and communication technology infrastructure. It propounds a sense of partnership between government and *Māori*, the indigenous people of New Zealand. These factors all contribute to New Zealand's ability to envisage itself as an ideal country within which to take a nationwide approach to library cooperation. A framework for how this may be achieved has been laid out by LIANZA in a document called *Towards a National Information Strategy.*

I will expand a little on the New Zealand environment, giving you a better idea of what fertile ground it would be for a nationwide approach to library cooperation, and explain how desirable and plausible such an approach is for New Zealand. I will also identify the challenges that will have to be faced before this goal is reached. An in-depth look at the document known as the *National Information Strategy* will follow. This is a living document which LIANZA reviews and updates regularly. To finish, I will share with you recent happenings such as the e-government project, the government directive that there be greater cooperation between libraries in the academic sector, and the new National Library Act. As each of these nationally focused library and information initiatives are achieved, New Zealand gets closer to making the National Information Strategy a reality–or at least to a stage where we can take a nationwide approach to library cooperation and beta test it for the rest of the world.

Let us start by considering New Zealand's size, probably its greatest asset in taking a nationwide approach to library cooperation. When one considers some of the statewide consortia and greater metropolitan library systems currently at work in the United States, compelling four million people and five hundred libraries to cooperate effectively should be relatively easy.

There are nationwide centralised systems for interlibrary loan, cooperative cataloguing, and school library support already in place–longtime stalwarts of the New Zealand library and information infrastructure. These are hosted and managed by the National Library of New Zealand and work well within a national framework. I use the term "well" loosely; a recent forum I attended for the purpose of discussing the interlibrary loan system clearly illustrated the adage that one cannot please all of the people all of the time. The basic fact remains, however, that it is easier to achieve consensus when there is a smaller number of participants. It is also easier to manage a system with a smaller number of participants.

Smallness in stature can also have its disadvantages. One of the main drivers behind library consortia is libraries' desire or need to have more leverage and bargaining power when purchasing monographs, serials, indexing tools and integrated library systems in the international market. New Zealand has to get the balance correct, because consortia with fewer members may be easier to manage, but it is the consortia with the power of numbers that are in the best position for bargaining with powerful vendors and publishers.

The academic libraries of New Zealand–particularly university libraries–are responsible for much of New Zealand's overseas purchasing power, especially for academic journals and electronic resources. Currently New Zealand university libraries do much of their purchasing of electronic resources through the Council of Australian University Librarians (CAUL). As its name suggests, CAUL is an Australian based consortium. Australia and New Zealand are neighbours (but still three and a half hours apart by plane) and, as in the case of CAUL, New Zealand is often invited to join Australia in projects. By partnering with a larger country, New Zealand university libraries have found they can purchase more electronic resources than they could alone. This raises two questions over whether New Zealand can conceivably adopt an initiative similar to the Canadian National Site Licensing Project: Under what circumstances might New Zealand university libraries consider moving from CAUL to a New Zealand based consortia, and, if New Zealand university libraries remain with CAUL, could New Zealand still form a consortium with enough purchasing power to negotiate with or even to attract vendors?

In July 2002, all library managers and schools were asked about their interest in the possibility of a nationwide library and schools consortium for the purchase of licences for electronic resources. Fewer than 20 percent of libraries responded. Only one university library responded. A second call for expressions of interest attracted a 42 percent response rate, again with little interest from university libraries but sufficient interest from polytechnic libraries, public libraries, school libraries, and government sector libraries to ensure a feasibility study. *Purchasing Electronic Resources: A National Approach* is a feasibility study currently in process which "will determine whether New Zealand libraries are ready for a consortium approach to electronic resources."[1]

Not surprisingly given its population, New Zealand does not have state-level government, and the central government has only one level of legislature. Public libraries still come under the jurisdiction of local authorities and private libraries are still subject to shareholders. But the National Library of New Zealand, the academic libraries, and the libraries of government bodies are all essentially under central governance. Without the complications of federal-state relations, the road to a nationwide approach to library cooperation is considerably simplified. New Zealand librarians are fortunate, too, in how accessible their politicians and decision makers are.

New Zealand has sound, up-to-date information communication technology. Geographically isolated, New Zealanders are very interested in the rest of the world. They have embraced emerging communication technology as a means of finding out more about the rest of the world, as a tool for corresponding with others overseas, and as a lucrative business opportunity. Thanks to different time zones, New Zealanders are working while Europe sleeps. For example, a London-based company might send a query to a reference librarian in New Zealand at the end of the business day and receive the answer on their desktop first thing the next morning.

The importance of partnership with *Māori*, the indigenous people of New Zealand, is less tangible but no less inherent to New Zealand's nationwide approach. The Treaty of Waitangi, signed in 1840, is New Zealand's founding document. One of the principles of the Treaty of Waitangi is that the government of New Zealand will work in partnership with *Māori*. In some areas this principle is stated in law; in others it is ingrained in culture. The nationwide approach in New Zealand involves working in partnership with *Māori*. An example of this is LIANZA's relationship with *Te Rōpū Whakahau*, the *Māori* Library and Information Workers' Group. This is a formal relationship agreement, which is reestablished each year at conference. There are places on the LIANZA council reserved for *Te Rōpū Whakahau* members and any documents or policies are written with full consultation. In August 2000, *Te Rōpū Whakahau* held a *hui*, a meeting to discuss the National Information Strategy document. Their input was fundamental to the drafting of the National Information Strategy.

This will have given you some idea of New Zealand and its library environment. It is in this environment that the seeds of the National Information Strategy were sown. It started a few years ago when the then government released a social policy paper called *Bright Futures*. It was a document about the path New Zealand would take to become a knowledge society; a document that did not recognise the role of libraries and librarians in building a knowledge society. This is where LIANZA got involved. ("LIANZA is the professional association that represents library and information professionals in New Zealand. The acronym LIANZA stands for the Library and Information Association of New Zealand *Aotearoa*.")[2] LIANZA held the attractively named LIPS–Library and Information Policy Summit–in December 1999. There were actually two LIPS. A second summit was held in July 2000. As a result of these summits, LIANZA committed itself to having an active voice in national policies relating to the library and information industry. It decided to take a holistic, nationwide, cooperative approach. The benefits of this were expected to be: the ability to use strength of numbers to ensure better lobbying and bargaining positions; the development of a more supportive and interactive library profession; the development of effective relationships with other related industries; the creation of a formal platform from which to launch cooperative library projects; and the creation of better synergy and consistency between library and information related projects.

Taking advantage of the change of government at the end of 1999, LIANZA positioned itself politically. LIANZA decided to take an inclusive approach, identifying all acts, regulations, and standards pertaining to libraries and information. It was a fruitful exercise, producing a wealth of information ranging from laws dealing with archives and heritage materials to legislation relating to the copyright of electronic resources. This formed the foundation for the National Information Strategy, admittedly quite vague and aimless in its raw form. Direction was achieved by clarifying the key principles of the strategy.

In establishing the core principles of the National Information Strategy, LIANZA is indebted to the United Kingdom for its National Information Policy and for the Keystone for the Information Age conference of April 2000.[3] The United Kingdom's policy incorporated the three principles of connectivity, content and capability. New Zealand adapted this to form our own three principles:

1. *Knowledge access* (*Te Kete Tuātea*): the infrastructure to communicate information through networks such as telecommunications and library systems. This is about ensuring the provision

of the tools which support the delivery of information: computer hardware and software; Internet access; librarians and information professionals. It is about ensuring that there is sufficient access to electronic and print resources in the places where people access information; home, work, and in the community;

2. *Knowledge content* (*Te Kete Aronui*): the access to information content through search tools and catalogues. This is about creating, acquiring, and identifying quality information content and providing bibliographic control so the content can be found and utilised; and
3. *Knowledge equity* (*Te Kete Tuauri*): the skills needed to turn information into knowledge such as literacy, computing skills, and information literacy skills. This is about supporting schools, public libraries, and community groups in assisting New Zealanders in acquiring the skills to use information effectively. It is about ensuring that information literacy skills are taught in all schools.

The theoretical framework of the National Information Strategy evolved. At its head would be a sponsoring cabinet minister. A Library and Information Commission would support the minister. It was the intention that a Library and Information Commission would spearhead any government initiatives relating to the library and information sector and represent the sector's views on more general initiatives. The Library and Information Commission would apply the three principles of knowledge access, knowledge content and knowledge equity when implementing these initiatives. The Commission would also encourage a nationwide approach from the library and information sector and provide a platform from which to manage nationwide library cooperation initiatives.

It was a relatively simple exercise to relate the knowledge access, content and equity principles to a number of the stated key objectives of the new government. The library and information industry has a lot to offer in support of a government that wants to increase the skill base of its citizens, strengthen its cultural identity, restore trust in government (through greater transparency and increased access to government information), and develop a growing and innovative economy. This has resulted in many lobbying opportunities for LIANZA such as making submissions on the National Library Bill and creating the Public Library Standards. The relationship between government and LIANZA has developed and there is a greater awareness of the National Information Strategy LIANZA is advocating.

So far, the New Zealand government has not adopted the National Information Strategy; however, its influence is evident. In May 2003 the new National Library Act came into place. The act "establishes the Library and Information Advisory Commission. This body has the brief of advising the minister on the rapidly changing field of libraries and information and of providing a national and international overview. This move supports a more outward looking National Library, empowered by the Act to work alongside other bodies with related aims."[4]

LIANZA and the library and information profession are increasingly recognised as stakeholders in a number of government initiatives. There are currently five main areas where we are trying to ensure that the principles of the National Information Strategy are being adopted, with varying levels of success. It should be noted that all of these strategies assume a nationwide cooperative approach.

The ICT in Schools Strategy is the government initiative for information and communication technology skills to be part of the high school curriculum. School libraries are keen to have greater involvement in this programme and to work towards knowledge equity for high school pupils. This aligns well with LIANZA's belief that "ICT skills should be taught in the classroom but practised in the school library as a laboratory for developing information/information literacy skills."[5]

The Connecting Communities Strategy is the government initiative to address the digital divide between the information rich and the information poor, and thus increase the skills of New Zealanders and build a knowledge society. LIANZA agrees that the digital divide needs to be addressed. E-mail and the Internet are part of many people's everyday lives, yet a significant number of New Zealanders do not have access to electronic information resources nor do they have the necessary skills to utilise this information. "LIANZA believes as part of the government Connecting Communities Strategies the public library system can be strengthened to provide equitable access to information to the community."[6] There is a role public libraries can play in helping New Zealand communities achieve knowledge access and knowledge equity.

The E-government Strategy is a government initiative that aims to "use the new technologies to provide people with more convenient access to government information and services, to improve the quality of the services and to provide greater opportunities to participate in our democratic institutions and processes."[7] The library and information profession has already had considerable input into this project, particularly in the areas of metadata and thesauri. The e-government project has made good progress: large amounts of government and government agency information are now available electronically, with effective search engines. This demonstrates the knowledge content principle. Many New Zealanders can access this information at home or at work, but for those who cannot it is essential that the Connecting Communities Strategy and the E-government Strategy work together. Again there is a role for public libraries to assist people with access to e-government information, knowledge access and knowledge equity.

The Heritage Information Strategy is a LIANZA initiative that identifies a need for "a co-ordinated policy, structure or infrastructure for managing heritage resources in libraries, archives, local government and museums."[8] It is about ensuring that all documentation relating to New Zealand, whether published or not, whether print or electronic, is collected and preserved as knowledge content and is accessible to all New Zealanders. This strategy aligns itself with the government objective to strengthen New Zealand's cultural identity.

The Intellectual Property and National Consortia Information Strategy is a LIANZA initiative designed to support research in New Zealand. This is the section of the National Information Strategy that deals specifically with academic and research libraries such as the Victoria University of Wellington Library where I work. "LIANZA argues that Government should act to ensure appropriate access for New Zealanders to the local and international knowledge resources needed to support innovation and the knowledge society."[9] The National Information Strategy makes a number of recommendations on how to achieve this, including: reviewing copyright legislation so that it is less prohibitive to education and research; creating an indexing and abstracting database of New Zealand research; negotiating national site licenses (as is being explored in the *Purchasing Electronic Resources: A National Approach* feasibility study mentioned earlier); and encouraging academic and research libraries to enter into cooperative arrangements.

This last recommendation fits neatly with the aforementioned government directive that there be greater cooperation between libraries in the academic sector and it also aligns with some of the recommendations made in a report commissioned by Council of New Zealand University Librarians (CONZUL) in 2002. This report is called, *The Big Picture: Opportunities for Potential Areas for Closer Collaboration among the New Zealand University Libraries. The Big Picture* is a significant document and to critique it would be a conference paper in itself.

Suffice to say, it identified many opportunities for closer collaboration. I expect that New Zealand university libraries will explore and adopt at least some of these in the future.

At present, the largest collaborative project New Zealand university libraries are involved in is CONZULSys–a shared integrated library system project among four of the university libraries, one of which is Victoria University of Wellington Library. The four libraries maintain separate databases but purchase common software and operate from a shared server. The rationale behind this project marries nicely with the key principles of the National Information Strategy–knowledge content and knowledge access. "This option was adopted to provide cost benefits and lay foundation for wider and easier access to academic/research information to serve the broader New Zealand research and heritage community."[10]

This briefly outlines the National Information Strategy, the principles and strategies underlying it, and what is currently happening of a nationwide collaborative nature in the library and information industry of New Zealand. The National Information Strategy is a wide-ranging, inclusive vision and encompasses all areas of the library and information profession. As a serials librarian working in New Zealand, how do I expect the current nationwide library initiatives to have an impact on serials work?

The academic libraries' shared integrated library system project is likely to result in better bibliographic control of serials, as it will be easier to share relevant information. It will also act as a convenient reference point for exploring complementary collection development policies and serial retention policies. In addition, it will provide greater common ground between the serials librarians in academic libraries, encouraging better networking and collegial support. There will be more cooperative ventures between New Zealand academic libraries: possibly a national shared storage facility; possibly a shared pool of cataloguing specialists for music and languages; possibly job swaps to share skills. This week LIANZA-TELSIG (Tertiary Education Libraries Special Interest Group) held a partnership conference: Cooperation, Communication, Collaboration, Conversation. I look forward to hearing the ideas from that and relating them to my role in serials.

PER:NA–Purchasing Electronic Resources: a National Approach will definitely have an effect on serials librarianship, providing that the feasibility study concludes that it is a viable model. New Zealand university libraries would then have to choose between CAUL, the consortia with Australian university libraries, and an inclusive consortium based in New Zealand. If they choose the latter, there will be some real challenges to work cooperatively with libraries from so many different sectors but there will also be real rewards in such a diverse network.

Likewise, a database which indexes and abstracts New Zealand's research output will definitely have an impact. Ease of access would increase use of serials published in New Zealand, which in turn would encourage a greater amount of New Zealand based publishing.

To date, the e-government project has had the pleasant effect of subsuming a number of government publications of a serials nature. Most newsletters and reports from government agencies are now available electronically, as are a number of official publications such as *Parliamentary Order Papers*. When the *1999 New Zealand Official Yearbook* was published in electronic format only there was a deal of controversy. Now serials librarians enjoy the convenience of electronic government publication while regularly reminding the publishing bodies of the importance of archiving past issues.

Even the ICT in Schools Strategy and the Connecting Communities Strategy are likely to have flow-on effects into the world of serials. After all, a country whose citizens have good access to information and the skills and interest to use it–a country that has a knowledge society–is a country where people are more likely to go on to higher education. And a strong academic sector will definitely need more serials.

NOTES

1. Fiona Rigby, "PER:NA-Purchasing Electronic Resources: A National Approach," *nz-libs listserv*, nz-libs@vuw.ac.nz (13 June 2003).

2. Library and Information Association New Zealand Aotearoa, "Towards a National Information Strategy," Nov. 2002, http://www.lianza.org.nz/text_files/nis_7nov02.pdf (6 Jun. 2003).

3. Ibid.

4. National Library of New Zealand, "What does the new National Library Act mean?" 1 May 2003, http://www.natlib.govt.nz/bin/news/pr?item+1051750597 (17 Jun. 2003).

5. Library and Information Association New Zealand Aotearoa, "Towards a National Information Strategy," Nov. 2002 http://www.lianza.org.nz/text_files/nis_7nov02.pdf (6 Jun. 2003).

6. Ibid.

7. State Services Commission, "E-government–A vision for New Zealanders," 1 May 2000, http://www.e-government.govt.nz/programme/vision.asp (17 Jun. 2003).

8. Library and Information Association New Zealand Aotearoa, "Towards a National Information Strategy," Nov. 2002 http://www.lianza.org.nz/text_files/nis_7nov02.pdf (6 Jun. 2003).

9. Ibid.

10. Council of New Zealand University Librarians, "CONZULSys Communiqué," Mar. 2002, http://www.conzul.ac.nz/CONZULSys%20(2).pdf (17 Jun. 2003).

REFERENCES

Council of New Zealand University Librarians. "CONZULSys Communiqué." Mar. 2002 http://www.conzul.ac.nz/CONZULSys%20(2).pdf (17 Jun. 2003).

Library and Information Association New Zealand Aotearoa. "Towards a National Information Strategy." Nov. 2002 http://www.lianza.org.nz/text_files/nis_7nov02.pdf (6 Jun. 2003).

National Library of New Zealand. " What does the new National Library Act mean?" 1 May 2003 http://www.natlib.govt.nz/bin/news/pr?item+1051750597 (17 Jun. 2003).

Renwick, Helen. "The Big Picture: Opportunities for potential areas for closer collaboration among the New Zealand university libraries." Jun. 2002. http://www.conzul.ac.nz/BigPicture.pdf (19 Jun. 2003).

Rigby, Fiona. "PER:NA-Purchasing Electronic Resources: A National Approach." *nz-libs listserv.* nz-libs@vuw.ac.nz (13 Jun. 2003).

State Services Commission. "E-government–A vision for New Zealanders." 1 May 2000. http://www.e-government.govt.nz/programme/vision.asp (17 Jun. 2003).

State Services Commission. "E-government Strategy–Home Page." Dec. 2001. http://www.e-government.govt.nz/programme/strategy.asp (17 Jun. 2003).

CONTRIBUTOR'S NOTE

Pauline La Rooy is Serials Librarian at Victoria University of Wellington, New Zealand.

Helping Manage the E-Journal Forest: Do You Need an Agent Any More? Part 1

Philip Wallas

Presenter

SUMMARY. The complexity of e-journal subscription management is requiring subscription agents to re-invent themselves to meet new demands. E-journal subscriptions have many more components, including licensing, registration, access, usage statistics, and archiving. By consolidating information and providing one-to-many and many-to-one flows of information, agents can provide efficiencies in operational tasks as well as simplifying the financial transactions. Agents also can add value in negotiations and in aggregating access to e-journals. Agents are making changes in processes such as speeding communications to publishers, partnering with third party content hosting services, and entering into discussions about standards for communication of electronic subscription information. This paper was presented as part of a panel that included presentations by Steve Bosch and Selden Lamoureux. *[Article copies available for a fee from The Haworth Document Delivery Service: 1-800-HAWORTH. E-mail address: <docdelivery@haworthpress.com> Website: <http://www.HaworthPress.com>]*

[Haworth co-indexing entry note]: "Helping Manage the E-Journal Forest: Do You Need an Agent Any More? Part 1." Wallas, Philip. Co-published simultaneously in *The Serials Librarian* (The Haworth Information Press, an imprint of The Haworth Press, Inc.) Vol. 46, No. 1/2, 2004, pp. 173-177; and: *Serials in the Park* (ed: Patricia S. French, and Richard Worthing) The Haworth Information Press, an imprint of The Haworth Press, Inc., 2004, pp. 173-177. Single or multiple copies of this article are available for a fee from The Haworth Document Delivery Service [1-800-HAWORTH, 9:00 a.m. - 5:00 p.m. (EST). E-mail address: getinfo@haworthpress.com].

http://www.haworthpress.com/web/SER
Digital Object Identifier: 10.1300/J123v46n01_18

At the 2002 NASIG conference, one of the plenary speakers warned subscription agents that they had better have some other line of business, implying that their existing business was going to disappear due to changes in scholarly publishing. That remark spurred me to propose a panel for this year's conference to explain some of the ways agents are reinventing themselves and to hear librarians discuss how they are and are not using agents.

WHY DO AGENTS EXIST?

Since I work for an agent my bias is obvious, so I'll keep my part of the presentation short. I offer my remarks as a reflection of the role of agents in general, not any particular agent. Agents exist to create efficiencies by managing one-to-many and many-to-one relationships. Aggregation and consolidation are our prime principles. The agent's core business has been to relieve the library and the publisher of certain back office operations. Working with an agent ought to cost less than doing it yourself.

All parties are coming to understand how e-journal subscriptions are different from print subscriptions: they are more complex; more a relationship, not just a transaction. What starts as a single event requires maintenance on both sides. Here's a generalized task cycle for e-journal subscriptions, with similarities to the print cycle but with additional requirements. Libraries need to *identify, select, negotiate for, license, order, pay for, register, access, integrate, administer, resolve problems, evaluate usage*, may need to *archive*, and need to *renew* their e-journal subscriptions.

Agents (and publishers, for that matter) are scrambling to meet the high expectations that libraries have for e-journals. How are we handling the cycle of tasks? I'll focus on a few areas where agents have made the most changes or provide the greatest value.

Identify. Agents have long maintained title databases to track title changes, price changes, ownership transfers and so forth. These databases have been expanded to list e-journals as well as publisher packages and even custom collections. Agents monitor when journals become available online and notify print subscribers.

Negotiate and license. Agents offer negotiation facilitation to streamline the request and offer process because they understand the demands of licensing and consortia deals. I have worked with dozens of publishers as they form their online pricing and packaging strategies, and draft licenses. Because agents have experience with the whole market, we can help publishers (and libraries) understand which approaches work and which are not well received.

Order. Agents have developed new e-journal order processing systems. What worked for print is too slow for online. When everything goes right, new e-journal orders go to the publisher and to the publisher's content host at the same time, often with expedited payment allowing access to be turned on in days instead of weeks. We now capture and include the customer contact name, e-mail address and, if we can get it, the publisher's customer subscriber ID in e-orders. Of course, everything does not always go right, but we're learning and participating in development of standards for the exchange of subscription information.

Payment. Agents consolidate financial transactions. Their invoicing experience and understanding of library needs have always been a strength, along with foreign currency capabilities and global offices.

Registration. Many publishers and content hosts describe the problem of subscribers who do not register for the online access they are entitled to, so online access goes unrealized. Agents have developed "back door" partnerships with content hosts so they can help libraries register for access, then help maintain any changes (in IP addresses, contact information etc.)

Access and integration. Many agents offer consolidated e-journal gateways–a single user interface to e-journal content from any source. These interfaces are not just searchable collections of metadata and links, but are "subscription-aware," so users know which content they own and which they can purchase by the article. Agents have also developed dozens of ILS interfaces and are able to provide durable URLs for OPACs. Agents understand and supply MARC records. Agents are also beginning to provide comprehensive A-to-Z services and OpenURL compliant link servers.

WHY LIBRARIES AND PUBLISHERS GO DIRECT

Why are some libraries and some publishers playing what someone has called "disintermediate thy neighbor" and bypassing agents? There are several reasons. Perhaps most common is the idea that the publisher can save the cost of the agent's commission. Yet publishers have frequently underestimated the costs and complexity of providing an e-journal service, beginning by making them available "free" with a print subscription ("it's so simple, we don't need an agent"). Now publishers find there really is no free lunch as they are challenged to provide detailed invoices, round the clock customer service, ILS and MARC record feeds and persistent e-journal links. Their systems are inadequate to meet these demands and their responses are, by nature, piecemeal. Should each of them develop the necessary systems? At what costs? Also, publishers are concerned that the involvement of a middleman might obscure important market signals as they experiment with terms, packaging and pricing for online journals. Libraries bypass agents because publishers encouraged it and agents didn't respond particularly well to licensing and consortia needs at first. Last year, an Ingenta Research Institute report quoted one librarian as saying agents had missed the boat on consortia e-journal licensing. I can personally testify that, whether we missed the boat or not, we are swimming very hard now.

JUST BECAUSE YOU CAN DOESN'T MEAN YOU SHOULD

Publishers are asking themselves what functions are truly a part of their core business. Many are deciding that they are not technology organizations, and are outsourcing their content hosting. Even some publishers who at first excluded agents from handling financial aspects of their online licenses have decided that the invoicing and collection roles, too, are best handled by a third party with economies of scale. For both publishers and libraries, thinking about core roles can lead to the recognition that just because the library or publisher can go direct, that is not necessarily the best course. What is the best use of your professional staff resources?

WHAT WE MUST DO BETTER

The new e-journal processes we have developed have to evolve from special projects to become an integral part of our operations, efficiently automated and with rich status communications back to libraries and customers. We must continue to support standards for licensing, linking, usage reporting, and exchange of subscription information. More generally, agents have not done a good enough job explaining the value they add and have not done a good enough job of explaining to libraries and publishers how agents make money. In light of the RoweCom collapse, the latter point takes on increased significance. We have to do a renewed job of explaining ourselves.

WHY LIBRARIES BENEFIT FROM USING AN AGENT

Agents continue to assist libraries in the following ways:

1. No single publisher can provide the overview information fundamental to making collection development decisions.
2. Focusing on Big Deals cannot meet important needs. Smaller publishers still publish a very large number of key titles; for example, the Brandon-Hill core titles for medical libraries are published by 61 different publishers, many of whom do not have the staff to deal directly with libraries.
3. No publisher service or content host is as comprehensive as agent gateways in providing a "subscription-aware" single point of access to your e-journal subscriptions.
4. Consolidating financial transactions continues to have the benefits it has always had: reduced administrative costs for the library and publisher and invoicing that meets your needs.
5. Agents are service organizations; publishers are not.

If you are convinced of the value of using an agent, do not assume that publishers automatically allow agents to be involved in a transaction. If you insist, almost all publishers will allow your agent to handle the financial transaction. Make their inclusion explicit in the agreement.

If you are persuaded that going direct is the best approach, understand the work involved to manage post-sale access, integration, administration, and other tasks and be sure who will be responsible for each of them.

CONTRIBUTOR'S NOTES

Philip Wallas is Director of Online Relations at EBSCO Information Services (E-mail: pwallas@ebsco.com).

Helping Manage The E-Journal Forest: Do You Need an Agent Any More? Part 2

Stephen Bosch

Presenter

SUMMARY. Electronic publishing is changing the business of serial publication. Yet despite tremendous growth in the volume of electronic publishing, traditional print publishing has not disappeared; consequently e-publishing has introduced more complexity into the environment, and current service needs co-exist alongside the need for new services required to manage e-publishing. Some believe that electronic publishing will be the end of the serial vendor or subscription agent; others are not so ready to mark their passing.

Assuming that the current commercial model will remain relatively unchanged as the basis for most scholarly communication, the roles of serial vendors or subscription agents will change, but the services they bring to the library and the publishing community will continue to prove valuable. Support will still be needed for paper subscriptions, and new services are needed to manage e-journals. Of course change is inevitable, and those service providers that fail to react to the changing environment will go out of business. Those that are able to develop new products will survive in the changed environment. If the basic business model transforms, and freely-accessible institutional digital repositories become the primary

[Haworth co-indexing entry note]: "Helping Manage the E-Journal Forest: Do You Need an Agent Any More? Part 2." Bosch, Stephen. Co-published simultaneously in *The Serials Librarian* (The Haworth Information Press, an imprint of The Haworth Press, Inc.) Vol. 46, No. 1/2, 2004, pp. 179-190; and: *Serials in the Park* (ed: Patricia S. French, and Richard Worthing) The Haworth Information Press, an imprint of The Haworth Press, Inc., 2004, pp. 179-190. Single or multiple copies of this article are available for a fee from The Haworth Document Delivery Service [1-800-HAWORTH, 9:00 a.m. - 5:00 p.m. (EST). E-mail address: getinfo@haworthpress.com].

http://www.haworthpress.com/web/SER

Digital Object Identifier: 10.1300/J123v46n01_19

nodes for scholarly communication, then the publisher/vendor/ library chain will become irrelevant. *[Article copies available for a fee from The Haworth Document Delivery Service: 1-800-HAWORTH. E-mail address: <docdelivery@haworthpress.com> Website: <http://www.HaworthPress.com>]*

INTRODUCTION

Vendors have been an important fixture in the library/publishing business model for a long time, but changes in the model are causing some customers to rethink that relationship. In a digital environment, why do we need to work with vendors? Up to now, the vendor's value-added services seemed fairly clear. Support for ordering, renewing, claiming, and invoicing was an important service that many libraries purchased from vendors without a large of amount of angst. Now, some of this service may appear unnecessary since many e-journals are bundled into packages that don't require the same amount of basic service support. Why not save the service charge and handle the order yourself? Why would a business developed to manage the acquisition of paper journals be needed in an environment where libraries buy electronic objects rather than physical ones.

There is not going to be a single answer to that question. Libraries will have their own set of needs and resources available to fill those needs. Continuing relationships with vendors will depend on how well vendors can change to meet an organization's needs. A small school whose serials are all tied up in a few bundles may have little need for a vendor, while a large library with significant paper subscriptions and a large number of e-journal subscriptions with small publishers might still need a vendor's services.

THE CURRENT SCENARIO

The current environment has not been favorable to serials vendors. There has been considerable contraction in the industry. The business runs on notoriously small profit margins and limited library budget growth; reductions in commissions from publishers, cancellations (mostly due to price inflation), and the costs of technological innovation have all contributed to volatility in the marketplace. There are fewer and fewer choices as companies are absorbed into larger corporations or go out of business entirely. A large full-service vendor may now:

- Maintain a comprehensive database of more than 240,000 serial titles
- Have an active working relationships with more than 65,000 publishers
- Provide services to over 50,000 libraries including academic, corporate, government and public libraries

It is important to note that vendors have had to develop a significant infrastructure and they have developed one-to-many relationships with both their customers and publishers. This will be an important point later.

Currently, the standard services that serial vendors supply for print orders include:

- New orders
- Invoicing and automation support for invoicing
- Order consolidation
- Database revisions
- Claiming/replacements
- Samples
- Renewal notices
- Cancellations
- Support for electronic ordering, claiming, publisher reports and other Electronic Data Interchange (EDI)
- Collection assessment and evaluation reports
- Reports (on price inflation, title distribution by country of origin, where titles are indexed, etc.)
- Management of memberships

Serial vendors supply the following standard services to publishers:

- Consolidating payments
- Sales data
- Marketing (e.g., vendors list titles in systems)

Vendors became partners in the serials distribution process because they were able to provide value-added services that reduced the costs of managing serials for both libraries and publishers. Obviously, to stay in business vendors must continue to reduce the costs to libraries for managing serials, especially the costs of managing electronic serials. In the past, the value of a vendor was determined by their ability to provide timely and accurate renewals, accurate invoices, quick processing of claims, timely and accurate placement of orders, and quality customer support. Currently, vendors are expected to maintain these services while providing new services that help libraries achieve similar cost efficiencies for the management of e-journals.

Electronic publishing is changing the current business model. Between 1996 and 2001 the Association of Research Libraries (ARL) Supplementary Statistics Reports indicated that reporting libraries increased their expenditures for electronic serials from approximately $15,000,000 to over $117,000,000.[1] One large serials vendor reports that subscriptions for electronic journals now account for nearly 15 percent of their business.[2] Some of vendor services may continue into the digital environment, but many may no longer be needed. Pushing the development of the electronic end of the business to an extreme (e.g., assuming that nearly all subscriptions are for e-journals) may result in changes in the following services provided by vendors:

- *New orders.* There will still be a need to support this activity.
- *Invoicing and automation support for invoicing.* If you are paying one-line invoices, the need for this service is possibly diminished.
- *Order consolidation.* If you are paying one-line invoices for large groups of customers, the need for this service is possibly diminished.
- *Database revisions.* This activity is useful to maintain library/vendor records. If there is no vendor, the need for this service is diminished.
- *Claiming/replacements.* This service will no longer be needed.
- *Samples.* This service will no longer be needed.
- *Renewal notices.* If you are working with large packages, the need for this service is diminished.
- *Cancellations.* If you are working with large packages, the need for this service is diminished.
- *Support for electronic ordering, claiming, publisher reports, and other EDI.* There will still be a need to support this activity, but it may not be vendor-specific.
- *Collection assessment and evaluation reports.* There will still be a need to support this activity.
- *Reports and projections on price inflation, reports on title distribution by country of origin, reports on where titles are indexed.* If you are working with large packages, pricing is in the contract and the need for inflation figures is diminished.
- *Management of memberships.* There will still be a need to support this activity.

This is a cursory look at potential changes. It is not, however, a realistic overview because most likely libraries are going to continue to collect some print journals for the foreseeable future. All of the above services will continue to be needed for at least part of the serials collection. At this time my own library spends about 33 percent of its serials budget on e-journals, whereas a review of the ARL figures in 2001 shows expenditures for electronic serials averaging 23 percent of overall expenditures for serials.[3] There seems to be a leveling off in growth after a period of extreme growth because many of the big serial publishers have already brought their packages to market. One can easily conclude that e-publishing has not made life simpler by reducing the need to process physical objects. It has done the opposite by layering another process over the existing ones with a continuing need for both. Managing serials is more complex, not less complex, in the current environment. This being the case, what other factors would lead libraries to question their business relationships with vendors?

PUBLISHER OR VENDOR–IS THAT THE QUESTION?

Recently, publishers have attempted to have subscriptions for e-only journals placed directly with the publisher and not through serial vendors. This pressure from some publishers to move away from the current business model has been part of the reason that we have to ask the question, does my library need a serials vendor? This represents a shift in the basic business model and this shift has major implications for all stakeholders including libraries, vendors, and other publishers

Many publishers assume they can stop using vendors to aggregate subscriptions in the electronic environment and that publishers can manage all accounts directly. Some go so far as to include savings from this shift in their business plans. Even when libraries have demanded that vendors handle the subscriptions, it is important to note that the publishers will no longer discount these renewal orders to vendors. Publishers are basically looking at a business model for e-journals in which packages are marketed and sold directly to libraries and the services of serial vendors are no longer used. Publishers don't expect to provide libraries with the standard services provided by vendors, however, nor any additional services.

When looking at the traditional set of services vendors provide libraries, there are real reasons why publishers should believe that in the e-publishing environment they can improve their profit margins and reduce the costs of their products to libraries by working directly with libraries. Because packages are bundled, there is no need for elaborate invoicing. There is no need for claiming. Renewals of continuing contracts are a snap. Customer service is handled directly by their staff without a "middleperson." Cancellations are minimized by contract stipulations and, since there are few transactions, there is no need for expensive technology to handle EDI. Libraries can save the costs of the service charge and, in some situations, receive a credit from the publisher for going direct. The publisher can save on the commission they formerly paid to vendors. On the surface this seems to makes sense.

When looked at globally, however, this shift may not be beneficial for libraries for multiple reasons. Some of the assumptions stated above may be erroneous. Some libraries may still need invoicing that can be electronically posted to individual e-journal titles. Some libraries allocate and expend funds at a fairly discrete level and this requires detailed payment information to chart expenditures against allocations. If libraries received one-line invoices for most publisher packages, expenditures could not be posted to discrete fund lines without significant manual intervention by libraries. Without expenses posted at a discrete level, it is difficult to allocate to individual fund lines and it would not be possible to monitor price changes and project inflation for fund lines again without significant manual intervention by libraries. The ability to track inflation and price changes for individual serial titles could be greatly compromised.

Detailed expenditure information would not be available through the one-line payment process. Subscription agents have invested resources in developing the proprietary interfaces needed to load financial data into a variety of library systems. Publishers won't do this. Subscription agents supply libraries with electronic invoices that allow the posting of payments with a minimum of effort. Libraries could change to accept one-line invoices or adjust internal systems and processes to manually post financial information. Increases in local processing costs or a loss of value-added services would have to be weighed against the savings from ordering packages direct from publishers.

If it ever became necessary to dissolve a bundled package, the unbundling process would be very difficult without a history of the basis for the package and its costs. Renegotiation of bundled packages will become more common given current budgets. Maintaining accurate title-level cost records provides a good basis for making decisions if it becomes necessary to reduce a package. Most libraries belong to a consortium. Subscription audits are the basis for creating many consortial agreements. The maintenance of accurate subscription records is critical for these audits. Without vendors, this work would have to be assumed somewhere, and most consortia and publishers do not have good systems for tracking this information.

There are additional reasons why this shift in the e-journal business model may not be good for libraries. The large packages from a few publishers would represent the bulk of the shift to vendorless transactions. The packages from a handful of publishers probably represent the bulk of the electronic serial expenditures reported by ARL libraries, but in all likelihood the actual number of subscriptions represented by the packages is much smaller. My local experience is that the big packages represent 25 percent of the dollar value of serials budget, but only 5 percent of the total subscriptions. Removing the orders for these packages from the mix means that the costs/service charges for the remainder of our subscriptions aggregated with serials vendors increase significantly. Essentially, we would be removing 25 percent of the dollar value from the account but leaving 95 percent of the work. The revenues for serial vendors are derived from the service charges levied customers, and from discounts received from publishers. Not all publishers can supply discounts, but the largest of these discounts have historically come from the larger publishers. In a direct marketing plan, these revenues are no longer part of the equation, and this will squeeze vendors and inevitably raise costs for libraries. Increased costs would have to be offset by reduced costs from the direct packages.

WHAT WOULD NEED TO BE DONE IN A WORLD WITHOUT VENDORS?

In a digital environment, some work such as claiming and replacing missing copies goes away, but other tasks such as basic financial processes will remain. It doesn't matter if a subscription is online or on paper, the publishers still want to be paid. The use of business-to-business software is becoming more common, but only the largest publishers are able to conduct a large portion of their business directly online with libraries. Smaller publishers don't have the resources needed to implement EDI to conduct their business. The parent organizations for most libraries do not have solid e-business systems in place to support serial purchasing activities.

In the past, subscription agents reduced the amount of checks that had to be cut, reduced the proofs of payments that had to be reproduced, and vendors made payments in foreign currencies. If direct purchase plans become the norm, local processing of financial transactions will increase and in many cases this will increase internal costs. My university isn't able to conduct much of its business in an electronic environment and it costs the central accounts payable unit $50-$100 to cut a check. It requires just about the same amount of effort and internal costs to produce a proof-of-payment voucher. My business office would not be pleased if I informed them that the library was changing its model and would now need to have the office cut an additional x,xxx checks per year with 10 percent of the checks paid in a foreign currency. Again, the savings achieved by not using a subscription agent would have to be weighed against the increased costs of absorbing some of the required processes. The situation won't be the same for all libraries. A small library that may make a few payments to a consortia for serial packages could save more dollars than a large library that had thousands of subscriptions it had to process internally.

Another service that would have to be absorbed locally is serials management reports. Agents provide their customers with important pricing and collection development reports. Vendors maintain large databases that allow them to track price changes and to provide comparative collection evaluation reports. Agents aggregate a large part of a library's business and are able to provide data and analysis that is used for budget allocation and collection assessment efforts. In a publisher-based purchasing model, this data collection and analysis is shifted to libraries. Data would have to be aggregated from several disparate sources to derive good expenditure, and collection management reports. Given the opportunity to reduce costs, this may be a trade off that is acceptable to some, but may not be feasible for others.

NEW SERVICE ROLES FOR SERIAL VENDORS

The traditional roles of vendors are changing and it is certain that some of their services will no longer be needed in the future. If publishers can make a case that the value-added services of vendors are no longer needed and that the savings garnered by ordering packages directly from publishers are greater than the additional costs incurred by a library, the publisher/vendor/library business model will change. Given this scenario, if vendors remain totally reliant on old service models, it is appropriate to question their future. The required services will diminish and revenue will diminish as well. Given tight margins, the financial viability of the business model would be doubtful. There may be some vendors who choose not to modify their service base but there will be others that will look upon changes in the publishing industry as opportunities to bring new services to market to replace those that will disappear. The vendors who make changes will probably survive or even thrive.

Commercial systems to manage most processes that involve purchasing electronic journals are nearly non-existent. This lack impacts libraries, users, vendors and publishers. Not having the tools to make the process work smoothly forces the participants to approach the process on an ad hoc basis, and to work on solutions to problems as they go. This is not cost-effective. Serial vendors are well positioned to bring systems and processes to market that could help manage e-journals. Vendors are able to bring additional features to management systems due to their relationships with publishers and the databases they have built as part of their business.

The management processes for e-journals could include:

- Acquisitions, including product identification, trials, terms, licensing, and order fulfillment
- Access, including registration, creation of bibliographic and metadata, linking and notification
- Account administration, including managing user IDs, passwords, IP addresses; managing content (titles added to or falling out of packages); providing pertinent information to users
- Problem resolution, including identifying and resolving access problems
- Renewals, including evaluation of use statistics and problem logs and cost benefit analysis

Serial vendors are in a position to use their current business infrastructure to build new services to manage serials in an electronic environment. Their databases of publisher information contain most of the information needed to support the process. They have gathered huge amounts of information on titles. Is the online free with print or is there a surcharge? Is a license required? If a license is required where can I get a copy? Who would it be returned to? Does the publisher work with consortia? Vendors' experience in building systems to move data between systems will also add value. Other aspects could include:

- Bibliographic, publisher, and title data available from internal systems
- Pricing, license, and registration terms

- Customer data
- Links to publisher's Web sites to automate registration
- Bibliographic and metadata records including holdings information
- Links to publishers to automate the troubleshooting process

Serial vendors could use these buildings blocks to provide systems that would help customers manage e-journals. These systems could gather all information needed from publishers concerning standard information required to acquire an e-journal including:

- Bibliographic and metadata information
- Stable URLs
- License terms
- Registration information
- Help desk/technical support information

An e-journal or e-resource management system would gather data such as customer account information, the customer's default licensing terms and preferred pricing models, the customer's requirements for linking, and the customer's requirements for public display of the terms for use; it would combine this data with the above information stored in the system to streamline the ordering process. The system could then track an order from trial, to license completion, to purchase, to access and linking completion and finally through the renewal process. The system could provide information that streamlines the process and in some cases the system could automate the process. Vendors have the basic building blocks for these types of systems but it will remain to be seen if they are successful in integrating current data structures and data warehouses into the data structures and data warehouses that could provide systems for managing e-journals.

Some vendors are pursuing service enhancements like these, but this is not the only area in which new services are being developed. The other side of e-journal management deals with access issues involved in e-journal management. Access services include:

- Platforms for aggregating content from multiple publishers
- Support for a variety of authentication methods including password, IP, or proxy servers
- Multi-level search engines
- Maintenance of URL's
- Providing extended linking or support for services like CrossRef

- Bibliographic records with correct holdings and URLs
- Support for customized search screens and viewing preferences
- Aggregated use statistics
- Links and management of pay-per-use e-journals or document delivery services

Some of these services are available from sources other than subscription agents. Serial vendors will not be the only group able to bring these services to the library community. Serial vendors will be able to aggregate these services with support for licensing and registration and the service needed to support paper subscriptions to bring a full menu of potential services for serials management to libraries. It would be reasonable to expect that most services offered by subscription agents would be priced based on libraries subscribing to the service, and a single service charge covering all services may be a thing of the past. Libraries could negotiate those services they needed; economies of scale could make these services less costly from subscription agents, but that would be determined by individual libraries looking at their needs.

CONCLUSION

Business models do change. There is no sense in sticking with one just because you are comfortable with it. All the stakeholders in the publisher/vendor/library relationship need to look at what brings value to the relationships in the current model, and how needed value-added activities can be maintained in an environment dominated by electronic publishing. The business relationship libraries developed with vendors reduced internal costs for conducting that business. Can a mix be found that supports the remaining paper-based business while integrating new processes for managing electronic serials? In an electronic environment claiming will disappear, but maintaining links and access will become the new claiming.

There will not be a simple answer to the question, "Do you need an agent any more?" Perhaps the real question might be, "Do you know why you would still need an agent?" With new ways of acquiring electronic publishing via bundled packages or consortial purchases, the answer to this question will be varied. Some libraries will continue to need vendors, others may not.

There are many reasons why vendors could continue to be valued service providers. They would provide support for financial functions, order management, licensing and registration management, and access management. Detailed invoicing that shows title by title what is subscribed to in a publisher's package is very important information to have. Keeping track of subscriptions and payment histories is actually more complicated in the electronic environment. When a link to an e-journal fails, it is just as important to be able to provide a subscription payment history. Orders will still need to be placed. There is a need for services to support the licensing and registration of e-journals and there is also is need to provide access management.

Yes, libraries have had to pay increased fees to agents to get these services, but because of economies of scale, vendors can provide these services more cheaply than libraries can through local processes. What should be looked at is the need for the service, and the potential savings that could be achieved by removing the vendor from the business model. If savings are significant, and the need for services low, then vendors aren't needed. Given the complexity of the publishing trade, I doubt that there are really many libraries that will be able manage their serials without the aid of a vendor in the near future.

NOTES

1. Association of Research Libraries, *ARL Supplementary Statistics, 2000-01* (Washington, DC: Association of Research Libraries, 2002), http://www.arl.org/stats/pubpdf/ sup01.pdf, 9 (21 Oct. 2003).
2. Swets Blackwell, *Press Release* (Nov. 27, 2002), http://www.swetsblackwell.com/press.htm (21 Oct. 2003).
3. *Machine-Readable Files of ARL Statistics Data*, http://www.arl.org/stats/ arlstat/mrstat.html (27 Oct. 2003).

CONTRIBUTOR'S NOTE

Stephen Bosch is Materials Budget, Procurement, and Licensing Librarian, University of Arizona, Tucson, AZ.

Hot Topics

Keith Courtney
Miriam Gilbert
Michael Markwith
Kim Maxwell

Presenters

Jerry R. Brown

Recorder

SUMMARY. What does industry consolidation mean for libraries, publishers, and vendors? The panel members were each given five minutes to talk about the state of mergers in the serials publishing industry from their perspective. They represented the viewpoint of a librarian, vendor, and publisher. This report paraphrases the conversation that filled this session with important ideas and concerns that need to be studied more thoroughly. Note: this report is based on the Saturday session only. *[Article copies available for a fee from The Haworth Document Delivery Service: 1-800-HAWORTH. E-mail address: <docdelivery@haworthpress.com> Website: <http://www.HaworthPress.com>]*

Anne McKee thanked this year's Program Planning Committee for trying some new formats. Attendees at previous conferences have asked for a hot topics session and these presenters agreed to do this session

[Haworth co-indexing entry note]: "Hot Topics." Brown, Jerry R. Co-published simultaneously in *The Serials Librarian* (The Haworth Information Press, an imprint of The Haworth Press, Inc.) Vol. 46, No. 1/2, 2004, pp. 191-199; and: *Serials in the Park* (ed: Patricia S. French, and Richard Worthing) The Haworth Information Press, an imprint of The Haworth Press, Inc., 2004, pp. 191-199. Single or multiple copies of this article are available for a fee from The Haworth Document Delivery Service [1-800-HAWORTH, 9:00 a.m. - 5:00 p.m. (EST). E-mail address: getinfo@haworthpress.com].

http://www.haworthpress.com/web/SER
Digital Object Identifier: 10.1300/J123v46n01_20

with only three weeks lead time. She introduced the speakers to the audience and explained the session guidelines. Each speaker had five minutes to speak and then the floor was opened for audience questions or comments.

Keith Courtney announced that, because there was insufficient time to prepare a paper, he was going to take parts of an article, "Merger Mania?" from *Scholarly Communications Report* as a basis for his comments on merger trends.[1] About 60 percent of the material indexed through Thomson ISI is now produced by Elsevier, Springer, or Taylor & Francis. This clearly rebuts the idea that scholarly publishing is essentially a cottage industry.

Historically, publishing mergers have resulted in higher prices. Publishers maintain that libraries benefit from mergers because larger companies will be able to take advantage of economies of scale and decrease costs. The resulting increased competition will keep prices down. Librarians worry that there will be little competition between the European publishers and, if they focus on profit (which is only to be expected), prices will rise.

Miriam Gilbert mentioned that this is her first NASIG conference. In the face of mergers and changes in the publishing business, each organization must concentrate on its core competencies. Small to medium-sized companies must find what they do best and concentrate on excellence. What can you do better? Passion and commitment aren't going to translate to your bottom line. Most small businesses claim excellent customer service as a hallmark of their company. How can a company be sure that's true? Is what they're doing contributing to the bottom line?

There's a real cultural difference between print and electronic publishing. You have to get your product to market and see how the customers react in order to learn what has to be done to get it right. Yesterday, Leigh Watson Healy talked about "e-mojo" in her plenary session. We have to have an edge and urgency to make these changes. We're all in this industry because of a love of a certain detail, correctness, and order, but there comes a time when we have to take a tough look at what we are doing and ask, What is the economic basis of it? All libraries are governed by budgets. None work for charities. What is the cost and what does the end user ultimately want?

Michael Markwith said that to prepare for his presentation he asked a number of people why mergers was a hot topic and received a group of mixed answers. His challenge was to decide what we were talking about in this meeting. Are we talking about publisher mergers? Are we talking about vendor mergers? Are we talking about library mergers (consortia purchasing)? He realized today that the answer has been delivered to his laptop every day. Every day the same e-mail messages arrive on three topics: Does size matter? Do you need money? Do you need people?

Yes, size can matter. No company is more committed to consolidation than WalMart. Proctor and Gamble built their sales office next door to the Benton, Arkansas, headquarters of WalMart. They've built offices that replicate WalMart stores, with shelves and walls where their products will be displayed in WalMart. Do you know why they've done that? Because twenty years ago, Proctor and Gamble's sales were 100 percent directly to the consumer. Today, 17 percent of their sales are to WalMart. That is something to think about.

The second email that keeps coming to his desktop: Do you need to consolidate now? In the business world the question is: Do we need money? Do investors need to be repaid for their investment in the businesses whether it's a publisher or a subscription agent or a bookseller? Considering the things that Leigh Watson Healy said in her plenary presentation about how technology is changing the information industry, it appears that the answer is "yes." The global context of technology drives our business. Technology has changed our roles. In fact, the globalness of technology breeds consolidation.

The third thing that keeps coming up on the desktop is: Are you looking for a partner? Instead of companies buying one another, maybe the way to go is to look for ways to set up partnerships. Despite what Keith read from *Scholarly Communication Reports*, perhaps it would be good for smaller companies that are focused on specific tasks to find ways to implement some form of *coopetition*. Coopetition is the term developed to identify the need for competitors to manage to cooperate so that the businesses can manage to survive.[2] Coopetition has become popular in many industries; perhaps it should become a bigger part of our industry. Companies will partner in a short-term relationship and then move on to meet changing needs in the library community. Instead of companies buying and merging, they should look for a partner to work with. That is an answer to consolidation. It keeps the options open for the smaller and independent operations.

Kim Maxwell stated that she would focus on vendors and subscription agents because, as a serials acquisitions librarian, she deals with subscription agents and vendors all the time. When she started at MIT in 1997, they had four major subscription agents and a couple of smaller ones. Now they have one subscription agent. Readmore Academic and Blackwell's Periodicals became Blackwell's Information Services.

Blackwell's Information Services merged with Swets Subscription Services to form Swets Blackwell. Swets Blackwell bought Martinez-Mienhoff International and stayed Swets Blackwell. There are some vendors who have remained constant. EBSCO is still EBSCO; Harrassowitz is still Harrassowitz; Everetts is still Everetts. At MIT, the majority of subscriptions have changed vendors in just the last five years. The speed of this change is surprising and worrying.

Ms. Maxwell went on to describe the book side of things at MIT:

> We have a lot of standing orders with Blackwell's Books (which had been Blackwell North America), and with Academic Book Center. They are now one company although they operate separately. Our money is still sort of in one place. I started to think about what this really means for us. What changes have I made or what changes do we see coming? There are always conversion issues when vendors merge. They have to merge two completely different systems and two completely different sets of services. I think that the reason Blackwell and Academic Book Center haven't completely merged yet is that they have two totally different approaches to approval plans. They haven't quite figured out how to merge those, so they're still operating separately. They're trying to figure out what their customers need. Everyone is re-creating themselves, creating new organizational cultures and new identities.
>
> Although not a consolidation, the death of Faxon/RoweCom got the attention of Financial Services at our university. We were not a Faxon customer so it didn't get their attention in that way, but we actually approached Financial Services to say we're about to plunk down 3.5 million dollars pre-payment money; we want you to know what's happening in the industry and we want to have a discussion with you about that. That office was never really involved in our decisions; we just didn't talk to them about that. There's a real focus now on protecting our money that wasn't there before. I think that our day-to-day level of comfort is still there, but I think there are some new relationships being built between people at a much higher level of the administration in the libraries and the financial administration of our institution.
>
> Everything I've said is kind of a knee-jerk reaction to what happens when vendors merge. But performance standards are something I'm ready to start drafting and talking about to our vendors. I have job descriptions and performance standards for every-

one on my staff. In a way, my vendors are part of my staff. I've contracted with them, hired them, or have some kind of agreement for them to provide a service to me. I need to let vendors know what I expect and how I think they're doing. I know plenty of libraries have done this. For me, watching what's happening and knowing that there are fewer and fewer companies with which I can do business means that I really need to talk to the vendors I do business with to make sure we're getting what we need.

Right now, am I making any changes immediately? No. Mostly because I don't have the staff to do that and I think that might be where a lot of libraries are caught. Everyone has budget cuts, hiring freezes, possible layoffs coming, or can't hire anyone new. That puts us in a bind because at the same time we want to be doing all these things, we don't have the staff to deal with them. This doesn't mean I'm not going to do something as I can. I think it raises the consciousness level. It's not just an acquisitions issue or serials problem any more. It's become an issue at really a much higher level in the administration of the library and something that they never talked to us about before but that they are starting to talk to us about now.

Anne McKee opened the discussion to the floor.

Katy Ginanni from Ebsco Information Services: Before I moved to the vendor side, I was a Faxon customer. Vendors do consider themselves part of, or an extension of, the library staff, and are really interested in being helpful.

Mike Markwith: I worked for Richard Abel in college. He was probably the first bookseller who focused on academia in the U.S. He created the approval plan in the 1950s. In the 1950s, his company was worth a couple of hundred thousand dollars, in 1967 it was worth two or three million dollars with maybe a hundred employees, and by 1972 it was worth 15 million dollars with six to seven hundred employees and a new office. The company grew too quickly and then the recession of the early 1970s happened and Abel ended up purchased by Blackwell. The sales were there; they just couldn't keep up.

Eleanor Cook: But how did it affect customers?

Mike Markwith: Oh, they got screwed! Some librarians held out for the dust to settle and Blackwell North America worked with them and eventually worked it out.

Dena Schoen (from Harrassowitz): I must disagree with Kim. I am not your staff; I'm your vendor. WalMartization of the product means a tendency to no longer work with customers. I came out of librarianship. I'm interested in serving my customers, not necessarily being your friend.

Miriam Gilbert: Kim did say something really important and that was the phrase "performance standards." Let's be really clear about what we expect from each other. We have to establish benchmarks so that everyone will understand what their responsibilities are in the relationship and can have some accountability.

Anne McKee: I think what's so interesting about this whole discussion is that (for those of you who remember when Abel went under) that's when you started hearing the phrase in the library industry, "all my eggs in one basket." For years there was talk about how libraries were going to diversify. Diversify subscription vendors, diversify book vendors. They were not going to have all their eggs in one basket. People have long memories, and it affected a lot. Just in the past few years, people were starting to think about putting more of their eggs in one basket. But the decision was made for them. Companies keep consolidating, so pretty much your eggs are all in one basket. But it's due to consolidation, not library decisions.

Mike Markwith: Is the problem fewer choices, or is the problem that the choices you have aren't meeting your needs? With size, money, and investment, these companies have staff and power and ways to create new products to create new services to meet new needs as library needs change, as technology changes. The question is, do you fear that there are too few choices or fear that people aren't listening to provide the services you need?

Marty Gordon: In a capitalist, laissez-faire environment (which we're not in now) more players, or at least a critical mass of players, ensure competition as long as there are no closed-door agreements among the players.

Emily: At ALA a few years ago, I looked around the vendor area and realized that all those people make a living from libraries. They are not partners with us. Who else are they going to sell their product to? As a profession, we do not use our clout to get changes we need. What can we do as a profession, a buying block, to get better service from the vendors instead of just accepting whatever models are offered?

Anne McKee: Librarians seem to ask for the wrong things. We need to reach a consensus about how to use our buying power.

Miriam Gilbert: Michael mentioned competition. This is one of my concerns. New initiatives seem to have more viability. Are you thinking of changes due to new ideas, like the Open Archives Initiative? Do publishers view that as a new form of competition since scholars may use open archives to self-publish?

We [Marcel Dekker] are aware of it. We are interested in knowing what librarians think. What does Open Archives mean for the university culture of scholarship? What does it mean for traditional publishers? I honestly don't know what it means. We're all wrestling with ongoing change and need to figure out ways to deal with it so that everyone survives.

Marilyn Geller: The reason you can't make a deal with the publishers is because we're dealing with a dysfunctional economic model. The problem is that the people paying are not the people using the product. You have no power in that situation.

Mary Page: We need to answer several questions about change. Who else is of a similar size that we can work with? What are the implications of these changes? What is it we really want? It's very important that we find answers. Everything has a price tag.

Reeta Sinha: We live in a state of anxiety in libraries. We're discussing document delivery directly to the user. This is another service that can lead to users feeling the library is irrelevant to their needs.

Phil Greene: There is no lack of competition in the subscription business. There may be fewer companies in business, but having fewer players does not mean the competition is less intense. Competition today is healthier than it's been in years. No one should have dealings with a vendor without checking the company's financial standing. Competitive pressures are causing people to think of competition in a new way; self-publishing is gaining popularity, quality of service and offering innovative services is coming along.

Anne McKee: Keith, I'm interested in what's going on in Britain and on the continent.

Keith Courtney: The Open Archives Initiative bypasses the peer review process. I think change is likely to start here in the U.S. and come to us.

Eleanor Cook: In the next couple of years, I expect to see articles and presentations about how libraries dealt with this issue.

Marilyn Geller: I'd like more discussion on the small versus large question. There is value in a small organization that can tailor services to fit its customers. How can small companies survive? Maybe Taylor & Francis can easily do URLs, but Marcel Dekker will find it harder. It takes lots of R and D, i.e., money, to take advantage of the new technologies, and develop new products. It seems that large companies can do the more expensive projects more easily than smaller companies.

Keith Courtney: There is still a need for small publishers. It's a shame there aren't more people out there to buy the small companies and keep them independent. All too many of them want to sell. Libraries tend to spend the bulk of their budgets with the big companies instead of supporting small companies.

Jodi Bussell: The destruction of quality bibliographic expertise because of mergers of subscription agents is causing the destruction of the standing order. All the e-journal business is going against standing orders.

Marilyn Geller: Standing orders are very expensive for small companies to do. The reason you're asking agents to do standing orders is because libraries get no respect in academia. The fact is, until we educate the provosts who are responsible for choosing the companies we work with, they will tend to continue working with the larger companies.

Dena Schoen: We are speaking in a vacuum. There are new models to cope with. We are asking agents to do what we have no money to do. We need advocates to educate vendors and develop new, needed services.

Cheryl Riley: Too many educational institutions haven't made good business decisions because we haven't wanted to be a business.

Anne McKee: Also, libraries haven't done enough marketing of their services and resources to convince our users and administrators that we hold an important place in our communities and offer valuable services to our users.

NOTES

1. "Merger Mania." *Scholarly Communications Report* 7, no. 5 (May 2003): 2-4.
2. Joe McGarvey. "Through the Looking Glass." *Inter@ctive Week* 7, no. 23 (6/12/2000): 59. http://search.epnet.com/.

CONTRIBUTORS' NOTES

Keith Courtney is Group Sales Director at Taylor & Francis and currently the Chair of the UK Serials Group. A former NASIG Board member, he has attended all the NASIG conferences. Miriam Gilbert is Assistant Vice President, Licensing and Consortia Sales at Marcel Dekker, Inc., a leading mid-sized STM publisher. Gilbert served as netLibrary's Senior Director, Publisher Relations; she was responsible for acquiring the content that formed the foundation of netLibrary's eBook collection. Michael Markwith is President of TDNet, Inc. He was previously at Swets & Zeitlinger, The

Faxon Company, and Blackwell North America. A little known fact about him is that as a graduate student at Berkeley, he regularly had lunch with Joan Baez. Kim Maxwell has been a serials acquisitions librarian at the MIT libraries since October 1997. She has been chair of the ALCTS Serials Section Acquisitions Committee for the past two years and is a member of the NASIG Continuing Education Committee. A past NASIG Student Grant Award recipient, she presented at the last two NASIG conferences, and is the desktop publisher for our print NASIG membership directory. Jerry R. Brown is Instructor of Library Services, Central Missouri State University.

[The recorder thanks Anne McKee for the biographical information on the presenters.]

WORKSHOPS

Case Studies in Electronic Serials Cataloging, or What Am I Supposed to Do With This?

Steve Shadle

Workshop Leader

Holley R. Lange

Recorder

SUMMARY. Shadle examined the CONSER recommended aggregator-neutral record, providing background on its development, as well as examples and discussion of records demonstrating the changes that are underway. He also included a brief discussion on electronic serials and integrating resources, with examples that served to clarify their differences. Lastly, there was discussion on title changes and buried title changes as they might appear in electronic serials, with suggestions on ways to most effectively handle them. *[Article copies available for a fee from The Haworth Document Delivery Service: 1-800-HAWORTH. E-mail address: <docdelivery@haworthpress.com> Website: <http://www.HaworthPress.com>]*

Electronic serials cataloging is a dynamic arena. Changes are occurring both in the items available to catalog and also in the guidelines and

---

[Haworth co-indexing entry note]: "Case Studies in Electronic Serials Cataloging, or What Am I Supposed to Do With This?" Lange, Holley R. Co-published simultaneously in *The Serials Librarian* (The Haworth Information Press, an imprint of The Haworth Press, Inc.) Vol. 46, No. 3/4, 2004, pp. 203-208; and: *Serials in the Park* (ed: Patricia S. French, and Richard Worthing) The Haworth Information Press, an imprint of The Haworth Press, Inc., 2004, pp. 203-208. Single or multiple copies of this article are available for a fee from The Haworth Document Delivery Service [1-800-HAWORTH, 9:00 a.m. - 5:00 p.m. (EST). E-mail address: getinfo@haworthpress.com].

http://www.haworthpress.com/web/SER
Digital Object Identifier: 10.1300/J123v46n03_01

recommended approaches for cataloging them established by such organizations as CONSER (Cooperative Online Serials Program, a component of the Program for Cooperative Cataloging). In his presentation, *Case Studies in Electronic Serials Cataloging, or What Am I Supposed to Do With This?* Steve Shadle addressed some of the current issues and upcoming changes in electronic serials cataloging. Mr. Shadle dealt primarily with records for electronic serials in the form of the aggregator-neutral record, its background and development, upcoming implementation by CONSER members, and provided examples of such records. He also described and gave examples of records that demonstrated title changes in electronic serials and the distinctions between electronic serials and integrating resources.

As companies began to provide electronic access to a particular journal title in their own package or aggregation of titles, catalogers were expected to find ways to provide access to these titles. For several years CONSER supported separate records for these types of serials. It soon became apparent, however, that another approach was needed as the number of these packages increased, providers were added, titles were dropped and sold, and companies changed hands and names. In this changing environment CONSER reexamined its guidelines, concluding that the differences between versions supplied by different providers did not reflect bibliographic differences in the item, but rather different licensing arrangements and access. The concept of the aggregator-neutral cataloging record came about in response to these changes, and because few libraries want to have multiple records for what is essentially one title. The aggregator-neutral record is, then, one record (separate from the record for the print resource) that can represent all manifestations of the same online serial; this is not a multiple version record, but one that will provide access to the electronic serial regardless of provider.

As of July 1, 2003, CONSER libraries will officially implement the guidelines for creating aggregator-neutral records. Cleanup of the many multiple records has already begun in OCLC, and it is estimated that this cleanup will take approximately two years. CONSER libraries will create records using the new guidelines. If multiple records already exist for a particular title, a CONSER or NSDP (National Serial Data Program) record will be chosen, edited (made neutral) as appropriate, and the remaining duplicate records will be reported to OCLC for deletion. If the only record available is one specific to a particular provider, it can be made neutral, with the appropriate URL added. The CONSER goal is to have a single serial record for all serials in aggregator packages.

These guidelines do *not* apply to full-text aggregator databases because coverage in these databases lack stability, and access to content in these databases is generally at the *article* level rather than the *title* level. Creating these aggregator-neutral records will not differ from other electronic serials cataloging, except that the 856/URL will apply to individual manifestations, so there may well be several 856 fields on any one record, and, as appropriate, title added entries may reflect titles on individual provider Web sites.

Following this more general introduction to the aggregator-neutral record, Mr. Shadle then turned to the following fields in the record itself: source of description; title (uniform title (130/240), title proper (245), and title added entries (246)); place of publication/publisher/date (260); frequency (310/321); numbering (362); a number of notes fields; provider added entries (710/730); and electronic access field (856). Specifics on the use of these fields are highlighted below.

Source of description: Information in the cataloging record is to be based on the most authoritative source, for example the publisher's site; if such access is not available, or another site has more coverage, that site may be used. The print record may also be used if these sources are not available, or, as a last resort, the record can be based on information found in another aggregation.

Uniform title (130/240): The name of the aggregator will no longer be used as part of the uniform title, although the same qualifier as needed for the print will be used; e.g., *Studies in English literature, 1500-1900 (Online : JSTOR)* will become: *Studies in English literature, 1500-1900 (Online); China journal (Canberra, A.C.T. : Online : JSTOR)* will become: *China journal (Canberra, A.C.T : Online).*

Title proper (245): As with cataloging records for print serials, the title for an electronic serial is transcribed from the first or earliest available issue. This will be preferred over the homepage title. If there are multiple titles presented (including the title for the corresponding print version), generally prefer transcribing the print version title so that print and online version records will collocate in the catalog and will be in sync when the title changes. Another way of describing this is "follow the pattern of the print, if possible."

Title added entries (246): If titles on the serial vary with different providers, the variants should be included; e.g.: *246 1 ǂi Issues from some providers have title: ǂa . . .*

Place of publication, publisher, date (260): The publisher/place in the 260 field will be from the first/earliest available issue for electronic serials; for digitized print serials this generally will be the publisher/ place as found in the print version. The transcribed date, as with other serial cataloging, will be from the first/last issue. Dates may well be those from the print version; digitization or online dates are generally not transcribed.

Frequency (310/321): The recorded frequency will relate to the title itself, and should apply to all versions.

Numbering (362): If the first issue is used for transcription, then the *362 0* is appropriate. If the first issue has been digitized, but is not available, the *362 1 Began with . . .* can be used. If it is not known whether the first issue is available, the *362 1 Print began with . . .* can be used. Electronic coverage notes will no longer be used, and OCLC will replace those with these *Print began with . . .* notes.

Notes (5XX): Many of the 5XX notes now appearing on these electronic serials will generally no longer be used in the aggregator-neutral record; these include the 500/550, Provider Note; 506, Access Restrictions Note; 516, Type of Computer File Note; and 538, System Requirements Note. Notes such as the following will be discontinued: *506 Restricted to institution with a site license to the JSTOR collection; 516 HTML (Electronic journal); 550 Digitized and made available by: Project Muse.* The *538 Mode of Access: World Wide Web* will be included. The 500 Title Source Note, however, will contain explicit information as to the source and description of the title being cataloged, for example, *500 Title from title screen (publisher's Website viewed Mar. 22, 2003).*

Provider added entries (710/730): These will no longer be needed, so headings such as: *710 2 Project Muse*, or *710 2 JSTOR (Organization)* will not appear on these neutral records.

Electronic location/access (856): These fields may be added to reflect individual access. Therefore a record might have multiple 856 fields (e.g., *856 40 ‡u http://www.jstor.org/journals/00393657.html*, as well as: *856 40 ‡u http://lion.chadwyck.com/StudiesinEnglishLiterature15001/ issues.htm*) in either OCLC or a particular catalog. Additional provider information may be added in the 856.

530/776/780/785: These fields will continue to be used in the aggregator-neutral record in the same way they are in other serials cataloging.

While the aggregator-neutral record is just that–a record stripped of provider information–which is usable by any library regardless of the source of its own record, it does not mean that individual libraries cannot choose to customize their own records. A library might wish to have access by provider by adding the appropriate 710 field, or a note in the body of the record. Shadle suggested that these local notes might be added in batch mode, driven by information present in the 856. Shadle then presented some detailed examples of how a record might change with the implementation of these guidelines. Undoubtedly, the CONSER Website (http://www.loc.gov/acq/conser/homepage.html) will be a useful resource for updated information as well as updated examples as these changes are implemented.

The final portion of Mr. Shadle's presentation was entitled *Case Studies,* and dealt primarily with examples that served as points of discussion as to whether the presented item should be cataloged as a serial or as an integrating resource. He also gave examples for decision making about title changes in electronic serials. For the serial/integrating resource discussion, examples included a publisher's Website, an online and frequently updated Website for a major newspaper, and an association Website. Shadle reminded us of the differences between an integrating resource (is material added, changed, or deleted via updates that do not remain discrete?) and a serial (does it have a succession of discrete parts, usually include numbering, and lack a predetermined conclusion?) and suggested looking at *LCRI* 1.0 as well as *CCM* 33.16 for clarification.

Finally, Mr. Shadle discussed title changes and buried title changes in electronic serials. There are three basic ways that these title changes might appear: (1) the title change appears as separate Websites, and has separate URLs for the earlier and later titles; (2) the title change appears on the same Website with the same URL used for the earlier and later title, but the earlier title still appears on the issues; and, (3) the title change appears on the same Website, having the same URL for the earlier and later title, but the earlier title has essentially disappeared from the site. In general, where there is confusion over title changes as evidenced in the electronic version of the serial, the pattern found in the print version can be used, and when all else fails, common sense in cataloging these materials should be the guiding principle.

Mr. Shadle's presentation was well received, with the level of interest evidenced by the number of people attending, and by the discussion and questions from the audience. Electronic serials continue to be a medium in flux, and Mr. Shadle presented this emerging information clearly, drawing on his expertise as a serials cataloger and a trainer in this developing field.

CONTRIBUTORS' NOTES

Steve Shadle is a serials cataloger at the University of Washington, SCCTP trainer (Serials Cooperative Cataloging Training Program) and speaker on issues related to e-serials. Holley R. Lange is a catalog librarian from Colorado State University.

Branching Out: The Importance of Networking in a Library Landscape

Jeff Slagell

Workshop Leader

Mykie Howard

Recorder

SUMMARY. What a feeling! Do you remember the point when you fell in love with the library profession? How about when you fell in love with serials work? Ponder on that feeling for a moment. Now, think of how you would feel if you lost your job because you fell behind the curve or because it was perceived that your talents, knowledge, and skills were no longer needed or valued. How can library professionals avoid the latter fate? The answer is networking. *[Article copies available for a fee from The Haworth Document Delivery Service: 1-800-HAWORTH. E-mail address: <docdelivery@haworthpress.com> Website: <http://www.HaworthPress.com>]*

As budgets decrease, as times get harder, and as many are losing jobs, who you know (as opposed to what you know) is more important than ever. The very energetic Jeff Slagell presented an excellent workshop

[Haworth co-indexing entry note]: "Branching Out: The Importance of Networking in a Library Landscape." Howard, Mykie. Co-published simultaneously in *The Serials Librarian* (The Haworth Information Press, an imprint of The Haworth Press, Inc.) Vol. 46, No. 3/4, 2004, pp. 209-213; and: *Serials in the Park* (ed: Patricia S. French, and Richard Worthing) The Haworth Information Press, an imprint of The Haworth Press, Inc., 2004, pp. 209-213. Single or multiple copies of this article are available for a fee from The Haworth Document Delivery Service [1-800-HAWORTH, 9:00 a.m. - 5:00 p.m. (EST). E-mail address: getinfo@haworthpress.com].

http://www.haworthpress.com/web/SER
Digital Object Identifier: 10.1300/J123v46n03_02

filled with great networking information and tips for any professional, not just the librarian. The location, Portland State University's Food for Thought Café, fit the topic. It had bright green walls and was decorated with buckets of twigs and branches. Growth and energy were all around.

Jeff began the session with the following quote (with some modifications) from Gordon Gekko played by Michael Douglas in the movie *Wall Street*:

> The point is, ladies and gentleman, greed is good. Greed works, greed is right. Greed clarifies, cuts through, and captures the essence of the evolutionary spirit. Greed, in all of its forms, greed for life, money, love, knowledge, has marked the upward surge of mankind–and greed, mark my words–will save not only you, but also the library profession.

In offering this quote, Jeff was not telling us to be greedy librarian cutthroats. Rather, he was trying to illustrate how vital networking is to our survival. Jeff warned about misconceptions often associated with networking in the 1980s when the term and activity were popular within the business profession. Networking is not an activity of greed. It is an activity of sharing: "How can I help you?" and "What can you teach me?" Networking involves the giving and teaching of your skills, similar to a mentor/mentee relationship, regardless of whether you are a seasoned professional or a newbie MLS grad.

To demonstrate the power and magnitude of networking, Jeff engaged his audience in an icebreaker activity, asking us to introduce ourselves and to say where we were born. In just a small crowd of about fifteen people, an internationally diverse instant network was immediately revealed: Lexington, Kentucky; Memphis, Tennessee; Louisville, Kentucky; Cincinnati, Ohio; Ottawa, Canada; Manchester, Iowa; Dunedin, New Zealand; and India were among the locations where workshop participants began their own personal networks. Most of the audience currently does not live in the same place where they were born and may have moved many places over time, increasing their network wherever they were. Although it is hard to realize it as it is happening, each stage of our life and each person we meet (personally and professionally) increases our own personal network and the rewards/results of networking accumulate over time.

So, why network? As the aforementioned words by Gekko in *Wall Street* emphasized, networking will save us. Networking (inside and outside of the library profession) is essential to our own professional survival as well as the survival of our profession. Things change. Professions change, especially the library profession. Positions change, and the people in those positions change. Nothing is ever certain. Only the fittest survive. Jeff provided many good reasons and explanations for networking, some of which can be found in Harvey Mackay's *Dig Your Well Before You're Thirsty*. We cannot survive on our own. We must keep in mind the fact that other people know things and people whom we don't. Likewise, it is imperative that we realize that networking reaps two types of rewards. Some networking rewards may be seen in the far distant future. However, the "magic mirror" principle suggests that you can also receive immediate rewards by obtaining immediate feedback and the synergetic bouncing of ideas between two parties.

For example, Jeff shared how his department created a serials database in Microsoft Access and he sent a copy to a colleague who was dealing with a similar problem. A short time later, the colleague e-mailed the database back to Jeff with some added features that Jeff had never thought of.

Networking involves taking advantage of other people's skills, knowledge, and abilities. As Jeff pointed out, there is no need to reinvent the wheel. But there is a need for us to gather all of the hard information (lectures, brochures, and handouts) and soft information (pertaining to character, morale, ambition and motivation) that we can. Soft information is a concept brought up in Simon Ford's article in *Library Association Record*, "The Art of Conferencing." Besides, networking is energizing! It allows us to get excited about and fall in love with the library profession and serials work all over again!

Have you ever felt silly or awkward walking up to a complete stranger and introducing yourself at a conference? Have you ever felt like a broken record at the end of the conference after repeating your introduction over and over again? Indeed, networking is generally difficult for most. One of the points made in Harvey Mackay's book is that networking is difficult because it is a learned behavior. In getting us started on learning this behavior and on the networking path, Jeff suggested the following: know your goals, identify relevant people, go deep versus broad, keep track, and maintain. As with all endeavors in life, it is important to know where you're going and what you're doing. Goals give us targets at which to aim.

For instance, my own personal goal for this year's NASIG conference (my first) was to network with other serials librarians all over the country for the purpose of support, learning, and sharing. My goal was definitely achieved, for I met a lot of great people who love serials work as much as I do. It was fun to see and network with serials people whom I have met in other settings: former supervisors, classmates, trainers, and trainees, as well as people I have met at other library conferences.

Although Jeff believes that one should always be "trolling the water" and that "antennae should always be up," he strongly suggests that we can benefit most from networking when we identify key people with whom we have something in common: same ILS, same vendor, same problem, etc. Jeff stressed, however, that networking is not a game of numbers. Going deep (quality networking with fewer people) as opposed to going wide (lower quality networking with many people) is more beneficial. As with most things, it is important to keep track and maintain any relationships resulting from networking. Otherwise, all networking will be done in vain. Just as information does not turn into knowledge unless you do something with it or put it to work, networking is not beneficial unless you track and maintain your contacts with follow-up.

Before ending the session, Jeff left us with some rules and pitfalls to help in our networking endeavors.

CARDINAL RULES OF NETWORKING

- Be yourself
- Strive for mutual benefit
- Always follow through
- Invest in the long term

FOUR COMMON PITFALLS OF NETWORKING

- Staying within your comfort zone
- Overcommitting
- Loss of perspective (taking things personally)
- Electronic communication temptations (reacting, treating people like machines, pretense, paranoia, getting overwhelmed, getting addicted, wasting time)

Not following these rules or succumbing to these pitfalls will surely lead to empty networking and wasting time and effort. Depending on the person, being yourself can be easy or hard. People can usually tell if you're being honest. So, be honest and forthright when networking. Also, don't be a selfish networker. Make sure each party gets something out of the networking. Do what you say you will do, because your reputation follows you. Also, be patient. As mentioned earlier, networking has both immediate and future rewards. The future rewards may come when you least expect it, but they may also be the most bountiful networking rewards you may receive (e.g., finding a job or being recognized by the profession).

In conclusion, Jeff Slagell indeed provided the attendees of his session with great food for thought in the Food for Thought Café. Growth and change are always good, although they may make us uneasy. Growth and change cause us to stretch our branches farther than we ever thought we could, leaving us shouting "What a feeling!" and getting great results in our careers.

RESOURCES

Ford, Simon. 1998. The Art of Conferencing. *Library Association Record* 100 (4): 194-195.

Mackay, Harvey. 1999. *Dig Your Well Before You're Thirsty*. New York: Doubleday.

CONTRIBUTORS' NOTES

Jeff Slagell is Assistant Director of Library Services at Delta State University. Mykie Howard is Serials Acquisitions Librarian at George Washington University.

Web-Based Trails and Cross-Campus Partnerships

Sharon Elteto
Maggie McVay-Lynch
Workshop Leaders

Elizabeth Parang
Recorder

SUMMARY. At Portland State University, librarians work closely with faculty in cross-campus partnerships. Sharon Elteto presented examples of the Web-based trails created by librarians to aid faculty in integrating library resources into instruction, and other trails created by librarians working with faculty to aid students in conducting research. Maggie McVay-Lynch demonstrated and guided workshop participants in the use of four electronic communication tools. *[Article copies available for a fee from The Haworth Document Delivery Service: 1-800-HAWORTH. E-mail address: <docdelivery@haworthpress.com> Website: <http://www.HaworthPress.com>]*

Workshop participants received a handout that reproduced the four PowerPoint slides available on the presentation Website. Sharon's portion of the workshop consisted mainly of presentation of products–the

[Haworth co-indexing entry note]: "Web-Based Trails and Cross-Campus Partnerships." Parang, Elizabeth. Co-published simultaneously in *The Serials Librarian* (The Haworth Information Press, an imprint of The Haworth Press, Inc.) Vol. 46, No. 3/4, 2004, pp. 215-219; and: *Serials in the Park* (ed: Patricia S. French, and Richard Worthing) The Haworth Information Press, an imprint of The Haworth Press, Inc., 2004, pp. 215-219. Single or multiple copies of this article are available for a fee from The Haworth Document Delivery Service [1-800-HAWORTH, 9:00 a.m. - 5:00 p.m. (EST). E-mail address: getinfo@haworthpress.com].

http://www.haworthpress.com/web/SER
Digital Object Identifier: 10.1300/J123v46n03_03

Web-based trails–created by Portland State University librarians and faculty; Maggie's portion consisted of a discussion of four electronic communication tools. Because this presentation conveniently took place in a computer lab in the PSU Library, the workshop participants had hands-on access to the Websites and electronic communication tools discussed. All of the Websites are linked from a page created for this presentation: http://web.pdx.edu/~mmlynch/webtrails.htm. The presenters brought a lot of experience to this project: Sharon Elteto has been employed by the PSU Library for 24 years, working as an instruction librarian since 1997. Maggie McVay-Lynch has 25 years experience in education and has recently concentrated on the distributed environment, developing over 60 online courses; she is the author of *The Online Educator*.

Sharon began the presentation by discussing current practices at Portland State University. Instruction activities are permeated with information literacy goals. Currently the most important activity is the creation of cross-campus partnerships. Working with the Office of Information Technologies, one goal of the Library is to educate faculty involved in distance learning, specifically with *WebCT*, on the importance of including library resources. Using a SMARTboard, Sharon called up the Website *Integrating Library Resources into WebCT* that was part of a 2002-2003 workshop series, *The Teaching Library*, co-sponsored by the Center for Academic Excellence. Other Center for Academic Excellence activities that involve the library include Scholarly Communication Workshops, Endnote Workshops and Focus on the Faculty presentations. Through these workshops, the Library plays a key role in educating faculty on dealing with plagiarism.

The PSU Library encourages "Partners for Presentations." Librarians from PSU received an award at LOEX of the West for most participants in one session. When queried, most of the NASIG workshop participants indicated a familiarity with LOEX of the West, a library user education conference. PSU librarians work with individual PSU faculty in co-teaching and creating Websites specifically for courses. Sharon called up one such Website, *Research Portfolio for Business Environment*, which includes general information on research, the research portfolio, grading, and required work samples. Each work sample is linked to a Webpage with further instruction, such as how to find company profiles and company history, or how to find journal articles. During the past year, the eight PSU instruction librarians conducted 365 library instruction sessions.

Next Sharon discussed the librarians' efforts to enhance information dissemination. One approach is through course modules in WebCT. Library skills are taught online for those who can't attend a regular class. Workshop participants were given a username and password to experience the use of WebCT in a course numbered Lib 410/510, Basic Library Skills for Research.

PSU Librarians also created a tutorial, *Research Survival Online*, that guides students from getting started to finding books, articles and Websites, evaluating sources, and finally writing and citing. Recently, a video was added to demonstrate use of one database. This video was created using Camtasia, a tool familiar to only one workshop participant. (I was able to locate information about Camtasia on the Web by performing a Google search.)

Another cross-campus partnership demonstrated was a resource aggregation that Sharon and an instructor had created on the topic of American women writers. This product included the syllabus, assignments, finding journals, finding books, finding articles, reference works, and Websites. PSU faculty are given instruction on creating electronic course reserves using durable links. Information is available on the library's Website to help faculty create a folder of links in *EBSCOhost* and add it to *WebCT*. Sharon and Maggie guided workshop participants through this process. A question arose as to whether students could access the course reserves from home; PSU makes this possible by the use of a proxy server. Several database vendors allow this type of durable link.

Next, Maggie took control of the SMARTboard and the workshop to discuss methods of enhancing communication. First she inquired about experiences of the workshop participants in using electronic communication tools. Some librarians don't use available electronic communication tools because of a lack of confidence. Oregon conducted a trial of *Ask a Librarian* throughout the state, with each university assigned a time to answer questions submitted via live chat. Maggie showed the PSU *Ask a Librarian* Webpage and talked about its use.

Careful planning is needed to carry on a successful discussion board, the next electronic communication tool presented. A course Q&A should be used to ask and answer questions specific to the course, and those types of questions should then be kept out of the discussion board. Maggie offered a number of tips for librarians in facilitating online discussions:

1. Make online discussions integral to the course activities and assignments. If you are teaching a class yourself this is easy; if you are a part of a larger class you need to work with the instructor to make sure there are specific objectives and assignments that include online discussions. Avoid having online discussions become what students may view as busy work.
2. To begin an online discussion, provide specific, clear writing prompts and questions related to readings, course activities, or course goals. Often, the key to a good discussion is a good question.
3. Participate in the online discussions yourself as a teacher. While you should not be expected to respond to every student's post, facilitating a discussion is not a spectator sport. Even brief participation in the discussions will help you familiarize yourself with your students' ideas, perspectives, questions, confusions, and insights. Model critical thinking for students. Affirm student participation with your attention and interaction.
4. For courses with a large number of students (or if you are using a universal board for many courses), spot check discussions and/or have TA's spot check with you. Encourage students to help each other and not to rely solely on your input to solve problems. You may also wish to form small groups or teams to encourage more group learning. Students will often work better in a structured, small group (three to five individuals) than in a very large class or a group with which they may not be familiar.
5. Draw positive attention (affirmation) to a thought-provoking post or a thoughtful reply during the online discussion.
6. To generate interaction (a) ask students to post a response and then respond to at least two other students' postings; (b) ask students to post a question of their own at the end of their post; (c) let students know that they should look not only to support each other's posts but also to offer differing views that may emerge during the discussion.
7. Students often need structure, so you may find that starting major topic threads (at least initially) helps get the discussion going.
8. Create a forum or discussion thread for casual conversation and questions. Use this forum at the beginning of the class as a place where students introduce themselves and respond to other students. Take the time to respond to each student. This type of forum helps build a community of learners and can alleviate some of the feelings of isolation distance learners sometimes feel.

Maggie stressed the importance of encouraging the faculty member to include the discussion board in a class. At this point the audience logged onto a PSU discussion board; about half of the workshop participants use *WebCT* at their institutions. After being reminded of the need to introduce a topic, everyone tried posting one message. Maggie noted that a discussion board is an example of asynchronous learning.

Chat sessions embody synchronous learning. Only a few workshop participants had previous experience with chatting on the computer, but soon all were busy chatting away. Maggie noted that "chat" becomes chaotic once the number of people in a session exceeds eight or nine. She indicated she had posted useful tips for facilitating chat on the workshop Website noted on the handout, http://web.pdx.edu/~mmlynch/webtrails.htm.

At PSU, *General Chat for All Courses* serves as a kind of electronic office hours. Again, Maggie has additional information available on the presentation Website. Originally Maggie and Sharon had envisioned a three-hour presentation and had prepared more material than could be covered in this workshop. Workshop participants mentioned and discussed experiences using the LSSI product that allows co-browsing during chat sessions. Additional discussion concerning *Ask a Librarian* type chat sessions centered on the problem of academic librarians who want to lead and teach versus public librarians who simply want to answer questions.

CONTRIBUTORS' NOTES

Sharon Elteto is Instruction Librarian at Portland State University. Maggie McVay-Lynch is Instructional Support Specialist at Portland State University. Elizabeth Parang is Serials/Electronic Resources Librarian at Pepperdine University.

From Catalogers to Ontologists: Changing Roles and Opportunities for Technical Services Librarians

Nathan Rupp
Workshop Leader

David Burke
Recorder

SUMMARY. In this presentation, Nathan Rupp discussed how the cataloging profession has evolved over the past few decades and whether Library and Information Science (LIS) programs are providing a sufficient educational background. As new formats for information resources and other technologies have developed, the tasks covered under the job title of cataloger have splintered, especially within the last ten years. Cataloging classes in LIS programs have changed, including their title, now usually called *Organization of Information* classes. These classes take a more generalist and theoretical approach to describing information materials, rather than simply drilling students in using MARC and *AACR2*. However, since these classes usually are not required and core courses absorb so many credits of the students, opportunities to take the courses are limited (let alone take additional classes to further cataloging skills).

[Haworth co-indexing entry note]: "From Catalogers to Ontologists: Changing Roles and Opportunities for Technical Services Librarians." Burke, David. Co-published simultaneously in *The Serials Librarian* (The Haworth Information Press, an imprint of The Haworth Press, Inc.) Vol. 46, No. 3/4, 2004, pp. 221-226; and: *Serials in the Park* (ed: Patricia S. French, and Richard Worthing) The Haworth Information Press, an imprint of The Haworth Press, Inc., 2004, pp. 221-226. Single or multiple copies of this article are available for a fee from The Haworth Document Delivery Service [1-800-HAWORTH, 9:00 a.m. - 5:00 p.m. (EST). E-mail address: getinfo@haworthpress.com].

http://www.haworthpress.com/web/SER
Digital Object Identifier: 10.1300/J123v46n03_04

[Article copies available for a fee from The Haworth Document Delivery Service: 1-800-HAWORTH. E-mail address: <docdelivery@haworthpress.com> Website: <http://www.HaworthPress.com>]

Nathan Rupp of Cornell University introduced this workshop by describing an odd discovery he made while browsing some library job advertisements. Dialog posted an advertisement for the position of "senior ontologist," a position title of which he had not previously heard. A closer look, however, proved that the actual tasks were essentially those of a cataloger, only with a salary of $90,000! This made him ponder how library cataloging jobs have changed over the past few decades and how Library Science programs have kept pace with those changes. Even within his own career, Rupp has been a technical services librarian, an electronic resources cataloging librarian, and a metadata librarian.

After examining the evolution of the job description for positions which involve describing information resources, Rupp noticed three trends. First there were catalogers who describe resources with pre-established standards, especially MARC and *AACR2*. Next came metadata librarians employing many optional description standards (e.g., Dublin Core), depending on the given material in hand. Most recently, the ontologist has arrived, creating definitions and relationships between items to describe them. To explore this evolution more thoroughly, Rupp analyzed job announcements. To evaluate how LIS programs are preparing aspiring technical services librarians, he analyzed the curricula of Library and Information Science programs from the past few decades and conducted interviews with LIS instructors.

For his review of job advertisements, Rupp referred to the back sections of *College & Research Libraries News* from the years 1972, 1982, 1992, and 2002. He examined cataloging and serials librarian positions, and in more recent announcements, Rupp looked over metadata and electronic resource librarian positions, too. Generally, the descriptions split between the position's responsibilities and the applicants' requirements.

In 1972, these positions were almost uniformly called catalogers, although some libraries did have specialized positions for serials. These positions were responsible for using *AACR2* and MARC to catalog materials in a number of different formats and languages. Since OCLC had just introduced its online shared cataloging system in 1971, few people worked directly with OCLC. Catalogers' responsibilities focused on serials and other "harder-than-books" formats, card catalog maintenance, and reclassification. Rarely did the positions include library automation in their descriptions. The requirements included working knowledge of cataloging standards, encoding, and classification schemes; the descriptions also called for applicants with "general computer skills," without defining which skills a given position required.

Ten years later, most libraries' cataloging departments used OCLC regularly, and many libraries at least planned to deploy an online catalog, if not actually using one yet. Naturally, the position descriptions changed to accommodate these developments. The responsibilities included online cataloging with OCLC, retrospective conversions, and implementing and maintaining an online catalog; increasingly the ads asked for prior experience in these tasks. The positions frequently required experience with using OCLC and online cataloging, and, increasingly, they requested some knowledge of database design and computer programming, too. The job titles had not changed much, although Rupp did find one advertisement for a "Head of OCLC Unit."

Although the trend toward increasingly automated library services accelerated over the next decade, libraries in 1992 remained untouched by the Internet. Electronic formats for materials were available predominantly through CD-ROM networks, and online catalogs replaced card catalogs in most libraries. Automation librarians split away from catalogers to maintain the proper functioning of the online catalogs and other electronic materials, but otherwise there was still little specialization. Serials catalogers became responsible for maintaining the holdings data of serials and multi-volume works, and catalogers often found themselves overseeing libraries' CD-ROM networks. Requirements for becoming a cataloger usually included knowledge of many computer applications, networks, and CD-ROMs; serials catalogers needed experience with automated serials control systems, too.

A few short years later, the World Wide Web became ubiquitous in libraries, and everything within changed, including cataloging. By 2002, classifieds advertised not just the various incarnations of catalogers; libraries sought electronic resources specialists and metadata specialists, too. As online materials pushed libraries to change acquisition policies from possession to access, some catalogers find themselves at least partly responsible for the management and registration of electronic materials. They also are responsible for keeping track of the new metadata systems; in addition to MARC and *AACR2* many employers now require some understanding of such new standards and classifications schemes as Dublin Core, FGDC, HTML, and XML. As more cataloging is performed by paraprofessionals, cataloging librarians increasingly need project management experience to work on team-based digital library projects. Of the decades Rupp analyzed, this last saw the most change in the profession.

Since technical services operations have changed drastically over the last 30 years, Rupp next asked the question, "Are LIS programs preparing professionals for these changes?" There are 56 ALA-accredited LIS programs in the United States, but most have dropped the word "library" from their titles, preferring the word "information." However, does the new title reflect actual changes in the curriculum to prepare students for the new expectations of employers, or are program changes purely cosmetic? The schools' core courses varied greatly in number (2-10) and content; Rupp found no pattern among the schools to identify what information every librarian needs to know. Furthermore, some LIS programs have dropped cataloging courses from their core classes. Cataloging and classification courses offered (whether part of a core or not) rarely are called such; many programs prefer the title *Organization of Information.* There appears to be no basic set of information in these courses common to most LIS programs.

For a closer look at how well library schools are preparing future librarians for the changed circumstances of technical services departments, Rupp interviewed the deans of several LIS programs from across the country. He asked them how technical services curricula had changed in the past few years, why had it changed, how had the changes affected graduates' prospects and career paths, and what future changes the curricula may undergo. He found that the changes in the courses went beyond a simple name change; these courses take a more theoretical approach to cataloging and classification rather than a practical one (e.g., focusing on using MARC and *AACR2*). They are meant to serve as a basis for a number of other topics in the fields of organizing information, knowledge management, or information architecture. Graduates encounter a wide variety of career opportunities, not only traditional technical services jobs. In these careers, they are asked to work with a number of other metadata schemes. The deans believe that their programs better serve the students by providing a basic background in the organization of information that they can apply to different situations that require various metadata schemes. Deans were also concerned that they could not adequately educate students on constantly changing standards. They felt that their time is better spent providing students with a background in the organization of information, leaving it to practitioners in the field to explain the rules, standards, and local policies to new employees. The more general background also provides students with a good basis for educating themselves about changes in standards and schemes. Lastly, the cosmetic aspect of the name change from *Cataloging and Classification* to *Organization of Information* was seen as enhancing the value of the courses to the LIS programs' parent institutions. With the advent of the World Wide Web, the organization of information was considered important to many fields, while cataloging and classification remained something germane solely to the library community.

Rupp found a couple of drawbacks associated with this change from *cataloging and classification* to *organization of information* classes. In some programs, there are few courses offered on the specific metadata standards to follow up classes on the basic, theoretical organization of information. In programs where there are follow-up classes, there may not be enough time, especially in short (one year) programs, to take them.

In the future, such courses will certainly maintain the generalized approach, with more specialized classes focusing on cataloging and classification, metadata, taxonomies, and ontologies building upon the theoretical foundation. Furthermore, such courses will likely incorporate teaching other skills such as project management, consulting, communication, and information technology, possibly in cooperation with other academic departments of a given university. To Rupp, the most intriguing development is the growing number of information science/digital library programs offered by institutions without traditional library science programs. Two programs he offered as examples are Johns Hopkins University's degree in Digital Libraries (http://www.jhu.edu/advanced/communication/concentrations.html) and Cornell University's interdisciplinary Information Science program (http://www.cis.cornell.edu/infoscience/). The LIS programs are changing along with the transformed positions available, although Rupp did not offer an opinion as to whether the programs have changed enough.

Since cataloging-related jobs are changing rapidly, Rupp concluded the presentation with suggestions for how individuals can get further education themselves. At the top of his list is attending workshops, making a plug for those offered by NASIG's own Continuing Education Committee (CEC) (http://www.nasig.org/education/cec/budget2003.htm). Particularly for those with limited travel funds, the CEC (among others) is also experimenting with providing opportunities for self-training through online tutorials. Of course, it is increasingly common for catalogers to enhance their knowledge and skills on the job and through networking with others. Lastly, Rupp gave a short list of journals for professional readings: *D-Lib Magazine* (http://www.dlib.org), *Cataloging & Classification Quarterly*, *Journal of Internet Cataloging*, and *The Journal of the American Society for Information Science and Technology* (*JASIST*).

Questions from attendees centered on the status of education for technical services positions. One person asked if Rupp had looked into the quality of online degree programs (a growing trend); he replied he had not. There was some discussion over the feasibility of libraries offering internships to local MLS candidates, but in a time of low budgets and even layoffs, many libraries find interns a luxury they cannot afford. Some people questioned whether it is worthwhile for cataloging courses to teach MARC and *AACR2*, both because of local adaptations and the constant and increasingly common changes in these formats. Overall, everyone showed at least some concern over how much these renamed degrees, even though they are ALA-accredited, are preparing students for their first job.

CONTRIBUTORS' NOTES

Nathan Rupp is Metadata Librarian at Cornell University, Mann Library. David Burke is Serials and Digital Formats Cataloger at Villanova University, Falvey Library.

Copyright Law: Fact or Fiction?

Janice M. Krueger
Workshop Leader

Karen Matthews
Recorder

SUMMARY. When the University of the Pacific purchased a new integrated library system there was a desire to make access to all types of materials more visible in the system. This required reviewing copyright law and determining the differences in the print and electronic environment. Licensing restrictions in the contracts for electronic databases and journals also influenced how the University of the Pacific would be able to handle these materials. *[Article copies available for a fee from The Haworth Document Delivery Service: 1-800-HAWORTH. E-mail address: <docdelivery@haworthpress.com> Website: <http://www.HaworthPress.com>]*

Copyright was originally designed to protect the copyright holder. There are three types of copyright: creative, providing full protection for original works; compilation, which includes items such as directories; and derivative works. There are also four types of use. These are:

[Haworth co-indexing entry note]: "Copyright Law: Fact or Fiction?" Matthews, Karen. Co-published simultaneously in *The Serials Librarian* (The Haworth Information Press, an imprint of The Haworth Press, Inc.) Vol. 46, No. 3/4, 2004, pp. 227-2332; and: *Serials in the Park* (ed: Patricia S. French, and Richard Worthing) The Haworth Information Press, an imprint of The Haworth Press, Inc., 2004, pp. 227-232. Single or multiple copies of this article are available for a fee from The Haworth Document Delivery Service [1-800-HAWORTH, 9:00 a.m. - 5:00 p.m. (EST). E-mail address: getinfo@haworthpress.com].

http://www.haworthpress.com/web/SER
Digital Object Identifier: 10.1300/J123v46n03_05

personal use, infringing use, fair use, and public domain. Copyright applies to all works no matter what the format.

FAIR USE DOCTRINE: TITLE 17, SECTION 107, U.S. CODE

Fair use is a limit on the copyright or marketing monopoly but not on the work itself. It allows the end user to use the work for personal reasons that may include aspects of teaching, scholarship, and/or research. When reviewing fair use there are four factors to consider. These factors are: purpose and character of use (will it be used for educational purposes?); the nature of the work (personal, compilation, or derivative); the amount and substantiality of the portion copied in relation to the entire work (the more copied, the greater chance of copyright infringement); and the effect of the use on the potential market for or value of the work. To stay within fair use guidelines, items put on electronic reserve must be requested by a faculty member for an educational program and must be only a portion of the item. Access also has to be limited by a password, and the student cannot be charged for this access. If the item will need to be used over a long period of time, then copyright must be obtained.

COPYING BY LIBRARIES AND ARCHIVES: TITLE 17, SECTION 108, U.S. CODE

Libraries and archives are permitted to make a single copy on request and they may make an archival copy of damaged, lost, stolen, or obsolete works (digital included). These libraries and archives have to meet certain requirements. They have to be nonprofit institutions, open to the public. The copied items must be owned by the library and housed in the general collection. Single copies are made at the request of the user and the copy becomes the property of user. Also, notices of copyright must be posted at the places where requests are made and on order forms that end users complete to request copies. This notice also has to be on the copies themselves.

FIRST SALE DOCTRINE: TITLE 17, SECTION 109, U.S. CODE

Once the copyright owner agrees to sell a copy of a work, the copyright owner cannot control further resale, lending, leasing, or rental of the copy. This permits libraries to: lend books, pamphlets, audiotapes, videotapes, periodical literature, compact discs, or DVDs; sell books and discarded items at book sales; and lend collections to other libraries and museums.

These copyright laws worked well in the print environment when libraries owned the materials. In this print environment there was also a relationship between the library or museum and the end user. In the electronic environment other issues are now involved. Libraries are now licensing access to materials that they do not own. Also, libraries are providing Internet access, acting as an ISP (Internet service provider) or OSP (online service provider). In addition, there are issues of distance education and providing access to these end users who are no longer physically in the library. Under the original copyright laws there was the user and the library as institution. Now there is the user, the distance education user, the library as institution, and the library as ISP or OSP. Do sections 107, 108 and 109 still apply?

SCENARIOS

Several different scenarios were discussed. In one example, an adjunct faculty member would like to provide access to e-journals for his class. Fair use would allow faculty and students to access these materials. Access through Blackboard would also be permissible since authentication is required to use it. However, the license would need to be reviewed to see if providing links is permissible. Many licenses are not as restrictive as in the past, so this may now be possible. However, many titles have persistent links at the journal level but not at the article level, with these article links changing over time. In this case it would not be possible to provide a link directly to the article. If the license does not allow coursepacks, the URL may be posted but it will not be possible to pull the work into the site. For journals accessed through a full-text database it may be acceptable to provide access through Blackboard. Check depending on the terms of the license. Check with the vendor. It is still not possible to put the entire work up on Blackboard under fair use.

In another scenario there is the question of whether the URL or link is copyrighted. Since it is not a fixed medium it cannot be copyrighted. However, it may be patented so others may not use the same URL for their resources. Deep linking into movie reviews is not acceptable according to court rulings since it undercuts advertising.

The third scenario discussed involved the use of coursepacks in class. A single copy for students would be fair use. Fair use would have to be applied to each excerpt that is included in the coursepack compilation. If the coursepack is going to be sold at the bookstore, however, permission would be needed in order to sell the coursepack.

In the fourth scenario, the library makes a copy and charges for the cost of the item. This would be okay under Section 108 since the library did not make a profit, so long as the library meets all other conditions of Section 108 (i.e., the library is open to the public, is a nonprofit organization, the item is owned by the library, the item has been requested by the end-user and will be kept by this end user).

DIGITAL MILLENNIUM COPYRIGHT ACT

The Digital Millennium Copyright Act has implications for fair use of electronic resources. It prohibits acts of circumvention and distribution of tools and technology for circumvention. It outlaws code-cracking devices, except in certain instances. It limits liability of ISPs or OSPs, gives "safe harbor" by limiting liability for such things as system caching, transient storage in the process of transmitting information on the Internet, linking to infringing sites, and placing infringing information on a system or network at the direction of the end user. It also limits liability of institutions or faculty using educational facilities for electronic publishing. Libraries have responsibilities when claiming "safe harbor," such as developing notification and termination policies.

THE TEACH ACT: TITLE 17, SECTION 110(2), U.S. CODE

This section lists requirements for instructors, institutions, and information technology officials. It provides guidelines for what may be mounted digitally with passwords and what information technology officials must do to protect these resources from being copied. It also determines who may have access. Two recommended Websites for information on the Teach Act are:

1. *Copyright Management Center's Overview of Copyright and Distance Education* located at: http://www.copyright.iupui.edu/dist_learning.htm

2. Laura Gasaway's *Teach Act Comparison Chart* comparing the old and new versions of Section 110 located at: http://www.unc.edu/~unclng/TEACH.htm

POINTS FOR CONSIDERATION

Some questions that need to be asked: Is the copy coming from material the library owns? Is the copy coming from a database that is subject to a license agreement and is it from a journal without a print subscription? Is the copy for an on-campus class or a distance education class?

Libraries still cannot copy an entire work digitally to put on reserve or to fill interlibrary loan requests. Interlibrary loan is still not possible in some electronic resource licenses. With libraries becoming ISPs or OSPs, they will have new responsibilities for service and for meeting requirements under the Digital Millennium Copyright Act.

COPYRIGHT LAW REFERENCES

Books

Crews, K. D. 2000. *Copyright essentials for librarians and educators.* Chicago: American Library Association.

Hoffman, G. M. 2001. *Copyright in cyberspace: Questions and answers for librarians.* New York: Neal-Schumann.

Articles

Balas, J. I. 2002. The laws, they are a changin'. *Computers in Libraries* 22, no. 5 (May): 42-45. Retrieved February 7, 2003 from Expanded Academic ASAP database.

Cheverie, J. F. 2002. The changing economics of information, technological development, and copyright protection: What are the consequences for the public domain? *The Journal of Academic Librarianship* 28, no. 5 (Sept.): 325-331.

Martins, C., and S. Martins. 2002. Electronic copyright in a shrinking world. *Computers in Libraries* 22, no. 5 (May): 28-32. Retrieved February 8, 2003, from Expanded Academic ASAP database.

Pike, G. H. 2002. The delicate dance of database licenses, copyright, and fair use. *Computers in Libraries* 22, no. 5 (May): 12-17. Retrieved February 8, 2003, from Expanded Academic ASAP database.

Shikolnikov, T. 2002. To link or not to link: How to avoid copyright traps on the Internet. *The Journal of Academic Librarianship* 28, no. 3 (May): 133-140.

Websites

Copyright Management Center, Kenneth D. Crews, director. http://www.copyright.iupui.edu/ (1 Oct. 2003).

Gasaway, Laura N. Copyright issues in cyberspace. http://www.unc.edu/~unclng/cyber-copyright1-04.htm (19 Feb. 2004).

Regents Guide to Understanding Copyright and Educational Fair Use, Board of Regents of the University System of Georgia, Office of Legal Affairs. http://www.usg.edu/admin/legal/copyright/ (1 Oct. 2003).

United States Copyright Office, Library of Congress. http://www.loc.gov/copyright/ (1 Oct. 2003).

Tutorials and Presentations

Harper, Georgia. Copyright crash course (Webcast). http://www.lib.utsystem. edu/copyright/ (1 Oct. 2003).

______There are also a number of streamlined presentations designed for the various roles of student, faculty, library, etc.

Hersey, Karen. Understanding Copyright Law and Fair Use of Resources for Teaching (Webcast). http://www.library.tufts.edu/fairuse/tutorialsIndex.html (1 Oct. 2003).

CONTRIBUTORS' NOTES

Janice M. Krueger is Electronic Resources and Serials Librarian at the University of the Pacific. Karen Matthews is Coordinator of Technical Services at Dana Medical Library, University of Vermont.

Electronic Content: Is It Accessible to Clients with "Differabilities"?

Cheryl Riley

Workshop Leader

SUMMARY. This workshop introduced the barriers and challenges clients with disabilities face when using electronic resources. It introduced screen-readers and used them to evaluate the accessibility of three aggregator databases: *EBSCOhost, INFOTRAC,* and *FirstSearch Electronic Collections Online*. Conclusions about the accessibility of each database were presented. *[Article copies available for a fee from The Haworth Document Delivery Service: 1-800-HAWORTH. E-mail address: <docdelivery@haworthpress.com> Website: <http://www.HaworthPress.com>]*

I want to share the results of a study of aggregator databases that I completed about two years ago. Before we look at the results of the study, I want to remind each of you of the number of individuals in America with a disability and specifically the number of first year, full-time students of four-year institutions with a disability. Each year a survey conducted by the Cooperative Institutional Research Program (CIRP) conducts a survey among a large sample of freshmen students. The survey is co-sponsored by the American Council on Education and

[Haworth co-indexing entry note]: "Electronic Content: Is It Accessible to Clients with 'Differabilities'?" Riley, Cheryl. Co-published simultaneously in *The Serials Librarian* (The Haworth Information Press, an imprint of The Haworth Press, Inc.) Vol. 46, No. 3/4, 2004, pp. 233-240; and: *Serials in the Park* (ed: Patricia S. French, and Richard Worthing) The Haworth Information Press, an imprint of The Haworth Press, Inc., 2004, pp. 233-240. Single or multiple copies of this article are available for a fee from The Haworth Document Delivery Service [1-800-HAWORTH, 9:00 a.m. - 5:00 p.m. (EST). E-mail address: getinfo@haworthpress.com].

http://www.haworthpress.com/web/SER
Digital Object Identifier: 10.1300/J123v46n03_06

the UCLA Graduate School of Education and Information Studies. In 2000, the most recent year for which data are available, results were received from 269,413 students representing 434 colleges and universities.[1] The responses were weighted to represent national enrollment patterns of the total 1.1 million freshmen in the United States. Questions on the survey ask students to self-report their disabilities; 6 percent of all first-time, full-time students enrolled for fall 2000 reported a disability. Between 1998 and 2000 the proportion of freshmen reporting disabilities averaged between 6 and 8 percent. Other resources indicate that one in five Americans has a disability; we are talking about a significant percentage of our population.

The Americans with Disabilities Act of 1990 (PL101-336) defines a disability as "a physical or mental impairment that substantially limits one or more major life activities; a record of such impairment; or being regarded as having such an impairment."[2] In 2001, the American Library Association (ALA) adopted the *Library Services for People with Disabilities Policy*, which states that "library policy, resources and services must meet the needs of all people."[3] Libraries Serving Special Populations (LSSP), a section of the ALA division of the Association of Specialized and Cooperative Library Agencies, focuses on serving populations with special needs.

Statistics show that 20.9 million Americans aged 15 and over have some type of work disability. Of that number, 5 million, or approximately one-fourth, have computers at home and 1.5 million have Internet access at home. Individuals without disabilities, on the other hand, are three times more likely to have Internet access at home.[4] Obviously, these statistics present compelling evidence that equal access to information remains a concern for those with disabilities.

Electronic resources should mean increased access to information for disabled users, since the very nature of the resource eliminates the biggest barrier for many of the disabled–transportation. Ideally, the World Wide Web should level the playing field for those with disabilities. Several authors have described the need for online information to be accessible. Various studies have evaluated the accessibility of specific Websites. Each of these studies used Bobby, an automated Web-accessibility assessment tool, to provide data about a site's accessibility. Five studies have focused on library Webpages. Schmetzke found that at the 24 most highly ranked schools of Library and Information Science (SLIS), 59 percent of the main campus library Webpages were accessible, but only 23 percent of SLIS pages.[5] Schmetzke also studied pages at the 13 four-year campuses in the University of Wisconsin system and found that 31 percent of the top-level homepages were free of major accessibility issues.[6] One year later, a follow-up study found 40 percent of the top-level homepages free of accessibility issues. Lilly and Van Fleet examined the colleges and universities on Yahoo's list of "America's 100 Most Wired Colleges" and found that only 40 percent of the library homepages were accessible.[7] An early study of higher education sites found that only 22 percent of front pages were accessible; one level beyond the front page, that number dropped to 3 percent.[8] To my knowledge, very little research has been completed about the accessibility of other online library resources. The only articles I am aware of are two special theme issues of *Library Hi Tech* from 2002. Unfortunately, that means that the data I am going to share with you is already outdated.

My primary research question was whether aggregator databases are accessible. The methodology I used included a manual check for adherence to the Web Access Initiative (WAI) design guidelines for the databases evaluated. The WAI, a section of the World Wide Web Consortium (W3C), publishes 14 design guidelines, with related checkpoints and priority levels. Specific items searched for included accessibility icons, browser preference statements, different user options (large print; frames/no frames; different style sheets; alternative color schemes), natural language indication, text equivalents for image descriptions, and clear navigation mechanisms. The databases evaluated were *EBSCOhost, InfoTrac Web Business & Company Profile ASAP*, and *OCLC's FirstSearch Electronic Collections Online* (*ECO*).

Each of the databases was evaluated with the assistive technology available in the James C. Kirkpatrick Library. The screen readers used in this study were *JAWS for Windows 3.7; ZoomText 7.0; OpenBook 5.0; L&H Kurzweil 1000*; and the *L&H Kurzweil 3000*. A screen reader works by beginning at the top left of the screen and reading aloud all texts and links. Figure 1 provides an example of information presented in columns across the screen.

FIGURE 1. Screen Readers and How They Work

Chapter 1	Chapter 2	Chapter 3
It was a dark and stormy night, and all through the house the thesis committee	Suddenly a shot rang out, then a shout, then a thump, then the sound of a car door	Then the Chief Inspector cried, "I know who did this dastardly deed and I will

A typical screen reader would read that information as Chapter 1; Chapter 2; Chapter 3; It was a dark and stormy Suddenly a shot rang out, Then the Chief Inspector night, and all through the, then a shout, then a thump, cried, "I know who did this. . . . As you can tell from this example, presentation is very important to the user dependent upon a screen reader.

Analysis of the databases for adherence to accessible design guidelines found that *EBSCOhost* offers both a frames and a no-frames option and that *ECO* offers different language options; *EBSCOhost* notes the best browsers for the site. Each of the databases indicates the natural language for the site, but not for individual documents. Hypertext markup language (HTML) provides elements to indicate when a different language, an abbreviation, or an acronym is used, but these elements are not routinely used. These elements become very important for a screen reader user because a screen reader will correctly pronounce non-English words, abbreviations, or acronyms when properly notified. The "alt text" descriptions are very cryptic in *EBSCOhost*, but excellent in *InfoTrac*. None of the aggregators display any accessibility icons, but all use consistent design and navigation. An especially helpful element was found in *InfoTrac*. *InfoTrac* includes a Top of Page link every five records within the results list. This navigation aid can be very helpful to someone dependent on a screen reader.

JAWS for Windows 3.7 was the first screen reader used to assess the accessibility of the aggregator databases. The frames version of *EBSCOhost* was casually examined since the no-frames version is intended to be the accessible product. As expected, the frames version read each frame separately beginning with the frame at the top left of the screen. Other issues noted were that the select button is placed before the databases button; the navigation bar information assumes product familiarity; information is not front-loaded (placing the link at the beginning of a line rather than at the end); images included with documents often have ineffective descriptions; and there is no easy way for the visually impaired individual to quickly determine whether the document retrieved is available in full-text or citation only.

Problems noted with the no-frames version of *EBSCOhost* were that the graphic linking to full-text is located before the description of the item. Most users require information about the article before they can determine relevancy to their specific need. It was difficult to determine the location within the database; additional prompts are needed to alert the visually impaired user. The visually impaired user needs an easy way to identify the results screen, the citation screen, the full-text of the document, or the e-mail screen. Another problem for the screen-reader-dependent user is that information is needlessly repeated. Once the user has determined that full-text is available and has selected the full-text, the citation and abstract information is repeated; this is problematic for the user who relies on the screen reader. Label descriptions are abbreviations and unintelligible when read out of context by a screen reader. The no-frames version provides fewer options for the user. There is no advanced search, expert search, options button, company directory, image collection, or select service button. All of these options are available in the frames version. Within the document, the natural language changes are not noted, meaning the screen reader tried to pronounce any foreign words in English, rather than switching to the correct language and pronunciation.

InfoTrac Web Business & Company Profile ASAP uses frames. Each frame is read separately and the cursor has to be in the frame for the screen reader to read the frame. The screen reader did not recognize abbreviations used on the pages and made no provision for highlighting search terms. On a positive note, either the mouse or the keyboard activated commands.

ECO is also designed with frames and presents the following problems for the screen reader. The navigation bar is always read first; a visually impaired user might not want to hear all those links each time a navigation bar is encountered. An accessible solution would be to provide a mechanism to skip the navigation bar. As with the other aggregators, too much extraneous information is listed before the article content. Finally, the information needs to be rearranged to allow for front-loading of links.

The next screen reader used was *ZoomText 7.0*. *ZoomText* is both a screen reader and screen magnification software. *ZoomText* does not recognize the frames version of *EBSCOhost*. The links in the no-frames version of *EBSCOhost* require a mouse click to activate the screen reader. Because many visually impaired users use the keyboard to activate commands, this requirement presents a problem. There is no prompt to enter search terms, something a blind user would most definitely need for independent searching. Another easily resolved problem is that side-by-side buttons are read as one button. The only problem encountered with the screen magnification option was that the image quality of the documents degrades significantly as magnification increases.

Both mouse and keyboard commands are usable in *InfoTrac Web Business & Company Profile ASAP*. The documents are legible at all levels of magnification. Problems encountered were that the controls do not have labels, meaning there is no prompt for the users; information is not front-loaded; and the screen reader does not translate the links and HTML correctly.

ECO was the least usable product with this software. The biggest drawback is the lack of text equivalents for images, labels, or command buttons. The "how to use" option is not available to someone with this screen reader because the document reader cannot convert .pdf files.

In order to be successful at using an aggregator database with *OpenBook 5.0* screen reading software, the articles must first be found and saved to the hard drive. Once the content has been saved, the software will scan the article and read it to the user. This approach was consistent for each of the aggregators examined. An additional barrier with *ECO* was that Java script is retained when saved as an HTML file, which results in a jumbled presentation.

The Kurzweil 1000 and Kurzweil 3000 screen readers presented limitations similar to those identified with *OpenBook 5.0*. Additionally, these products do not recognize HTML. Consequently, a client reliant upon this software would not be able to access these aggregator databases.

In summary, there are several points that stand out about the aggregator databases and accessibility. First of all, none of these aggregator databases uses accessibility icons. *EBSCOhost* offers different user options and *ECO* different languages. In addition, many features available in the text versions of the databases lack equivalents when used via screen readers. Among screen readers, *JAWS* appears to provide the best solution for using aggregator databases, with *ZoomText* a viable alternative. Users dependent upon other screen readers will likely need mediated searches. Scanning, reading, and writing software is not presently useful for accessing aggregator databases. Accessibility is often a judgment call. Bowman found the accessibility of *OCLC FirstSearch* and *InfoTrac Web* mildly reduced using *WindowEye*,[9] while I found them significantly reduced using *JAWS*.

Other findings report that accessibility was significantly reduced in *Proquest Research Library*.[10] *Lexis-Nexis* had minor problems that mildly reduced accessibility. McCord et al. found *OVID* to be very accessible; *Cancerlit, Hazardous Substances, MSDS, Medline Plus*, and *Toxline* presented mild reductions in accessibility; and accessibility was significantly reduced for *Electric Library Plus* and *PubMed*.[11]

Recommendations to the profession are that we must work collegially and proactively to educate content providers about the necessity of following accessibility guidelines. They should eliminate non-essential and duplicated information and front-load the information. Secondly, interfaces should first and foremost enhance information functionality;

we should check this functionality by testing database/screen reader interfaces with both blind and visually impaired users. Two important questions to ask about new electronic resources are: Can the resource be accessed with adaptive computer technologies? Is the electronic resource evaluated for accessibility before procurement? By asking these questions we can develop a committed approach to advocacy for service to this segment of our population. I truly believe that we do not have accessible products because we have not educated publishers about what our disabled clients require.

AUDIENCE REACTION

The first question was whether mental disabilities were under-reported. The answer is that they are probably even more under-reported than physical types of disabilities because of the stigma American society attaches to mental disorders. A standard figure used by the disability community is six percent; if we use this figure, then libraries need to make six percent of everything accessible–computer stations, materials, etc. The next question asked was, What makes a Webpage inaccessible? Unfortunately, there wasn't enough time to cover that question because it is an entire workshop in itself, and each Webpage is dependent upon the content in that particular page. The third question referred to the code for the natural language and asked if you didn't simply put in a language code. The answer was yes–it is very simple to code for natural language changes and there is a NISO standard for the language codes. Discussion then focused on front-loading, which means putting the link at the front of the sentence rather than the end. The screen reader reads the link and any description put in the "alt.text" tag. Other comments agreed with my assertion that content is inaccessible due to a lack of knowledge of the requirements. The information from this workshop will be shared with designers because it is information that has not previously been considered. Another participant works with a blind physics professor and that professor spent a good deal of his time talking with publishers about why he cannot read their journals. Ron Stewart, Director, Northwest Center for Technology Access at Oregon State University, recently completed a study of the accessibility of the databases at Oregon State University. He made an extremely thorough comparison of each online database available at Oregon State University and presents his conclusions online (available at http://tap.oregonstate.edu/research/ahg.htm). The final comment was from a participant aware that *Medline* recently published a list of requirements for online content; however, the W3C guidelines were not mentioned. Because *Medline* is a government product, they are required to conform with Section 508 standards. The W3C guidelines are more comprehensive than the Section 508 standards.

NOTES

1. C. Henderson, *College Freshmen with Disabilities: A Biennial Statistical Profile* (Washington, D.C.: American Council on Education, 2001).

2. *Americans with Disabilities Act of 1990*, Public Law 100-336, *U.S. Statutes at Large* 104 (1990): 327.

3. American Library Association, *Library Services for People with Disabilities Policy*. Council Document # 24 (2001).

4. H. S. Kaye, *Computer and Internet Use among People with Disabilities*. Disability Statistics Report 13 (Washington, DC: U.S. Department of Education, National Institute on Disability and Rehabilitation Research (2002).

5. A. Schmetzke, *Web Page Accessibility on University of Wisconsin Campuses: A Comparative Study* (a Web site created to accompany a presentation at the Wisconsin Association of Academic Libraries conference, Madison, WI, April 15, 1999). http://library.uwsp.edu/aschmetz/Accessible/UW-Campuses/contents.htm (1 Oct. 2003)

6. A. Schmetzke, *Web Page Accessibility on University of Wisconsin Campuses: 2000 Survey Data* (a Web site created to publish the most recent data on Web page accessibility at University of Wisconsin campuses, along with some other information pertinent to the issue. The data were collected between March 24 and March 31, 2000, and they were first presented at the Wisconsin Association of Academic Libraries (WAAL) conference, Fond Du Lac, WI, April 12, 2000). http://library.uwsp.edu/aschmetz/Accessible/UW-Campuses/Survey2000/contents2000.htm (1 Oct. 2003).

7. E. B. Lilly and C. Van Fleet (1999). "Wired But Not Connected: Accessibility of Academic Library Home Pages," *The Reference Librarian* 67/68 (1999): 5-28.

8. Cyndi Rowland, "Accessibility of the Internet in Post-secondary Education: Meeting the Challenge" (paper presented at the WebNet World Conference on the WWW and Internet, San Antonio, Texas, Oct. 31, 2000). http://www.webaim.org/articles/whitepaper.htm (1 Oct. 2003).

9. V. Bowman, "Reading Between the Lines: An Evaluation of WindowEyes Screen Reader As a Reference Tool for Teaching and Learning," *Library Hi Tech 20* (2002): 162-168.

10. S. L. Byerley and M. B. Chambers, "Accessibility and Usability of Web-based Library Databases for Non-visual Users," *Library Hi Tech 20* (2002): 169-178.

11. S. McCord., L. Frederiksen and N. Campbell, "An Accessibility Assessment of Selected Web-based Health Information Resources," *Library Hi Tech 20* (2002): 188-198.

CONTRIBUTOR'S NOTE

Cheryl Riley is Professor and Librarian at Central Missouri State University.

Planning for New Growth in the Forest: Cultivating New Serialists for the Future

Selden Durgom Lamoureux
Workshop Leader

Susan Davis
Recorder

SUMMARY. A greater percentage of librarians are approaching retirement age than the general working population, and there is particular concern that specific expertise such as that needed to work with serials will be lost. So there is a great need to attract new professionals and for a better understanding of serials issues throughout the profession. Lamoureux offered a number of practical suggestions current serials professionals can follow to cultivate the next generation of serialists. Among the ideas explored were internships, mentoring, guest lectures, and networking. *[Article copies available for a fee from The Haworth Document Delivery Service: 1-800-HAWORTH. E-mail address: <docdelivery@haworthpress.com> Website: <http://www.HaworthPress.com>]*

This workshop opened with an explanation of why Lamoureux proposed this topic and its relevance to NASIG. She noted the "graying" of the profession, especially worrisome because more librarians are ap-

[Haworth co-indexing entry note]: "Planning for New Growth in the Forest: Cultivating New Serialists for the Future." Davis, Susan. Co-published simultaneously in *The Serials Librarian* (The Haworth Information Press, an imprint of The Haworth Press, Inc.) Vol. 46, No. 3/4, 2004, pp. 241-244; and: *Serials in the Park* (ed: Patricia S. French, and Richard Worthing) The Haworth Information Press, an imprint of The Haworth Press, Inc., 2004, pp. 241-244. Single or multiple copies of this article are available for a fee from The Haworth Document Delivery Service [1-800-HAWORTH, 9:00 a.m. - 5:00 p.m. (EST). E-mail address: getinfo@haworthpress.com].

http://www.haworthpress.com/web/SER
Digital Object Identifier: 10.1300/J123v46n03_07

proaching retirement age than is true of the general population. And even if replaced, many new hires will not have the special skills traditional to librarianship. Lamoureux recommended reading Stanley Wilder's article "The Changing Profile of Research Library Professional Staff" for more specific demographic information showing just how great the challenge to replace librarians and their skills is.[1] Lamoureux believes there is a great need to attract new librarians to the profession and for a better understanding of serials issues within the profession. There are very few library schools that actually teach a serials course, so it is difficult for students to become aware of the opportunities in serials librarianship. Her goal for the workshop was to develop some concrete action points that NASIG as an organization or even individual NASIG members could implement.

Lamoureux believes that internships are a key method to expose library school students to the benefits of serials work, or at least to offer them a greater appreciation of how serials knowledge can benefit librarians regardless of position. Other possibilities for providing valuable pre-professional experience in serials are: graduate assistantships, independent studies, and fellowship programs. Paula T. Kaufman's article "Where Do the Next 'We' Come From?" lists other steps that may help recruit promising students into librarianship:[2]

- Be creative in recruitment
- Hire talent rather than skills
- Design jobs around people and *then* train
- Offer Internship and Development Programs
- Promote librarianship as a career in elementary and high school
- Seek diversity
- Mentor

The Alumni Association at the University of North Carolina, Chapel Hill sponsors a week-long mentor program that Lamoureux cited as an example of a successful mentor program. She noted that it's also important to mentor paraprofessionals. Her library has seven full-time serial assistant positions, and in the past four years there has been fairly high turnover. Of the ten staff that have come and gone, five have gone on to library school.

Besides working in the library at UNC, Lamoureux teaches a serials course for the library school. In her course she tries to create awareness of serials by a variety of methods and recommended these to the audience:

- Guest lecturers (Marcia Tuttle is usually her first guest)[3]
- Mentoring
- Creating opportunities to attend conferences (Lamoureux served as a reference for one of this year's NASIG Conference Student Grant winners)
- Teaching a serials course

Lamoureux noted that she had problems finding good readings for her students as part of her preparation for this course. She found very little about vendors and would like to see more cooperative efforts to share course planning ideas and suggested reading lists.

She also identified some ways to keep serialists in serials, for example, the discussion lists *liblicense-l*, *SERIALST*, and *ERIL-L*. Continuing education is very important to keep up with new developments and to learn or enhance skills. She also listed a number of conference opportunities for networking and continuing education such as NASIG, the Charleston Conference, North Carolina Serials Conference, and ALA.

As a conclusion to the presentation portion of the workshop, Lamoureux described a number of possible actions that NASIG or individual NASIG members could take to create greater awareness of and interest in serials librarianship:

- Create a bibliography
- Create a Web-based serials course
- Create a template for a serials lecture course
- Develop a distance education course
- Establish a clearinghouse for student opportunities at libraries, vendors and publishers
- Network within NASIG to create a project list for independent studies
- Create one- or two-year internships for recent graduates

She conducted a short, informal survey of the audience to stimulate the discussion portion of the workshop. A total of seventeen respondents indicated that 85 percent work in a library, while 15 percent are vendors or publishers. Two-thirds of those who work in libraries are academic librarians. Sixty percent live within a couple hours drive of a library school, and 36 percent have been guest lecturers in a library school course. One person was seriously considering teaching a serials course! And finally, two respondents are actively involved on continuing education committees in NASIG or ALA or both. Other comments from the audience included a need for more serials collection development perspective in library school, and more information about public service for serials. One publisher noted that they were not very successful getting applicants for their internships.

Lamoureux's enthusiasm for serials work was evident throughout the workshop. The audience was very engaged during the discussion period; unfortunately time ran out before some recent graduates in attendance could offer their perspective. Clearly, Lamoureux identified a number of opportunities for serialists to serve as "ambassadors" in efforts to recruit good people into the profession and develop the next generation of great serialists.

NOTES

1. Stanley Wilder, "The Changing Profile of Research Library Professional Staff," *ARL*, 208/209 (2000): 1-6. http://www.arl.org/newsltr/208_209/chgprofile.html (16 July 2003).
2. Paula T. Kaufman, "Where Do the Next 'We' Come From?" *ARL*, 221 (2002):1-4. http://www.arl.org/newsltr/221/recruit.html (16 July 2003).
3. To understand why Marcia is so significant to serials librarianship see: "Marcia Tuttle: A Tribute on Her Retirement," *Serials Review*, 23:2 (Summer 1997): 1-30.

CONTRIBUTORS' NOTES

Selden Durgom Lamoureux is Serials and Electronic Resources Librarian at the University of North Carolina at Chapel Hill. Susan Davis is Head of the Periodicals Section at the University at Buffalo, State University of New York.

When the Rug Comes Out from Under: Managing Change, Technology, Information, and Staff

Althea Aschmann

Workshop Leader

Gail Julian

Recorder

SUMMARY. Change is inherent in modern organizations. Various models that managers may follow in order to promote change within the organization were discussed. The change process should involve planning, two-way communication, participation by staff, and constructive feedback. *[Article copies available for a fee from The Haworth Document Delivery Service: 1-800-HAWORTH. E-mail address: <docdelivery@haworthpress.com> Website: <http://www.HaworthPress.com>]*

Althea Aschmann provided insight into change gained from her personal experiences as a manager and conveyed the ideas of several authors with expertise as change agents. Ms. Aschmann encouraged audience participation throughout the presentation, beginning with her

[Haworth co-indexing entry note]: "When the Rug Comes Out from Under: Managing Change, Technology, Information, and Staff." Julian, Gail. Co-published simultaneously in *The Serials Librarian* (The Haworth Information Press, an imprint of The Haworth Press, Inc.) Vol. 46, No. 3/4, 2004, pp. 245-251; and: *Serials in the Park* (ed: Patricia S. French, and Richard Worthing) The Haworth Information Press, an imprint of The Haworth Press, Inc., 2004, pp. 245-251. Single or multiple copies of this article are available for a fee from The Haworth Document Delivery Service [1-800-HAWORTH, 9:00 a.m. - 5:00 p.m. (EST). E-mail address: getinfo@ haworthpress.com].

http://www.haworthpress.com/web/SER
Digital Object Identifier: 10.1300/J123v46n03_08

query to the audience: "Why change? What's wrong with the card catalog?"

The audience was cautioned not to use change as a way to address personnel issues, to cover up problems that are not being resolved or to simply undertake change for change's sake. Change should be undertaken in order to achieve a desired goal or outcome (e.g., improve efficiency, reduce obsolescence, provide a new service, or to focus on an organization's core business). Various catalysts may drive a change; these catalysts may be voluntary or mandated. Change may occur incrementally, or radically, as in a "paradigm shift." Change may be driven by new technologies such as the Internet, an integrated library system or bibliographic utility migration, or by the availability of resources in new formats. Economic factors could lead to downsizing or result in unfilled positions. Changes in management or administrative personnel could affect the vision of the institution. Regardless of the catalyst for change or the speed at which change occurs, it is a process which requires planning and two-way communication with those personnel who will be affected. Several models for change were discussed.

The first of the change models discussed was Eliyahu Goldratt's "Theory of Constraints." Goldratt emphasizes the need to identify and reduce the constraints or bottlenecks that impede progress toward goals. He recommends devising practical solutions to identified problems and engaging personnel in becoming part of the solution. Once the constraints are removed, improvement in the system follows until additional constraints develop, and the change process repeats. Althea Aschmann illustrates the process in Figure 1, adapted from Goldratt's work.

Spencer and Adams emphasize the fear of the unknown that is often associated with change and the need to leave the past behind. They note a downward trend, or pit, in the process before change is accepted and incorporated into the institutional structure. Althea Aschmann illustrates Spencer and Adams' "Stages of Change" in Figure 2.

Robbie Champion's "Change Journey" in his *Tools for Change Workshops* starts the cycle with "change imminent," and shows a path similar to that of Spencer and Adams, including a dip or valley before change is accepted by the institution and eventually becomes routine.

Much of the discussion of the change models revolved around the work of Rosabeth Moss Kanter and her "Formula for Success." Kanter advocates involving personnel affected by the change as much as possible. However, she warns of the risky business of asking staff for input if decisions have already been made or if their input will not be consid-

FIGURE 1. Goldratt's Theory of Constraints: Continuous Movement

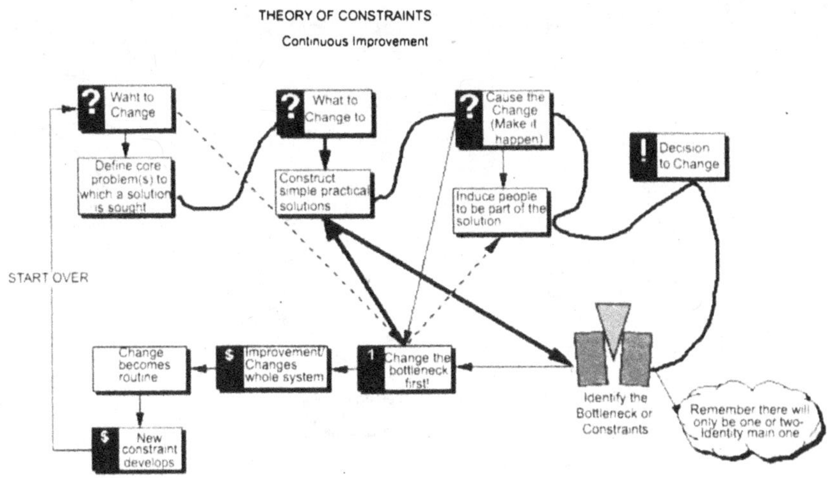

ered. It is important to realize that change takes time and morale is enhanced by giving employees a clear indication of what the change entails and how they will be affected. Kanter advises taking small steps or breaking a large change into smaller more manageable parts. It is important to realize that conflict can occur as change is assimilated. Emotions may play a pivotal role in either a positive or negative way. Encouragement of staff, praise for both current and previous accomplishments, acknowledgement of staff contributions, and avoidance of criticism of risk takers facilitate smooth transitions. Past experiences can provide a frame of reference by linking the old with the new, and may provide a sense of safety during the transition. Constructive feedback is essential for letting employees know what they are doing right and what needs to improve. Listening to employees, particularly those who actually perform the tasks that will be affected by the change, allows the free exchange of ideas between management and staff. Listening helps managers stay informed about problems and concerns. Respecting long-time employees helps them feel valued. Job security is often a concern in times of change. It is important to assure people that

FIGURE 2. Spencer and Adams' Stages of Change/Transition

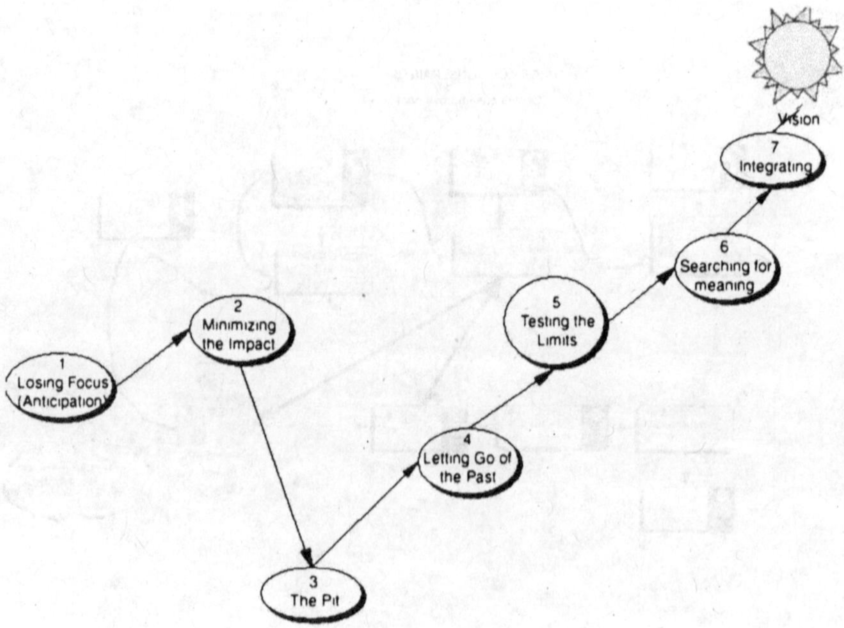

Figure created by Althea Aschmann

their jobs are safe, if that is indeed the case. Honesty and respect go a long way toward promoting trust and collaboration in an organization. There may be employees who will be unable to make the transition, despite being given a fair chance. Handling these situations honestly, quickly, and compassionately is in everyone's best interest.

Adapted by Althea Aschmann from ideas in Kanter's work, Figure 3 outlines the most common reasons Kanter lists for resisting change.

Communication is crucial for effective change. The rumor mill should not be the primary channel of communication during the change process. Being prepared to deal with the uncertainties that employees may feel and realizing that not everyone is the same helps managers provide effective employee support. People have different work and learning styles. The speed at which change can be accepted or embraced varies with individuals. Variations in the ways people process informa-

FIGURE 3. Reasons for Resisting Change

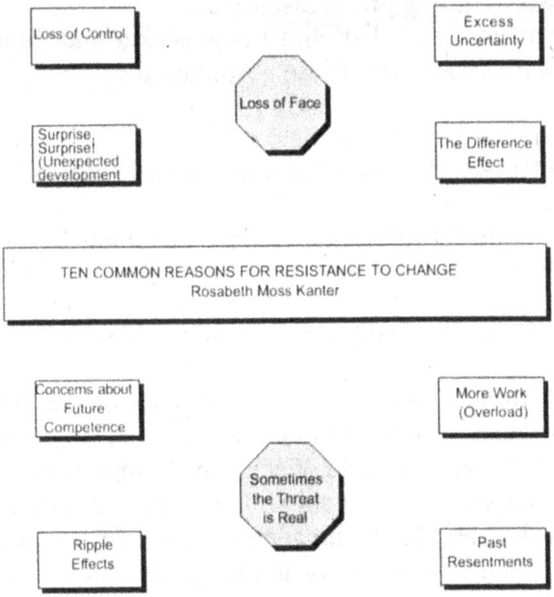

tion need to be taken into account. Everyone needs to watch for signs of burnout caused by increased stress resulting from the combination of change and overwork. Being prepared to deal with burnout as soon as early signs appear helps keep an organization healthy.

In addition, Ms. Aschmann acknowledges the ideas of Barbara Herrin of the American Association of School Librarians. Ms. Herrin's self-development model outlines an individual's process for gaining perspective on and coping positively with change. Her recommendations include looking at the whole as well as the parts, taking risks without being afraid, and developing working relationships with others.

In current times, change is often determined or carried out by the actions of a team or group. Both individuals and groups process information. Adequate time for the collective processing of information is necessary. Participation on a team may be an unfamiliar experience to many. An effective team depends upon the cultivation of collaborative behavior and the effective interpersonal skills of its members. Sufficient time is required for group dynamics to play out in order to build trust and positive relationships during group discussions.

Ms. Aschmann concluded with Longenecker and Simonetti's *Five Absolutes That Get Results*. These absolutes are:

- Get everyone on the same page;
- Prepare for battle; equip your operation with tools, talent, and technology;
- Stoke the fire for performance/Create a climate for results;
- Build bridges on the road to results–nurture relationships with people;
- Practice continuous improvement and renewal.

Discussion from the audience was limited due to time constraints and the volume of material covered in the presentation. Audience members were concerned about the role of long-time employees in the change process. Change may make them feel as if the work they've done for years is not valuable. Ms. Aschmann emphasized the importance of acknowledging their contributions and using the talents they've developed over the years to contribute toward the change process. Ms. Aschmann emphasized the importance of managers being 100 percent behind changes. If a change is mandated, being honest with employees about the circumstances surrounding the change helps everyone come to terms with it. Some mandated changes may be positive. The audience contributed the idea that a mandated change could result in a team building exercise for the organization as employees bond in order to address the change.

A bibliography prepared and distributed by Ms. Aschmann lists works of the authors whose ideas were discussed in the presentation.

BIBLIOGRAPHY

Champion, Robbie. *Tools for Change Workshops*. National Staff Development Council, 1993.

Covey, Stephen R. *The Seven Habits of Highly Effective People*. New York: Simon & Schuster, 1990.

DeGraff, Jeff and Katherine A. Lawrence. *Creativity at Work: Developing the Right Practices to Make Innovation Happen*. San Francisco, CA: Jossey-Bass, 2002.

Goldratt, Eliyahu M. *The Goal*. 2nd rev. ed. Great Barrington, MA: North River Press, 1986.

Goldratt, Eliyahu M. *What Is This Thing Called Theory of Constraints, and How Should It Be Implemented?* Great Barrington, MA: North River Press, 1990.

Kanter, Rosabeth Moss. *The Change Masters: Innovation for Productivity in the American Corporation*. New York: Simon and Schuster, 1983.

Kanter, Rosabeth Moss. "Managing the Human Side of Change." *Management Review* (April 1985): 52-56.

Kanter, Rosabeth Moss. *When Giants Learn to Dance: Mastering the Challenge of Strategy, Management, and Careers in the 1990s*. New York: Simon & Schuster, 1989.

Levesque, Paul. *Breakaway Planning: 8 Big Questions to Guide Organizational Change*. New York: AMACOM, 1998.

Lipman-Blumen, Jean and Harold J. Leavitt. *Hot Groups: Seeding Them, Feeding Them, and Using Them to Ignite Your Organization*. New York; Oxford: Oxford University Press, 1999.

Longenecker, Clinton O. and Jack L. Simonetti. *Getting Results: Five Absolutes for High Performance*. San Francisco, CA: Jossey-Bass, 2001.

Nanus, Burt. *The Leader's Edge: Seven Keys to Leadership in a Turbulent World*. Chicago: Contemporary Books, 1989.

Reed, Peter J. *Extraordinary Leadership: Creating Strategies for Change*. London, Eng.; Milford, CT: Kogan Page, 2001.

Schwartz, Peter. *The Art of the Long View*. New York: Doubleday, 1996.

Spencer, Sabina and John Adams. *Life Changes: Growing Through Personal Transitions*. San Louis Obispo, CA: Impact Publishers, 1990.

Vance, Mike and Diane Deacon. *Break Out of the Box*. Franklin Lakes, NJ: Career Press, 1996.

Wurman, Richard Saul. *Information Anxiety*. New York: Doubleday, 1989.

WORKSHOP LEADER'S ACKNOWLEDGMENT

Ideas taken from my lecture notes in Psychology of Information course lecture by Dr. Barbara Herrin, at Emporia State University (Kansas), summer 1995.

CONTRIBUTORS' NOTES

Althea Aschmann is Head of the Cataloging Department at Virginia Tech. Gail Julian is Head of the Acquisitions Unit at Clemson University.

Tools for Tenure Trailblazing: Planning Productive Paths for Green Serialists

Claire Dygert
Markel Tumlin

Workshop Leaders

Marsha Seamans

Recorder

SUMMARY. Claire Dygert and Markel Tumlin presented an overview of the tenure process by providing definitions, history, and factors for success. While stressing that the process and requirements vary from institution to institution, they outlined six factors for success which included: (1) succeeding in the application process; (2) putting a file/dossier together; (3) developing your academic career; (4) finding a mentor; (5) the importance of collegiality; and (6) understanding the political culture of your institution. *[Article copies available for a fee from The Haworth Document Delivery Service: 1-800-HAWORTH. E-mail address: <docdelivery@haworthpress.com> Website: <http://www.HaworthPress.com>]*

Claire Dygert and Markel Tumlin began this workshop, *Tools for Tenure Trailblazing: Planning Productive Paths for Green Serialists,*

[Haworth co-indexing entry note]: "Tools for Tenure Trailblazing: Planning Productive Paths for Green Serialists." Seamans, Marsha. Co-published simultaneously in *The Serials Librarian* (The Haworth Information Press, an imprint of The Haworth Press, Inc.) Vol. 46, No. 3/4, 2004, pp. 253-256; and: *Serials in the Park* (ed: Patricia S. French, and Richard Worthing) The Haworth Information Press, an imprint of The Haworth Press, Inc., 2004, pp. 253-256. Single or multiple copies of this article are available for a fee from The Haworth Document Delivery Service [1-800-HAWORTH, 9:00 a.m. - 5:00 p.m. (EST). E-mail address: getinfo@haworthpress.com].

http://www.haworthpress.com/web/SER
Digital Object Identifier: 10.1300/J123v46n03_09

by referencing a June/July 2003 article in *American Libraries* in which Mark Herring and Michael Gorman address the questions, "Do academic librarians need tenure and what has been gained from having the ability to earn tenure?"[1] This particular workshop was not designed to debate the merits of tenure, but rather to share experiences, point out some of the differences that might be found among institutions, and provide some insight into the process of gaining tenure.

As a starting point, the presenters provided some definitions and a brief history of tenure and the tenure process. Using the *Encyclopedia of Education* (*EE*), they provided the following definition: "Academic tenure is the academic teacher's or researcher's claim to or guarantee of the permanence of the position to which he has been appointed by a college or university."[2] The *EE* continues the definition by pointing out that there is sometimes a distinction made between "permanent tenure" and "security of employment," with the latter term used for scholars and researchers that are not granted full faculty appointment. Tenure can be enforced by law through the educational code, by contract with the institution, by moral commitment or practice, and/or de facto.

The concept of tenure began in 19th century Germany as a means to seek freedom within the teaching profession. In 1915, the American Association of University Professors (AAUP) was formed and in 1940 that body issued its *Statements on Principles of Academic Freedom and Tenure*. Even though the AAUP has no power to enforce claims to tenure, many colleges and universities have adopted or at least observe that standard.

Building on the AAUP principles, the Association of College and Research Libraries (ACRL) developed the *Model Statement of Criteria and Procedures for Appointment, Promotion in Academic Rank, and Tenure for College and University Librarians*.[3] The model was approved in 1973 and revised in the late 1980s. It is not recognized by all universities, and there are some deviations in institutional practices. For example, some institutions may require a second master's degree. Within institutions that grant tenure to librarians, there is a very high success rate, upwards of 90 percent, and there seems to be very little effect on turnover rate, except perhaps where there are really strict publication requirements.

The requirements for tenure vary by institution, but the core areas are generally: librarianship/primary responsibilities, professional development, and service to the library and university. The requirements are not always equally distributed among those three areas. Preparation of a successful file or dossier that documents progress in each area is essential.

After providing the background information, Dygert and Tumlin continued their presentation by expanding on the factors for success. They identified these factors as: (1) succeeding in the application process; (2) putting a file/dossier together; (3) developing your academic career; (4) finding a mentor; (5) the importance of collegiality; and (6) understanding the political culture of your institution.

The process begins with applying for a position within a tenure-granting institution. As the applicant, you should carefully research the institution to which you are applying and you should write your cover letter in direct response to the position advertisement. Keep information about the job or jobs for which you are applying handy and be prepared to receive a telephone screening interview. One of the questions you can expect to answer is how you can fulfill tenure requirements.

As part of the tenure process, you will have to build a file/dossier. As you progress, it is helpful to document your activities at the time they are completed, and to maintain your curriculum vitae in an ongoing fashion. Save everything that may be useful in building your file. Some other tips provided were: don't be afraid to ask for help or input, especially from those who have already gone through process; plan carefully for the future; and solicit outside letters of support for your activities. Finally, the presenters cautioned to leave yourself plenty of time to prepare your final dossier; it will take more time than you think.

Moving on to the third factor for success, Tumlin and Dygert discussed developing your academic career. Participation in professional organizations, including committee involvement, is important. Many institutions require some degree of publication. Grant writing is looked on very favorably within colleges and universities. Working outside your primary area of responsibility can enhance your performance. As a last point, the presenters stressed that it is important to create your own opportunities.

The fourth and fifth factors for success involve networking–finding mentors and developing collegiality. Mentoring, whether formal or informal, whether a single person or multiple people, can be very beneficial, especially in the preparation and presentation of the dossier. Collegiality with tenured and non-tenured librarians, both on your campus and off-campus, as well as with non-library faculty, is important. The general rules of collegiality demand such things as good manners, good citizenship, and following through on committees and tasks.

Finally, a good dossier is not enough in and of itself for success in tenure seeking; it is critical to be aware of the political culture within the institution and within the library. In every organization there are unwritten rules and interpersonal relationships that must be recognized and respected.

Before opening the floor to discussion, Dygert and Tumlin offered two final comments. First, your institution wants you to succeed. Second, while you are pursuing tenure you cannot champion a "non-tenure" viewpoint. Markel Tumlin also distributed a bibliography that he had compiled of additional readings. The bibliography includes sources that provide overviews of tenure in academe, survey research on tenure and its impact, the official ACRL statement on tenure, items that describe some mentor programs, sources on problematic issues of publishing requirements and/or similar professional activities, articles with helpful tips, and two articles that provide strong arguments against tenure for librarians.

Following the presentation, there was discussion and a sharing of experiences by the workshop participants. One point of discussion included how to keep people motivated and working after they are tenured. Participants offered insight on variations in practice at different institutions. The content of this workshop was very useful to those of us in positions seeking tenure.

NOTES

1. Herring, Mark Y. and Michael Gorman, "Do Librarians with Tenure Get More Respect?" *American Libraries*. 34 (2003): 70-72.
2. *Encyclopedia of Education*. 2nd ed., s.v. "Academic Freedom and Tenure" (by Philo Hutcheson).
3. Association of College and Research Libraries, "Model Statement of Criteria and Procedures for Appointment, Promotion in Academic Rank, and Tenure for College and University Librarians," *College & Research Libraries News*. 48 (1987): 247-54.

CONTRIBUTORS' NOTES

Claire Dygert is Serials & Electronic Resources Coordinator at Bender Library, American University. Markel Tumlin is Associate Librarian at the University Library, San Diego State University. Marsha Seamans is Senior Serials Catalog Librarian at the William T. Young Library, University of Kentucky.

Policies and Procedures Manuals in Technical Services: The Forest, the Trees, and the Critters

Stephanie Schmitt

Workshop Leader

Sandra Barstow

Recorder

SUMMARY. The purpose of this workshop was to emphasize the importance of written procedures manuals for technical services, using anecdotal evidence to demonstrate the difficulties that can arise when workplace policies are not documented. In the subtitle of the workshop, the forest represents the big picture (having any kind of written policies or procedures); the trees represent the policies to which the staff can refer in doing their work; and the critters are items not normally addressed in manuals, the absence of which can cause unexpected problems for unwary managers. *[Article copies available for a fee from The Haworth Document Delivery Service: 1-800-HAWORTH. E-mail address: <docdelivery@haworthpress.com> Website: <http://www.HaworthPress.com>]*

[Haworth co-indexing entry note]: "Policies and Procedures Manuals in Technical Services: The Forest, the Trees, and the Critters." Barstow, Sandra. Co-published simultaneously in *The Serials Librarian* (The Haworth Information Press, an imprint of The Haworth Press, Inc.) Vol. 46, No. 3/4, 2004, pp. 257-262; and: *Serials in the Park* (ed: Patricia S. French, and Richard Worthing) The Haworth Information Press, an imprint of The Haworth Press, Inc., 2004, pp. 257-262. Single or multiple copies of this article are available for a fee from The Haworth Document Delivery Service [1-800-HAWORTH, 9:00 a.m. - 5:00 p.m. (EST). E-mail address: getinfo@haworthpress.com].

http://www.haworthpress.com/web/SER
Digital Object Identifier: 10.1300/J123v46n03_10

OVERVIEW OF LIBRARY PROCEDURES DOCUMENTATION

Stephanie Schmitt began the workshop by discussing the results of an informal, unscientific online survey she conducted in the spring of 2003. She received 219 responses, of which 88 represented technical services departments. Of the technical services department respondents, almost 66 percent reported having an up-to-date procedures manual, with almost 7 percent having no manual at all, and 27 percent being in the process of either creating a manual or rewriting an existing manual. The Yale Law Library falls into the second category, having a selection of procedures guides but not a whole procedures manual, although Schmitt mentioned that they are preparing a disaster plan in response to the bombing which occurred on May 21, 2003.

The second survey question was related to the frequency of reviewing and updating technical services procedures manuals. Over 27 percent were reviewed at least once a year, with another 26 percent being reviewed every 1 to 3 years. More than 3 years passed between reviews for 13.5 percent, with the remainder having an unknown review cycle.

The next question determined the level of staff awareness of the procedures manuals in technical services departments. In 27 percent of the cases, staff were assumed to be accountable for the content of their manuals but reviews were not conducted; another 11 percent had routine reviews, either in the process of training new people on all existing policies or training all staff whenever there was a new policy; 10.5 percent had manuals available but no attempts were made to ensure they were reviewed; and the remaining respondents were unable to surmise the level of their staff's awareness. It was interesting to note that over 93 percent of the respondents provided online access to at least part of their policy manuals.

The next section of the survey requested information about the types of coverage provided in the manuals. Over 82 percent of the manuals included general procedural information; 83 percent included general policies; almost 85 percent included administrative information and regulations; 76 percent included technology and systems information; and almost 57 percent incorporated disaster plans. The handout provided by Schmitt included URLs for examples of online manuals which covered the various types of information well.[1]

PROBLEMS CAUSED BY LACK OF DOCUMENTATION

Having discussed the forest and the trees, Schmitt moved on to the critters, which in the forest environment are things that jump out unexpectedly at hikers but in the workplace environment are topics not included in procedures manuals. The lack of documentation can lead to problems with employees, some of which may result in court cases. One example of workplace critters is the failure to be aware of the provisions of Title 7 of the Civil Rights Act of 1964 relating to discrimination on the basis of race, sexual orientation, and, more recently, religious beliefs. Technical services staff members who are uncomfortable with processing certain types of materials may complain about having to deal with the materials or may decide to sabotage the effort to add the materials by putting the items at the bottom of an endless stack of materials to be processed, or by covering the objectionable part of the material with a bookplate or security tag. A manager who fails to take these objections seriously may be subject to a legal action by the employee.

There are other critters in the technical services workplace as well. They may include censorship in the collection development selection process, perhaps including using fiscal constraints to justify not purchasing certain types of materials even though they have been requested by patrons. Another problem might be taking away the right of a staff member to travel using institutional funding, depending on the destination of travel. There may be issues involving patron rights to have the personal information they provide protected from sabotage, hacking, and identity theft. And finally, there may be disasters, whether defined as acts of God, acts of random crazy people, or terrorism.

As an example of the difficulties that can occur when an institution does not have well-documented policies and procedures, Schmitt described the aftermath of the recent bombing at the Yale Law Library. A pipe bomb detonated in a stairwell at 4:38 p.m. on May 21, 2003. At that time, five of the seventeen technical services staff were working in their department including one person who was only ten yards away from the explosion site. Schmitt showed several photographs of the damage that ensued, including a lot of broken glass, damage to ceilings and walls, 450 water-damaged books, and other scenes of destruction. The staff were evacuated, leaving everything behind including the emergency contact list, which made it difficult to determine the chain of command or what to do next. No one except the librarian was allowed back into the building for several days and in the meantime crews cleaning up after evidence was collected disposed of damaged materials without keeping a record of what was tossed. Although a reverse inventory might be able to ascertain which library materials were lost, artifacts which had been loaned to the library for display remained unaccounted for due to a lack of any kind of listing of what was in the collection.

In addition to the loss of materials and infrastructure, administrative problems arose due to the lack of formal documentation of personnel policies relating to involuntary leave. The staff in technical services were denied access to the workplace for six work days. The rest of the library staff returned to work after two working days. During the time when each department was denied access to its respective work area, those employees on scheduled leave were granted a reprieve and did not have to use accrued leave time. This decision did not follow policy and for a period of time it caused confusion on the part of management and staff, as well as a concern by management that it would lead to unrest. In this situation, a policy was set aside to meet the needs of highly unusual circumstances.

WORKPLACE DISCRIMINATION AND HARASSMENT

In the second part of the workshop, Schmitt discussed the issue of workplace discrimination and harassment based on lack of a formal policy delineating the means by which an employee has the right to appeal work assignments that violate his or her religious beliefs. As an introduction to this part of the workshop, Schmitt displayed photographs of several books, periodicals, and videos that some people have found to be offensive. These items included *The Turner Diaries*, two Ku Klux Klan pamphlets that had been donated to the library, *The Anarchist Cookbook*, *Playboy* (in print and microfiche), *Dirty Pictures*, some books on the art of Mapplethorpe, *In Good Conscience*, the videos *Taxi Zum Klo*, *I Am Curious Yellow*, and *The Tin Drum*, and the magazines *The Advocate*, *Vanity Fair* (with a pregnant Demi Moore on the cover), and a *Sports Illustrated* swimsuit issue. She asked the attendees to think about whether any of these materials would be offensive to their staff, and how they would react to an objection by a staff member who did not want to process the materials. Schmitt explained that the manager must confront issues of religion, race and gender when the staff person feels discriminated against or harassed by having to deal with certain library materials. The code of libraries may state that we do not endorse censorship in any form in libraries, but to ensure that such a statement includes prohibition of censorship by staff, procedures must be in place to explicitly address these concerns. Schmitt cited several recent articles from the American Law Reports that address this issue.[2]

DISCUSSION

In the question and answer period that followed the presentation, someone asked why there need to be written policies for dealing with discrimination and harassment within a department, rather than relying on informal policies at that level. Schmitt explained that courts have ruled against employers that do not have a written policy stating that staff are required to work with or sell materials they find offensive on religious grounds, although she did not cite any court cases that dealt with this situation in a library environment. The manager must accommodate the request if it is based on religious belief, rather than being just a preference of the employee not to work on certain types of materials. Another workshop attendee added that when dealing with an employee who is objecting to certain work assignments, the manager should document every encounter as it occurs, not retrospectively. This action will protect the manager from a later charge of hostile work environment or harassment.

The session was well received by the audience. The opportunity to discuss the provocative topics introduced by Schmitt was limited by the minimal time allotted to the workshop (only 45 minutes) as well as the fact that there was another workshop scheduled in the room only 15 minutes after the end of this one. It was clear that the participants would have liked to continue the discussion at some length, had they been able to remain in the room. Despite these logistical difficulties, this workshop covered a very important topic and the participants were made well aware of the importance of well-documented procedures, as well as being provided with some URLs for excellent examples to assist them in preparing manuals if they have not already done so.

NOTES

1. For examples of online manuals including various types of coverage, see the following URLs, which Schmitt provided in a handout during the presentation (All URLs accessed July 23, 2003.):

Process (Procedures)

- Cornell University Library. http://www.library.cornell.edu/tsmanual/home.html
- Stanford University Law Library. http://llts.stanford.edu/deptmanual.html

General Policies

- Acqweb's Directory of Collection Development Policies. http://acqweb.library.vanderbilt.edu/acqweb/cd_policy.html

- University of Illinois at Urbana-Champaign. http://www.library.uiuc. edu/techserv/
- University of Texas at Austin. http://www.lib.utexas.edu/admin/cird/cird.html

Regulations/Administrative (Travel, Personnel Policy Manuals)

- University of Chicago. http://uhrm.uchicago.edu/policy/index.html
- University of Chicago Employee Handbook. http://uhrm.uchicago.edu/reference/ehbook/ubook.html
- Yale University. http://www.yale.edu/ppdev/PersPracWeb/TOC.html (access restricted to Yale University on-campus users only).

Technology/Systems

- ARL SPEC Kit 218. http://www.arl.org/spec/218fly.html
- University of Minnesota OIT Policy/Laws. http://www1.umn.edu/oit/security/policy.shtml

Contingency (Disaster Plans)

- Harvard University. http://preserve.harvard.edu/emergencies/plan.html
- Library of Congress.*http://www.loc.gov/preserv/pub/seibert/*
- Resources on Emergency Evacuation and Emergency Preparedness. *http://www.access-board.gov/evac.htm*

2. Schmitt provided the following citations for those wishing to pursue the legal issues of religious harassment and accommodation:

Beckley, Gloria T. and Paul Burstei. "Religious Pluralism, Equal Opportunity, and the State." *The Western Political Quarterly* 44, no. 1 (March 1991): 185-208

Bourdeau, John A. "Individual Liability of Supervisors, Managers, or Officers for Discriminatory Actions–Cases Postdating the Civil Rights Act of 1991." 131 A.L.R. Fed. 221.

Campbell, Andrew M. "What Constitutes Employer's Reasonable Accommodation of Employee's Religious Preferences Under Title VII of Civil Rights Act of 1964." 134 A.L.R. Fed. 1.

Shields, Marjorie A. J. "Necessity of, and What Constitutes, Employer's Reasonable Accommodation of Employee's Religious Preference Under State Law," 107 A.L.R. 5th 623.

Stephenson, Jr., David J. "What Constitutes Religious Harassment in Employment In Violation of Title VII of Civil Rights Act of 1964." 149 *American Law Reports* Federal 405 (149 A.L.R. Fed. 405)

CONTRIBUTORS' NOTES

Stephanie Schmitt is Manager of Serials Services at the Yale Law Library. Sandra Barstow is Assistant Director for Administrative Services at the University of Wyoming Libraries.

Paving the Way for Print Repositories Through Electronic Access

Mary Jo Zeter

Jeanne Drewes

Workshop Leaders

Michael A. Arthur

Recorder

SUMMARY. Mary Jo Zeter and Jeanne Drewes from Michigan State University presented an overview of the state of print repositories. The presenters provided a brief history of the move toward print repositories, outlined reasons for inclusion of print serials, and discussed the impact that electronic formats are having on print repositories. Ms. Zeter and Ms. Drewes discussed initiatives by the Center for Research Libraries and provided specific recommendations for the planning and development of a national repository system. *[Article copies available for a fee from The Haworth Document Delivery Service: 1-800-HAWORTH. E-mail address: <docdelivery@haworthpress.com> Website: <http://www.HaworthPress.com>]*

[Haworth co-indexing entry note]: "Paving the Way for Print Repositories Through Electronic Access." Arthur, Michael A. Co-published simultaneously in *The Serials Librarian* (The Haworth Information Press, an imprint of The Haworth Press, Inc.) Vol. 46, No. 3/4, 2004, pp. 263-267; and: *Serials in the Park* (ed: Patricia S. French, and Richard Worthing) The Haworth Information Press, an imprint of The Haworth Press, Inc., 2004, pp. 263-267. Single or multiple copies of this article are available for a fee from The Haworth Document Delivery Service [1-800-HAWORTH, 9:00 a.m. - 5:00 p.m. (EST). E-mail address: getinfo@haworthpress.com].

http://www.haworthpress.com/web/SER
Digital Object Identifier: 10.1300/J123v46n03_11

INTRODUCTION

Throughout the years, librarians have planned and implemented off-site storage for print and nonprint materials. With this workshop the presenters reviewed the history of off-site storage, provided reasons for inclusion of print serials within repositories, discussed the impact that electronic access is having on shared repositories and described current cooperative programs involving the Center for Research Libraries (CRL), and the Committee for Institutional Cooperation (CIC). Ms. Zeter and Ms. Drewes addressed key issues related to the creation of print repositories and provided specific recommendations.

MOVING TOWARD PRINT REPOSITORIES

Ms. Zeter began her comments on the history of print repositories with a broad review of the problems that led to the need for repositories. From the early years of the profession, librarians felt that materials worth keeping should be accessible. Space limitations quickly created a need for off-site storage. Storage space needed to be safe and inexpensive. Low use materials were candidates for off-site storage; however, off-site storage presented a challenge for user access in an effective and efficient manner. Storage facilities were generally located away from the library, and thus patrons experienced problems with easy access to the materials; however, environmental conditions could be ideal with closed stacks facilities.

With the push toward storage facilities, low use periodicals were often selected for storage. This trend toward storage of low use periodicals, rather than de-accessioning, was based on the need for longevity and continued access for future use even if the amount of usage declined over time. The other impetus for storage of low use periodicals was based on the feeling that archiving was an essential function of libraries.

Today, agreements between various partner libraries are creating local and regional repositories in an effort to provide common access to materials. This allows libraries to cancel print or cease binding for a savings of time and money. This scenario would be acceptable if a *designated* member institution took responsibility for the preservation of those print materials.

IMPACT OF ELECTRONIC ACCESS

The level of confidence that a library has in the long-term availability of electronic access is an important factor in deciding whether or not to store or cancel print holdings. Electronic access opens the door for archiving print in shared print repositories, leading to savings in space and staff time, with no inconvenience to patrons. The responsibility to preserve print journals is based on considerations of ownership vs. rights of access to electronic versions, variations between print and electronic versions, longevity of media, and the artifactual value of print.

CRL AND PRINT REPOSITORY PROJECTS

The Center of Research Libraries (CRL) is an early example of a regional depository utilizing collective management and ownership of a collection of research materials. CRL began in 1949 as a repository for ten midwestern universities and has now grown to over 100 members. The CIC/CRL Reference Books Archive was an early cooperative print repository project initiated in 1998, in which superseded reference serials titles were selected by librarians at CIC institutions (universities in the Midwest Big Ten Conference plus the University of Chicago) for transfer to CRL. The long-term goal of the project was to minimize the redundancies of these seldom-consulted volumes among member libraries, thereby freeing valuable shelf space.

CRL is now testing a distributed model of print serials retention for JSTOR journals, with funding from the Andrew W. Mellon Foundation. Three CRL member libraries have partnered with the Center to test a model whereby long-term preservation and access is assured through a system of access repositories backed by *dark* (that is, highly secure) repositories.

LIGHT AND DARK REPOSITORIES

Light or *dim* access repositories are intended for collections that may allow on-site use, circulation and scanning or photocopying for interlibrary loan purposes. A dedication to service is essential for this level of repository and the focus is on accurate holdings records and the ability to provide materials. *Dark* repositories are for archival copies where access to the materials is not the intended purpose. Rather, these repositories offer a high degree of security and preservation with long-term protection and limited access to specific items.

The focus of dark repositories is on security and environmental conditions. Optimal climate control, proper temperature and humidity levels, effective air filtration systems and ultraviolet light control are essential. Security measures include closed stacks, and theft and hazard prevention systems such as sprinklers. A written disaster response plan should be mandatory to ensure recovery and restoration of materials in case the need arises.

INFORMATION SHARING STRATEGIES

Key to any move toward a national repository system is the development of a mechanism for information sharing on the status of repository holdings. This could include new holdings symbols to be used in the bibliographic utilities to identify an item's repository status. It was also suggested that there be a Web registry outlining the contractual terms and conditions of the repository. Such a system could include links from the bibliographic records directly to the Web registry.

Trust is an essential ingredient for the successful development of a national print repository system. Written contracts strengthen confidence that materials in repositories will be safe and available as needed. This step will further assure librarians and make them comfortable with not only eliminating the purchase of some new materials, but with the weeding process as well when space is needed.

CONCLUSION AND DISCUSSION

This workshop provided a history of library off-site storage and specific recommendations for the establishment of shared print access in any future move toward a national repository system. Discussion included questions and comments about the impact on shared repositories as more libraries move to electronic-only subscriptions. The presenters emphasized that this trend underscores the need for specific institutions to take responsibility for archiving the print so that important scholarly information is preserved. The discussion also included comments about a specific regional repository. An attendee alluded to her experience with the development of a regional repository by stating that the users at each institution had quite different goals, and she emphasized that rules and guidelines for member libraries need to be strict. The presenters addressed a question regarding participation in a national repository system by smaller libraries with limited funds. They emphasized that each library could be responsible for preserving selected materials.

This workshop provided many issues to think about regarding the long-term preservation of print serials. Particularly as publications move increasingly toward electronic formats and libraries reduce print collections, the benefits of cooperative print repositories are being recognized.

SELECTED BIBLIOGRAPHY

Bridegam, Willis. 2001. *A Collaborative Approach to Collection Storage: The Five-College Library Depository*. Washington, D.C.: Council on Library and Information Resources. Also available online at http://www.clir.org/pubs/abstract/pub97abst.html.

Center for Research Libraries. 2002. Towards a National Hard Copy Strategy. *FOCUS* 21(3): 1-5. Also available online at http://www.crl.edu/info/focus/Focus%20in%20pdf/302focus.pdf.

Kisling, Vernon N., Stephanie Cornell Haas, and Pamela S. Cenzer. 2000. Last Copy Depository: Cooperative Collection Management Centers in the Electronic Age. *Collection Management*. 24 (1/2): 87-92.

McCormick, Edith. 1999. NYPL, Columbia, Princeton Cooperate on Storage Site. *American Libraries*. 30(5): 16-17.

Nichols, Stephen G. and Abby Smith. 2001.*The Evidence in Hand: the Report of the Task Force on the Artifact in Library Collections*. Washington, D.C.: Council on Library and Information Resources. Also available online at http://www.clir.org/pubs/abstract/pub103abst.html.

Nitecki, Danuta and Curtis L. Kendrick. 2001. *Library Off-site Shelving: A Guide for High-Density Storage*. Englewood, Colo: Libraries Unlimited, Inc.

O'Connor, Steve, Andrew Wells, and Mel Collier. 2002. A Study of Collaborative Storage of Library Resources. *Library Hi Tech*. 20(3): 258-269.

Oud, Joanne. 2001. Eliminating Duplication in a Shared Storage Facility: Practical and Political Issues. *Against the Grain* 13(3): 1, 20, 22. Also available online at *http://www.against*-the-grain.com.

Reilly, Jr., Bernard F. with research and analysis by Barbara DesRosiers, Center for Research Libraries. 2003. *Developing Print Repositories: Models for Shared Preservation and Access*. Washington, D.C.: Council on Library and Information Resources. Also available online at http://www.clir.org/pubs/abstract/pub117abst.html.

CONTRIBUTORS' NOTES

Mary Jo Zeter and Jeanne Drewes are from Michigan State University. Michael A. Arthur is Assistant Head of Acquisitions Services at Ball State University.

Reinventing Acquisitions with a "Forget-to-Do" List

Ann McHugo
Carol Magenau
Workshop Presenters

Jeanne M. Langendorfer
Recorder

SUMMARY. Many changes have occurred in our work in the last few years. In the Dartmouth College Library Acquisitions Department, there was new work to do without additional resources; in fact, there were fewer people. How could the acquisitions staff manage this situation? McHugo commented that their then-new director gave them the title of their presentation by suggesting that they would just "have to forget to do" some things. Here they present the strategies they developed to meet the challenge. *[Article copies available for a fee from The Haworth Document Delivery Service: 1-800-HAWORTH. E-mail address: <docdelivery@haworthpress.com> Website: <http://www.HaworthPress.com>]*

The background for this challenge facing the Acquisitions Department staff is that the new director was focusing on digital collections, bringing about an accelerated growth in activity related to digital resources. In addition to ordering digital resources, which in itself re-

[Haworth co-indexing entry note]: "Reinventing Acquisitions with a 'Forget-to-Do' List." Langendorfer, Jeanne M. Co-published simultaneously in *The Serials Librarian* (The Haworth Information Press, an imprint of The Haworth Press, Inc.) Vol. 46, No. 3/4, 2004, pp. 269-273; and: *Serials in the Park* (ed: Patricia S. French, and Richard Worthing) The Haworth Information Press, an imprint of The Haworth Press, Inc., 2004, pp. 269-273. Single or multiple copies of this article are available for a fee from The Haworth Document Delivery Service [1-800-HAWORTH, 9:00 a.m. - 5:00 p.m. (EST). E-mail address: getinfo@haworthpress.com].

http://www.haworthpress.com/web/SER
Digital Object Identifier: 10.1300/J123v46n03_12

quires more time and attention, staff had to link to Web resources, review and negotiate licenses and develop collections of digital journals. Staff reductions really affected department staff as they faced the transition from print to digital. Budget constraints forced managers to make choices.

Dartmouth College Library is an Ivy League school with 4,000 undergraduate students and 1,000 graduate students. It has a $6.5 million acquisitions budget, covering a medical school, engineering school, and business school, as well as the arts and sciences departments. There are thirty subject bibliographers, six libraries and a storage facility, several hundred funds, twelve major vendors with more than 600 total vendors, 6,500 periodicals, 20,000 current subscriptions, and 23 acquisitions staff, one of whom is part-time. Two staff work with digital resources full-time; another 7 staff work with digital resources part-time.

The goal was to support a growing collection of digital resources. To meet the challenge, staff would have to be redeployed and retrained. This would make it possible to support new directions for the department. In addition to the focus on building a digital library, the Acquisitions Department was assigned to manage two public service areas to assist users with periodicals, and newspapers and digital resources.

The management team developed some strategies to present to the staff and asked them for more ideas. The strategies agreed upon were to transform tasks by changing the way the task is accomplished, transfer the work to another department, or terminate the work. These reinventions were hard on everyone; change is difficult.

Changes that impacted direct services to users–bibliographers, faculty, and library staff–were the hardest. Reducing or transforming their services to this group was difficult to accept. The work done by the Acquisitions Department for bibliographers was based on a long tradition. Now bibliographers were taught to produce, review, and evaluate the regular, routine financial reports that Acquisitions staff previously provided them. Routing of review journals was transformed and transferred. The creation of lists of newly acquired digital resources was transferred to the IT area. Faculty and administrators were taught to set up electronic journal alerting services, transforming the table of contents service by terminating the photocopying and distribution of paper tables of contents and using online services. The newspaper retention program was transformed by reducing back holdings of print for many titles.

Support services, the technical processing activities that make up much of the work of Acquisitions, were also affected. Trigger (or tickler) files for materials not available on standing order, or wanted only intermittently, were discontinued. Some titles were transferred to a helpful vendor willing to work with such materials, some transitioned from print to online, and some the bibliographers decided to cancel altogether. Remaining titles were turned over to bibliographers for them to firm order as needed. A free Web service called *WatchThatPage* (http://www.watchthatpage.com/) is useful for alerting bibliographers to new editions of titles that are advertised at stable Websites.

There were other changes in direct support services. One was the termination of claiming; they decided to respond to questions and problems "just in time," rather than "just in case." Acquisitions staff would take a passive role by not performing systematic claiming unless the title fit specific criteria. This decision was reached after much discussion, including discussion about the ethical dimensions that were part of their stewardship of resources. In the end, it was decided that the time spent in the past was not warranted for the future. Other reinventions were: cease keeping histories of claim responses and checking in monographic series; transfer, transform or terminate check-in; and transform gift order records to reduce the amount of time spent in gifts processing.

Two questions by the presenters were available at the door and then asked during the presentation:

- How have you managed to redeploy staff to accommodate working with electronic resources?
- What services have been dropped at your institution that were difficult for you to accept?

Magenau responded first that she was not personally comfortable with all the changes they had to make but that she experienced personal growth from meeting the challenge. Their anxiety was eased as they learned that some problems did not occur because the library moved so quickly into the online environment.

Future directions for acquisitions work include copyright management, digital publishing, linking services, license management, digital access management, use statistics, and public service. McHugo and Magenau ended by asserting that "change is here to stay!" and wished us good luck with the reinvention process.

The session was so crowded that an adjoining room was opened up and more seating made available. The presentation was enthusiastically received by the audience. Many questions were asked at the end of the presentation.

QUESTIONS AND ANSWERS

Q: *What is the staff role in managing usage statistics? Please describe.*

A: The Acquisitions Department is the library connection with the publisher. We receive the usage data for digital resources by e-mailing to get the statistics or by setting up regular reports from the publisher, collecting and archiving the data. A liaison in IT puts the data on a Website for bibliographers to analyze, though there is a small but growing role for Acquisitions in analysis in putting the statistical information into a profile to help bibliographers make decisions about renewals or cancellations.

Q: *Were staff redeployed within the unit or to other units?*

A: Staff were redeployed within the unit. Generally, staff are being redeployed from print workflows to digital workflows. We are indirectly taking on work that other units do or have done, expanding boundaries unofficially.

Q: *Due to changes in functions, are job descriptions being rewritten?*

A: Yes, as it is possible. We were encouraged to push the parameters of the job as much as possible, but due to budget constraints, there isn't much we can do at Dartmouth to raise pay. Position descriptions are written in a manner that generally accommodates the reality of change in the workplace. An audience member commented that due to changes in work, she was successful in upgrading the positions of several workers and retooling the binding position to handle electronic resources. Another suggestion was to use open positions to work in upgraded skill requirements.

Q: *Do you know the cost benefits that came from terminating or transforming work?*

A: No. We did not conduct a cost-benefit analysis of the changes we have made and continue to make. We don't have the resources to do that.

Q: *Describe how check-in is not being done.*

A: Check-in takes a huge amount of time and check-in accuracy doesn't matter if the item is not available when the user wants it. The presenter referred to an article in the literature by Rick Anderson and Steven D. Zink.[1] Audience members raised the issue of stewardship of resources, with other attendees presenting a variety of viewpoints without any resolution. Dartmouth is not checking in digital resources.

Q: *Has there been a problem with the auditors?*

A: No. We keep complete financial records, which are the main concern of our auditors. The auditors do not track physical library materials.

Q: *What are you asking your agents/vendors to do?*

A: We ask them to do more and more, such as providing us with quicker turnaround on setting up digital subscriptions, creating lists by publisher for us, etc. The vendors are responsive, but they can't provide these services for nothing. As a result, we see increased service charges.

Q: *How did you change the table-of-contents service?*

A: We used mostly freely available services, but kept some commercial services that were already in use.

Q: *How are you handling bundled packages (print and electronic)?*

A: We throw away the print if we have agreed that the electronic source is reliable.

Q: *How is that going?*

A: We don't tell the faculty that we are tossing print. The new director mandated a single format. We do try to sell some of it but there is not much of a market except in the scientific/technical/medical area.

Q: *What are your operations costs?*

A: We try to keep it as little labor intensive as possible. We won't get more staff, but we will get more work. We must identify strategies for meeting library goals within the realities of the staffing resources we have.

NOTE

1. Rick Anderson and Steven D. Zink, "Implementing the Unthinkable: The Demise of Periodical Check-in at the University of Nevada," Library Collections, Acquisitions, and Technical Services 27, no. 1 (Spring 2003): 61-71).

CONTRIBUTORS' NOTES

Ann McHugo and Carol Magenau are from Dartmouth College Library. Jeanne M. Langendorfer is Coordinator of Serials, University Libraries, Bowling Green State University.

Electronic Resource Management and the MARC Record: The Road Less Traveled

Paula Sullenger

Workshop Leader

Anne Mitchell

Recorder

SUMMARY. This workshop was a case study on the use of MARC fields to record access and licensing data for electronic resources at Auburn University. The presentation touched on Auburn's overall philosophy toward electronic resources, the factors that motivated development of their current approach to electronic resource management, and an assessment of the project to date. Although the project was implemented quite recently and is not yet fully comprehensive, it is regarded as a success and will undergo further development. *[Article copies available for a fee from The Haworth Document Delivery Service: 1-800-HAWORTH. E-mail address: <docdelivery@haworthpress.com> Website: <http://www.HaworthPress.com>]*

[Haworth co-indexing entry note]: "Electronic Resource Management and the MARC Record: The Road Less Traveled." Mitchell, Anne. Co-published simultaneously in *The Serials Librarian* (The Haworth Information Press, an imprint of The Haworth Press, Inc.) Vol. 46, No. 3/4, 2004, pp. 275-280; and: *Serials in the Park* (ed: Patricia S. French, and Richard Worthing) The Haworth Information Press, an imprint of The Haworth Press, Inc., 2004, pp. 275-280. Single or multiple copies of this article are available for a fee from The Haworth Document Delivery Service [1-800-HAWORTH, 9:00 a.m. - 5:00 p.m. (EST). E-mail address: getinfo@haworthpress.com].

http://www.haworthpress.com/web/SER
Digital Object Identifier: 10.1300/J123v46n03_13

BACKGROUND

Effective management of administrative data for electronic resources (such as access restrictions, passwords, contact information, and cancellation policies) has become a major issue for libraries. Auburn University Libraries have chosen to record e-resource management data in the holdings records that appear in the library catalog. Paula Sullenger, Serials Acquisitions Librarian at Auburn, described how and why her library arrived at its present solution to the electronic resource management challenge. To provide a context for Auburn's e-resource management strategy, Sullenger described a similar catalog-based solution that her library has used to provide access to e-journals. Her example illustrates both the pragmatic, single-database approach that Auburn has preferred in the past, and the precedent of interdepartmental collaboration that has been essential to the success of the electronic resource management project. In particular, Sullenger recognized the contributions of Cataloging IT Specialist Jack Fitzpatrick, who has provided ongoing technical support, and Head of Cataloging Henry McCurley, whose ideas have been the catalyst for the project.

When electronic journals emerged in a major way in the mid- to late-90s, many libraries were uncertain whether to catalog e-journals or provide access to them through a separate list, particularly where the volatile, high-volume aggregator databases were concerned. Auburn's philosophy that "a library resource is a library resource" led logically to their decision to catalog their entire electronic collection at the title level. They employed the single-record model for electronic journals, with separate holdings records for each print, microform, and full-text electronic version of a journal; all were attached to a primary bibliographic record for that journal. The electronic journals list that can be accessed from Auburn's library homepage is generated directly from the library catalog. Specialized coding in the 710 field identifies the aggregator or collection where the journal appears and whether that version is acquired by subscription, is freely available, is available in conjunction with a membership or print subscription, or is part of an aggregation. The following example indicates that the journal has an online version (QEJ) that is part of an aggregation (K), in this case JSTOR:

710 02 $aQEJK$bJSTOR

This coding is the basis for the A-Z list, which displays the journal title, source title, and coverage dates. The list is virtually indistinguishable from commercially available A-Z services, but the library has to maintain only one data set.

THE PATH TO E-RESOURCE MANAGEMENT

For the acquisitions unit, electronic databases and e-journal collections created a host of new licensing and access data to be managed. Auburn identified approximately ten elements of essential information to record about the resources, including whether the resource provides full-text, whether it was an individual or consortial purchase, type of authentication, number of simultaneous users, and restrictions for off-campus use, interlibrary lending, and e-reserves. The library initially considered recording access and licensing information in the notes area of the acquisitions record, but decided against this option based on concerns that the e-resource management notes would be difficult to disentangle from the payment-related notes already in the records.

At the 1999 NASIG conference Sullenger learned about ERLIC, an external license management database developed at Penn State. Tired of rummaging through paper files to answer questions about a particular subscription or license, she decided to create her own license management database in Microsoft Access, linked to the pertinent payment information that already existed in the catalog through the bibliographic ID number. The e-resource database had a public interface for use by the public services librarians who also needed access to information about passwords, simultaneous user limits, and renewal dates. Although the database was a major improvement over cumbersome paper files, it still required librarians to gather information from two separate sources. Most information about electronic resources already resided in the catalog; couldn't the license terms live there too?

The catalog-based approach provides a number of advantages over maintaining a separate database. Every other piece of information about the resource, from the URL to the coverage statement to the payment data, was already incorporated into the catalog. Auburn's librarians were both familiar with the interface and accustomed to using the catalog as the central point of reference for the library's resources. Perhaps more importantly, the MARC format is fielded, standards-based, and in almost universal use in libraries, minimizing concerns about platform and software dependency that would make a future migration difficult.

Auburn's electronic resource management data were ready for MARC. But was MARC ready for them?

Enthusiasm for the project was high, but the existing ILS technology was not as cooperative as Sullenger would have liked. Auburn was using Endeavor's Voyager, a relatively young system. At that time, it was prohibitively difficult to retrieve certain kinds of MARC data from the catalog to the extent that would be necessary to implement the project. Auburn continued to push Voyager to develop the e-resource management functionality they were looking for, but the technology gap temporarily brought the project to a halt. The idea was revisited when, in 2002, Voyager introduced global update capabilities, making the MARC records more accessible than ever before. At last it was feasible to use MARC to manage electronic resources.

In summer 2002, around the same time as Voyager's upgrades, presentations about electronic resource management at ALA and NASIG motivated Sullenger to resume development of the project. Spurred by the extensive ARL licensing survey, Sullenger conducted an inventory and review of the existing electronic resource licenses, and cleaned up her Access database to ensure that all of the appropriate information was current and correct. Meanwhile, the cataloging unit was deciding how the holdings records could be suited to their data management needs. Cataloging staff recommended using fields 995 and 997, which are designated for local use and are, therefore, fully customizable. Sullenger had previously recorded 10-15 data elements that she said have been sufficient for the library's management needs up to this point, but the system is flexible enough that more could be added if necessary. The 995 field is used to record administrative information that is strictly for acquisitions use (such as the ARL type, confidentiality requirements, and cancellation policy). This field is necessary for management and reporting purposes, but does not display to the public. The 997 field contains the public data used by the reference librarians, including when the subscription began, access restrictions, number of simultaneous users, off-campus availability, restrictions on use of the resource for interlibrary loan, e-reserves or course packs, and the procedure for acquiring additional logins for classroom use.

Once a decision had been reached about which subfield to use for each piece of data, the old Access database was output as an Excel file, converted to MARC data, and loaded into the system. After the initial load, Sullenger began using the "data planter," a secondary interface programmed in Visual Basic, to enter e-resource management data directly into the holdings record. When she needs to retrieve data for reporting purposes, another program known as the "data reaper" can retrieve data from the specialized holdings fields.

OUTCOMES

Auburn's reference librarians have been impressed with the new system and would like to see it developed further but there are still some obstacles to overcome. The original Access database was specifically for resources that Auburn had licensed and paid for; it did not include free electronic resources such as locally created resources or databases available through the Alabama Virtual Library. Because the old database used payment records as a linking point whereas the new system is holdings-based, Sullenger also has to resolve those cases where the payment and administrative data are connected to an umbrella title instead of its component databases. For example, the METADEX product consists of nine separate parts, but there is only one payment record in the system. A more intractable problem is that confidential payment and password information cannot be placed in the public catalog.

Auburn is currently considering several potential enhancements to their license management tool. One such enhancement would incorporate individual journal licenses, which at present exist entirely in paper form, into the system. Sullenger also mentioned the possibility of tracking "negative decisions," the reasons why a particular electronic resource was *not* purchased, so that the record of the consideration process could be more readily accessible. Finally, the library is investigating the feasibility of integrating usage statistics into the existing data structure.

DISCUSSION

A short question-and-answer period followed Sullenger's presentation. The questions largely pertained to the specific workflows involved in the project. In response to a question about how much maintenance is necessary to keep up this kind of system, Sullenger noted that because the conversion was so recent, they have not had a chance to assess the maintenance phase. In her experience, however, license terms remain relatively stable, so she does not anticipate that maintenance will become a major problem. Another audience member inquired about how Auburn deals with journals covered by multiple licenses. At present, the license terms are entered only at the database or collection level, so seeing the license terms for a particular journal is a multi-step process of looking up the journal, seeing that it is part of a collection, and then looking up the collection to see the terms. A final question had to do with how the data elements were selected. According to Sullenger, she decided on what elements to include largely on the basis of requests from other librarians, and that method has been acceptable so far.

CONCLUSIONS

Sullenger concluded the question-and-answer session by remarking on some of the major advances taking place in electronic resources management. She noted that the Digital Library Federation's forthcoming electronic resource management specifications will be an interesting development to watch for. Commercial electronic resource management tools are beginning to emerge in the marketplace as well, and are likely to alter the e-resource management landscape considerably. Sullenger suggested that libraries unable to afford a commercial system consider a local solution like the one Auburn has achieved, and expressed confidence that until a commercial system is developed that can be as readily customized and as seamlessly integrated with the catalog as what her library has already developed, the MARC-based solution will continue to be the best fit for her library's needs.

CONTRIBUTORS' NOTES

Paula Sullenger is Serials Acquisitions Librarian at Auburn University. Anne Mitchell is Metadata Coordinator at University of Houston Libraries.

From Survival Hike to a Walk in the Park: Training Guideposts to Lead the Way

Rene J. Erlandson
Workshop Leader

Robert J. Congleton
Recorder

SUMMARY. Rene J. Erlandson discussed the basic characteristics of all training programs and the basic principles for designing and implementing a training program. *[Article copies available for a fee from The Haworth Document Delivery Service: 1-800-HAWORTH. E-mail address: <docdelivery@haworthpress.com> Website: <http://www.HaworthPress.com>]*

Erlandson began by introducing four essential provisions needed to develop and implement a good training program. The first two elements are planning and organization. In addition, it is necessary to have flexibility. You must determine the skill levels of the trainees and target your training sessions towards those skill levels. You must also be ready to redesign an area of the program that is not working. And finally, while communication is important in all areas of our workday lives, it is particularly important when designing a training program. You need to communicate with your prospective trainees, trainers, and administra-

[Haworth co-indexing entry note]: "From Survival Hike to a Walk in the Park: Training Guideposts to Lead the Way." Congleton, Robert J. Co-published simultaneously in *The Serials Librarian* (The Haworth Information Press, an imprint of The Haworth Press, Inc.) Vol. 46, No. 3/4, 2004, pp. 281-286; and: *Serials in the Park* (ed: Patricia S. French, and Richard Worthing) The Haworth Information Press, an imprint of The Haworth Press, Inc., 2004, pp. 281-286. Single or multiple copies of this article are available for a fee from The Haworth Document Delivery Service [1-800-HAWORTH, 9:00 a.m. - 5:00 p.m. (EST). E-mail address: getinfo@haworthpress.com].

http://www.haworthpress.com/web/SER
Digital Object Identifier: 10.1300/J123v46n03_14

tion. You should keep the lines of communication open between you and those who will be affected by your training program. Communication between the various groups affected by the training program will assist you in designing a training program that will meet the needs of everyone involved. You will need to use all four of these important skills: planning, organization, flexibility, and communication, as you go through the four stages of setting up and completing a successful training program.

STAGE ONE: ASSESSMENT AND EVALUATION

Determine whether or not a training program is needed. Has something changed or will something be changing that requires the training of staff in order to facilitate or implement the change? Keep in mind that a training program will not alleviate all problems within an organization. Shortages of staff or interpersonal problems among the staff will not be addressed by a training program. Use an assessment form to list the changes that will require new/additional training.

Once you have determined that a training program is needed, you need to define the expected outcome of the training. Visualize how you expect your staff to function after they have completed the training program. Think about how your department or organization is going to operate after the training program has been completed. Break down the overall training goal into specific skills that each trainee should acquire from the program.

Determine what you would consider an adequate competency level for each of the skills taught in the training program–the criteria the staff needs to meet to actually be competent in that skill. For example, in a training program designed to teach staff how to create a text file in Microsoft Word, the goal would be creating the text file. The skills needed to meet the goal would be the ability to open the program, create a new document, manipulate fonts, use italics or bold, and save the document. The level of success in learning these skills determines the competency level of each trainee. If after completing the training program a trainee cannot do each of these skills, they would have a below average competency for the training program's goal. If a trainee can successfully do each of these skills, they would be considered competent. If a trainee can also do additional skills such as adding numbered lists or inserting tables, they would be expert/advanced.

Write down your goals, specific skills, and competency levels. This will give you a document that you can refer to throughout the training development process.

Determine the date when training must be completed. Be specific and write it down. This is your "drop dead" date. If you are implementing a new system, new software, or purchasing an online new service, a date has probably been determined. If you are implementing a departmental training program that is not constrained by any outside deadline, you must decide on a firm date for completing the training. Create a time frame for each stage of the training program by working backwards from the drop dead date.

Identify groups and individuals who will be affected by the training. Identify potential trainees as well as individuals who already have expertise in this area and could be used as additional trainers. Write down the names of the potential trainees. Be specific. You will need to determine the current competency level of every trainee in each of the skills focused on in the training program. Create a training needs assessment tool/document to distribute to each potential trainee. The training needs assessment document should list every skill expected to be covered in the training program. The assessment tool should delineate what is the acceptable competency level for each skill and provide a way for the potential trainees to rank their own competency level for each skill. The document should include an area where participants can indicate their preferred training method. Some people do not like to work in large group training sessions; they prefer one-to-one. One-to-one training preferences cannot always be accommodated, but if you are dealing with only five or six people, it may be possible to provide a one-on-one training experience for them. Also indicate on the document an exact date by which you want the form returned to you as well as an address to use for returning the form. Distribute the training needs assessment tool to all prospective trainees. Have them complete the form and return it to you. Your training program sessions should be based on the information provided by the completed forms. You should be able to decide on the number of training sessions needed, and the competency levels addressed in each session.

Build support and consensus for the training program. Often this can be done by approaching potential trainees and showing them how the training will make their job experience better; i.e., what the training will do for them. Most people want to do a good job. If there is an area in which they are deficient, most people are open to having additional training if they are allowed time away from their current job for the training.

STAGE TWO: DESIGN YOUR TRAINING PROGRAM

Use the needs assessment tool to determine the training levels needed within your program. How many individuals are at the beginner level? How many at the intermediate level? How many are already at the acceptable competency level and do not need training? Also identify those individuals who may have expertise in the area and whom you may tap as trainers or coaches for those individuals at the beginning level. Then determine the number of training sessions needed.

Specify the desired outcome for each training level. Write it down. You need to create a document based on the skills you delineated at the assessment phase. The document should lay out what trainees can anticipate learning from the training session(s). The document will help you assess whether or not you met the goals of the training program once the program has been implemented and completed.

Create a timeline. You have your drop dead date and you know how many training sessions you need and at what level. Now you need to plug those training sessions into a time frame, working backward from your drop dead date. It is best to train people at the point when they will begin to use the skills they learn. If you are going to train people on a new online system or computer related system, don't train them six months before you are going to bring up the system. Nobody is going to remember the training. It is better to have a lot of training sessions a few weeks just before the system is brought up. If possible, set up a test database with a sample of your own records for hands-on training. This way staff will know how their data will look in the system rather than being surprised when they begin to use the real system.

Develop your training material. Create training material such as manuals and hands-on in-class exercises for the trainees who will be attending the sessions. Create a cheat-sheet or quick and dirty notes on one piece of paper that the trainees can quickly consult at their work stations after the training sessions. Training manuals and scripts must also be created for your trainers. This will ensure that every trainer is covering the exact same material in each training session. You do not want people going to multiple training sessions and getting different information.

Create an analysis instrument. In order to obtain consistent information from program participants, you must create an analysis instrument. Most often this instrument will be a survey. However, if the training program involved only a handful of people, you may be able to interview each individual one-on-one. If you do decide to interview participants, develop the questions beforehand to assure that everyone is asked the same questions. If you are doing a larger training session, you will probably opt to use a survey approach whereby at the end of the training session each participant is handed a form asking questions related to the training program.

STAGE THREE: IMPLEMENTATION

Select an appropriate site. If you are doing online training with hands-on exercises, make sure that site has enough computers for all the participants, and that the appropriate software or online connections are available at the time of training. A training site should be easily accessible for all trainees and have adequate amenities (lighting, heating/cooling systems, etc.)

Create an environment at the training site that does not have a lot of distractions. If you have windows, you will want to turn the blinds down. If you are having sessions in the afternoon after lunch, you do not want to turn the lights down because people will fall asleep. If you are doing training that is related to workflow and you are not walking them through a hands-on experience online, making it feel like a group activity can be done by changing the layout of the room such as by putting the chairs in a circle so that they are all together and you are not lecturing to them.

Practice the training script. Do the hands-on exercises. If you find a flaw in the training program, be willing to rewrite it. Have every trainer practice the training script at the site where their session will be given. Multiple trainers practicing at multiple sites will help to discover "bugs" in the script or site before the actual training sessions begin.

Once you have practiced the program and redesigned it, then "just do it." Whenever the date comes up in your timeline, go ahead and do the session. Few training sessions go without a hitch. You learn from the problems and adjust for the next session. Just be willing to jump in and get your feet wet.

STAGE FOUR: ANALYSIS

After you have done the training, hand out your analysis tool or conduct the one-to-one interviews. Gather the completed survey or interview data. Look at the responses and determine what changes to the training program would make it better. Analyzing the surveys is a great way to find areas for more training. Many times individuals will know an area that they are deficient in and write it on the survey. Use the analysis tool to improve your training program and also augment the training program with additional sessions.

ALTERNATIVES TO IN-HOUSE TRAINING

There are alternatives to in-house training. One of them is coaching or mentoring wherein someone works with one to five individuals on a one-to-one basis. There is also continued special development by professional organizations. The annual meetings of NASIG, ALA, CONSER, and state library associations have professional development sessions. Using sessions provided by professional organizations can augment in-house training programs. Another alternative is distant learning. Many of the online vendors, such as Voyager or OCLC, offer online tutorials for their products.

ONGOING TRAINING

Remember that training is ongoing. Sometimes institutions and individuals within institutions think that since all the staff has been trained, they will not have to go through the training program again. But there is always new staff coming in, jobs change, people move around or are assigned new responsibilities. Having some kind of ongoing training program in place will assist you as new staff is hired or individuals are reallocated. You can train them systematically instead of having them work for three months without really knowing what they are doing.

CONTRIBUTORS' NOTES

Rene J. Erlandson is Senior Newspaper Cataloger at the University of Illinois at Urbana-Champaign. Robert J. Congleton is Serials Librarian at Rider University.

Starting with an Empty Map: Benchmarking Time and Costs for Serials Operations

Nancy Slight-Gibney
Mary Grenci
Workshop Leaders

Lisa S. Blackwell
Recorder

SUMMARY. Nancy Slight-Gibney and Mary Grenci from the University of Oregon Libraries presented the results of a time/cost study conducted during 2002 to measure resource utilization associated with all aspects of technical services operations performed in the University of Oregon Libraries Acquisition and Catalog Departments. This workshop focused on the data gathered regarding serials operations across the departments. The overall goal of the study was to provide a solid research foundation that could be used to support process and budgetary decisions that would best support the mission of the Libraries. The workshop concluded with an audience participation discussion regarding possible interpretations of the research results. *[Article copies available for a fee from The Haworth Document Delivery Service: 1-800-HAWORTH. E-mail address: <docdelivery@haworthpress.com> Website: <http://www.HaworthPress.com> © 2004 by The Haworth Press, Inc. All rights reserved.]*

[Haworth co-indexing entry note]: "Starting with an Empty Map: Benchmarking Time and Costs for Serials Operations." Blackwell, Lisa S. Co-published simultaneously in *The Serials Librarian* (The Haworth Information Press, an imprint of The Haworth Press, Inc.) Vol. 46, No. 3/4, 2004, pp. 287-293; and: *Serials in the Park* (ed: Patricia S. French, and Richard Worthing) The Haworth Information Press, an imprint of The Haworth Press, Inc., 2004, pp. 287-293. Single or multiple copies of this article are available for a fee from The Haworth Document Delivery Service [1-800-HAWORTH, 9:00 a.m. - 5:00 p.m. (EST). E-mail address: getinfo@haworthpress.com].

http://www.haworthpress.com/web/SER
Digital Object Identifier: 10.1300/J123v46n03_15

BACKGROUND

The University of Oregon Libraries include an estimated 18,000 current serials subscriptions as part of a research collection of 2.5 million volumes supported by an annual budget of approximately 5.8 million dollars. Not surprisingly, in light of the current economic climate, the materials budget has been flat in recent years, which is expected to continue in the foreseeable future. A cost-savings proposal to purchase shelf-ready approvals provided the impetus to design and implement a comprehensive Technical Services cost/time study.[1] Additional benefits of such a study include the ability to update job descriptions and performance standards as well as identify processes to be improved or eliminated. Similar studies were conducted in 1982 and 1997; however, no serials data were collected for either earlier study. A literature review failed to uncover any cost/time studies specific to serials.

Technical Services in the Libraries is subdivided into the Acquisition Department and the Catalog Department. All serials functions for the Libraries are divided between the two departments with the exception of Law library serials subscriptions, where related operations are handled by Law library staff.

The Acquisition Department includes five FTE paraprofessionals whose activities are primarily related to serials (check-in, claiming, etc.). The head of the department, Nancy Slight-Gibney, two additional paraprofessionals, and a staff supervisor also assist with serials activities (e.g., placing new orders and processing payments). The department handles pre-order process tasks (vendor assignment; searching, printing, and mailing purchase orders), receiving, payment, and maintenance tasks (claiming, canceling, and updating records utilizing vendor reports, processing rush orders).

The Catalog Department includes one professional cataloger, Mary Grenci, and three paraprofessional catalogers whose primary responsibilities are serials cataloging. Other department members periodically assist with cataloging serials. An end processing unit is responsible for labeling, bindery activities, etc. The department is responsible for new cataloging (e.g., copy and/or original cataloging, record enhancements, check-in/item record creation), authority control (e.g., creation of NACO, SACO, and local records), retrospective conversion (does not include Conser, PCC, NACO, or SACO verification), and related support tasks (e.g., withdrawals, reinstatements, transfers, added copies/locations, reclassification.)

METHODOLOGY

The research team next described data collection issues to be considered in the study:

- Sampling: sample days (taken from *ALCTS* guidelines) were March 11-22 and April 29-May 10[2]
- Unit of measure is the title, but this can still produce different results. For example: in acquisitions, one title ordered includes all variant titles; in cataloging, one title cataloged is one bib record, and associated bib records are each counted as a title
- Overhead calculation formulas: scalable calculations based on individual and/or team expenditures, specific cost centers or the entire department (excludes firm budget expenditures: electricity, phones, etc.)

Making clear distinctions between the process categories of each department proved problematic. For example, title changes for serials might be considered record maintenance (acquisitions) or new record creation (cataloging), or belong in both departments. Strong arguments were generated for clearly identifying and separating monograph related tasks from activities specific to serials. This will be kept in mind when designing future cost analysis studies.

Theoretically, lumping activities together into larger categories should make data collection easier; however, splitting the processes into smaller units could enhance data analysis. The team chose to define broad categories and identify specific tasks within each category as much as possible. Once consensus on the process categories and associated tasks was achieved, the team was able to create worksheet templates for both departments to record time spent on activities. To provide consistency in data collection across multiple studies, the worksheet (Figure 1) was adapted from the 1997 study.[3]

RESULTS

The Acquisitions Department analyzed the survey data and found that 7.5 percent of departmental staff time (.9 FTE) is used for check-in. A projected $40,000 annual savings (salary and benefits) could be achieved if check-in and claiming were discontinued. Careful consideration should be given to the ramifications of such a strategy. Discussion focused on the current policy of claiming and replacing missing issues

FIGURE 1. Serials Acquisitions Times and Cost

a. Pre-order process and order record creation. Pre-order sorting and problem solving, vendor assignment, searching and ordering, pre-order updating, and related activities for:	No. done	Time spent (minutes)	No./ hour	Unit cost
New serials or standing orders	56	475	7	$5.65
b. Record and order maintenance process. Claiming, canceling, updating records with reports from vendors, resolving complex problems for:	No. done	Time spent (minutes)	No./ hour	Unit cost
Serials and standing orders	3409	10224	20	$1.80
Serial replacements/backsets	68	305	13	$2.76
c. Receiving process. Opening periodicals mail and boxes, serials check-in, checking receipts, updating records.	No. done	Time spent (minutes)	No./ hour	Unit cost
Opening periodicals		1825		$0.21
Serials check-in	4292	7745	33	$0.86
Check-in of items with invoices	248	573	26	$1.34
Serials labeling	4351	2537	103	$0.09
Receiving serial replacements and backsets	5	35	9	$4.46
Searching unidentified receipts (snags)	202	736	16	$1.76
d. QuickCat process for:	No. done	Time spent (minutes)	No./ hour	Unit cost
Documents-serials	57	1045	3	$8.44
e. Payment/accounting process. Reviewing invoices, keying payment into III system, Banner work (campus Oracle system), reconciling, resolving payment problems, printing accounting reports for:	No. done	Time spent (minutes)	No./ hour	Unit cost
Serials and standing orders	1968	1756	67	$0.63
Budget/payment reconciling		356		$0.02
Filing Invoices		269		$0.02
Accounting reports		579		$0.02

whenever possible. According to the most recent LIBQUALL survey, the faculty at the University of Oregon places a very high value on the retention of complete journal runs. A compromise solution was implemented to discontinue claiming missing issues, beyond routine claiming, for journal titles that are electronically archived. Department staff are alerted to this procedure by a note added to the e-record of a title. All other titles continue to be claimed and replaced, if possible, to facilitate complete binding.

Upon completion of the study, the Cataloging Department reevaluated the criteria for records accepted "as is" for depository items. In addition, Mary noted that for new cataloguing non-CONSER records are especially time consuming. This is because the situation would be particularly complex for the decision to be made to create a non-CONSER record. This could potentially lead to misleading results if not properly distinguished (Figure 2). Retrospective conversion processes were altered to eliminate unnecessary steps. For example, prior to the study, the 780 and 785 fields in both the old card catalog and online were searched for related titles. After the study, a policy was implemented to restrict searching to electronic records. It became clear that the inventorying process for retrospective conversion was inefficient and costly (Figure 3). A more efficient method was devised and implemented.

Both the Acquisitions and Cataloging Departments found that approximately 25 percent of total time is devoted to necessary administrative tasks (Figure 4).

This benchmarking of administrative activities is highly valued by the technical services staff. Prior to the study, the staff felt that the potential existed for these essential tasks to be overlooked and thus not

FIGURE 2. Materials Processing and Conservation Unit Time and Cost

New cat./recat. tasks	# done	Avg min./unit	Avg #/hr	Avg cost/unit
NACO	7	14.71	4.08	$ 5.98
SACO	3	3.33	18.02	$ 1.26
Local authorities	2	39.00	1.54	$14.68
All authorities	***12***	***15.91***	***3.77***	***$ 6.25***
CONSER upgrade & enhance	73	39.21	1.53	$14.82
CONSER original	9	55.56	1.08	$21.76
Upgrade & enhance, non-CONSER	17	19.47	3.08	$ 7.33
Original, non-CONSER	1	93.00	0.65	$34.88
Copy cataloging	194	14.47	4.15	$ 5.46
FastCat	19	10.58	5.67	$ 3.38
All bibliographic recs	***313***	***21.71***	***2.76***	***$ 8.18***
Total serial titles	***313***	***22.32***	***2.69***	***$ 8.42***

FIGURE 3. Serials Cataloging Time and Cost

Retro. con. tasks	# done	Avg min./unit	Avg #/hr	Avg cost/unit
Copy	460	8.08	7.43	$ 2.91
Original	16	11.06	5.42	$ 4.44
Total for both	***476***	***8.18***	***7.33***	***$ 3.06***
Searching related titles	294	3.57	16.81	$ 1.31
Barcodes	1103	0.99	60.61	$ 0.26
Inventorying holdings	2308 vols.	1.07	56.07	$ 0.22
Total for above	***3705***	***1.24***	***48.39***	***$ 0.32***
Total serial titles	***476***	***17.87***	***3.36***	***$ 5.44***

FIGURE 4. Serials Cataloging Time and Cost

Administrative tasks	*Hrs (out of 700)*	*% of Time*
Non-library meetings	39.33	% 5.62
E-mail	23.57	% 3.37
Other library meetings	15.72	% 2.25
Consulting outside dept.	10.85	% 1.55
Workshops	8.83	% 1.26
Dept. meetings	6.12	% 0.87
External committee work	3.10	% 0.44
Keeping stats	54.07	% 7.72
Various other	11.88	% 1.70
Total for all admin.	*173.47*	*% 24.78*

properly budgeted for in any effort to revise existing processes based on study results.

CONCLUSION AND DISCUSSION

The workshop leaders concluded the session by inviting discussion of the study results. It was generally concluded that the study is a valuable addition to benchmarking studies in technical services. Similar studies reported in the literature focus on monographic cataloging, ILL activities, and technical services operations; however, the researchers are aware of no studies that benchmark serials operations costs. It is hoped that libraries conducting similar studies will be encouraged to report their results so that meaningful trends and standards for serials operations may be identified.

NOTES

1. University of Oregon Library, "Cost/Benefit Analysis for Shelf-Ready Books: University of Oregon Library, 2001/2002," http://libweb.uoregon.edu/acqdept/taskforce/progress.html (28 July 2003).

2. Association for Library Collections and Technical Services, Technical Services Costs Committee, "Guide to Cost Analysis of Acquisitions and Cataloging in Libraries," *ALCTS Newsletter* 2, no. 5 (1991): 49-52.

3. University of Oregon Library, "Tally Sheet, 1997," http://libweb.uoregon.edu/acqdept/taskforce/ 1997tallysheet.doc (28 July 2003).

CONTRIBUTORS' NOTES

Nancy Slight-Gibney is Head of Acquisitions at the University of Oregon Libraries. Mary Grenci is Serials Catalog Librarian at the University of Oregon Libraries. Lisa Blackwell is Assistant Librarian, Grant Morrow III, M.D. Library, Columbus Children's Hospital.

Is It Working: Usage Data as a Tool for Evaluating the Success of New Full-Text Title Access Methods

Joanna Duy
Eric Pauley

Workshop Leaders

Wendy Highby

Recorder

SUMMARY. Using data captured by the North Carolina State University (NCSU) Libraries' in-house tool, the *E-journal Finder*, as well as locally gathered e-resource usage data, researchers Joanna Duy and Eric Pauley[1] proceeded to answer two research questions: did the E-journal Finder make a difference in the amount of use of the libraries' full-text databases? And, how do people search with the tool? The researchers ascertained that, following the implementation of the E-journal Finder, the access to information increased, particularly in full-text databases. *[Article copies available for a fee from The Haworth Document Delivery Service: 1-800-HAWORTH. E-mail address: <docdelivery@haworthpress.com> Website: <http://www.HaworthPress.com>]*

[Haworth co-indexing entry note]: "Is It Working: Usage Data as a Tool for Evaluating the Success of New Full-Text Title Access Methods." Highby, Wendy. Co-published simultaneously in *The Serials Librarian* (The Haworth Information Press, an imprint of The Haworth Press, Inc.) Vol. 46, No. 3/4, 2004, pp. 295-300; and: *Serials in the Park* (ed: Patricia S. French, and Richard Worthing) The Haworth Information Press, an imprint of The Haworth Press, Inc., 2004, pp. 295-300. Single or multiple copies of this article are available for a fee from The Haworth Document Delivery Service [1-800-HAWORTH, 9:00 a.m. - 5:00 p.m. (EST). E-mail address: getinfo@haworthpress.com].

http://www.haworthpress.com/web/SER
Digital Object Identifier: 10.1300/J123v46n03_16

Joanna Duy described the origins of the project. The E-journal Finder was developed at NCSU Libraries in the spring of 2001 and released for use to the public in October 2001. Its genesis sprang primarily from the reference librarians' desire to provide easy title-level access to journals in full-text databases. The ultimate research goal was to attempt to objectively evaluate the impact of this full-text title access tool.

The central question pertaining to the development of the E-journal Finder was: How can we provide title-level access for e-journals within full-text databases in a manner that is clear and easy for patrons to use? Several options were considered. One possibility was for the full-text database e-journal titles to appear in the catalog. But at that time, Serials Solutions did not yet offer MARC-ready records, so this would not have been an easy solution. Also, e-journals were viewed as a new and different beast, and staff wanted to be sure to provide the access to full-text e-journals and their access points in a clear and simple display. Due to the availability of Serials Solutions data, and enthusiasm and programming knowledge on the part of staff in the Distance Learning Services Department, an in-house tool was developed for conducting e-journal title searches.

Eric Pauley elucidated the technical aspects of the E-journal Finder (http://www.lib.ncsu.edu/eresources/ejfinder/). It presents the patron with a simple search box for a known item search. In the list of results, two levels of availability are indicated: full issue coverage with the start date (and end date when applicable), or selected coverage. Behind the scenes, a user's query goes to a Web server. The server runs ColdFusion software that allows it to open a connection to a database. In this case, it opens the connection to a Microsoft Access database containing Serials Solution data (one large table of all serials e-holdings). ColdFusion looks up any matching titles in the database and sends them back to the Web server. The Web server sends the data back to the user in the form of an HTML file. Pauley then described the maintenance of the E-journal Finder data. The comma-delimited file, updated every two months by Serials Solutions, is imported into Access. Then some local editing of the data is performed before the old data set gets overwritten with the new data.

An audience member asked a question regarding server set-up. Pauley responded that at NCSU the ColdFusion server was already in place. He remarked that the same type of tool could be developed with PHP, SQL, or any other scripting language. He noted that the technical challenges were fairly minor. The greater challenge was refining the tool to match users' needs.

Duy then discussed the methodology for investigating the impact of the E-journal Finder's implementation. She related the researchers' approach toward their first research question: Did the E-journal Finder make a difference in the usage of NCSU Libraries' full-text databases? The intended purpose of the tool was to give improved access to the titles in the full-text databases. Did access increase?

Duy described the researchers' methods. Twenty-four full-text databases (such as *InfoTrac* and *ProQuest* databases) were designated as the experimental group. Local usage data were gathered for this group of full-text e-resources. Vendor data was not used because not all vendors collect session-level usage data in the same manner. Access was counted for this project whenever a database was accessed from the E-journal Finder, the catalog, or from anywhere from the NCSU Libraries' Webpage. Duy acknowledged the limitations of this data; this counting mechanism did not measure whether or how well the information matched the patron's need.

Practical experience and a review of the literature indicated that, in general, library e-resource usage is always climbing. Duy and Pauley wanted a research model that accounted for this tendency and could objectively determine whether the tool had impact. Thus, two non-full-text indexing and abstracting databases were used as the control group: *WebSPIRS* and *Web of Science* databases, which comprise twenty-five separate databases, available through these two platforms. The researchers assumed that the E-journal Finder implementation would not influence the usage of these non-full-text databases.

The usage of the experimental group of full-text databases and the usage of the control group of non-full-text databases were compared before and after the implementation of the E-journal Finder. The percentage change of hits per month was calculated. Usage of the experimental group of full-text databases increased by 152 percent, whereas usage of the control group of databases (*WebSPIRS* and *Web of Science*) increased 7.1 percent and 12.5 percent, respectively, for an average of 9.8 percent. The wide variation between the experimental and control groups indicates that usage of the full-text databases had increased more than might be expected over a normal 14-month period. Although the researchers cannot prove how much of the extra traffic came through the E-journal Finder, they have proven that the libraries' full-text databases experienced greater use since the implementation of the tool.

Duy then posed a question for further research. Reference librarians anecdotally indicate that full-text databases are usually more popular than indexing and abstracting databases. She hypothesized that perhaps full-text databases might exhibit a steeper rise in usage than non-full-text databases regardless of whether there was an E-journal Finder release. The researchers are interested in comparing their results with those of other institutions to further analyze the impact of the E-journal Finder. The dramatic increase in usage seems to confirm affective and anecdotal evidence recounted by librarians regarding the popularity of the tool. Duy noted that in her experience with patrons she saw that they really loved the E-journal Finder. It gave them a novel way to approach the databases.

In the next segment, Pauley addressed users' behavior as well. He focused upon a second series of research questions and its corollaries:

- How much were patrons using the E-journal Finder?
- In what ways were patrons using the E-journal Finder?
- What were the effects of changes in search functionality?
- How did patrons' searches succeed, and how did they fail?

This part of the study covered the time period from October 2001 to April 2003. During that period, the E-journal Finder processed 699,562 searches. Numbers of sessions and/or users were not measured. Average searches per month totaled 36,819 (about 1,000 to 1,500 per day). At its inception, the interface was designed to provide three ways of searching: a "starts with" title search; a keyword search (words contained anywhere in title); and an alphabetical listing (A-Z, 26 lists, including both aggregators and subscriptions). Initially, server logs indicated that the three types of searching were equally popular. In the Spring 2002 semester, title searches increased in popularity. Browsing an alphabetical list remained fairly popular as well, but less so than the title search.

In Fall 2002, the search interface and the mechanism of searching was changed at the suggestion of a librarian in the following way: in the event the "starts with" title search failed to harvest results, the system was programmed to default to keyword searching. Thus, if "journal of behavioral" brought up no results, it would automatically convert to a Boolean "AND" search of the terms "journal" and "behavioral." A beneficial side effect of this change in search functionality was the tool's ability to better handle journal title abbreviations. Previously, if someone had entered "j biol inorg chem," in the title search, they would have gotten no hits. With the automatic keyword search, however, the tool puts a truncation symbol next to all the terms and then combines them with the Boolean "and," resulting in a correct hit for the *Journal of Bio-*

logical Inorganic Chemistry. It is estimated that title abbreviations are used in approximately 13 percent of searches, so this new search functionality will almost certainly improve results for users who search with abbreviations.

What were the overall effects of this change in search functionality? The researchers defined success in this case as the production of a list of titles. Success was measured by examining server logs to determine how often a list of titles occurred as a result of a search. The frequency of "no hit" results decreased by 23 percent after the change in search functionality, indicating that searchers were at least getting *some* results. Pauley provided the audience with curious and amusing examples of searches from the logs, but he concluded that the majority of information seekers are knowledgeable; they know the tool should be used for e-journal title searches.

Duy presented further details about search results. Information gleaned from a random analysis of search logs for one hundred "no hits" entries revealed anecdotal evidence about search strategies. Analysis indicated that 40 percent of the failed searches were for journal titles that the library had in print, but not electronically (hence, these titles would not be in the E-journal Finder). The user would be offered the chance to submit the search to the library catalog. In about 10 percent of searches, the title existed but was not available locally in traditional or electronic formats. Seven percent of the searches were for misspelled e-journal titles. Database names (for example, *ERIC, Dissertation Abstracts*) appeared in about 7 percent of the failed search entries.

In summary, Duy stated that the usage of the NCSU Libraries' full-text databases increased two and one-half times following the release of the E-journal Finder. Approximately 70 percent of the searches produced some results. The auto keyword searching improved the search process, particularly when abbreviations are used. As with most research studies, questions are answered but new questions are raised. Did the tool accomplish the intended goal of making e-journals in full-text databases more accessible to users? It appears so, but Duy cautioned that they must be careful about interpretation. This study did not measure actual user satisfaction. Conversation with the user or an interactive button that asked the user about satisfaction would be necessary to gauge whether users actually found what they were looking for.

Duy and Pauley's research served to objectively confirm librarians' intuitive and anecdotal observations about full-text title access. Librarians "know" that patrons love full-text databases; the researchers proved that usage significantly increased. The experiment's design, using an experimental group of full-text e-resources and a non-full-text control group, effectively dealt with the tendency of e-resource usage to increase as a matter of course. The implementation of the NCSU Libraries' home-grown E-journal Finder offered a unique opportunity to study the before and after effects of a new e-resource tool. Locally collected usage data for the Libraries' electronic resources, and more in-depth usage data in the form of the E-journal Finder search logs provided valuable and concrete anecdotal information for analysis.

A short question-and-answer session followed the presentation. Questions ranged from concerns about pragmatic implications, such as maintenance, to queries regarding cutting-edge linking technology and its relationship to the E-journal Finder. The presenters noted that the E-journal Finder requires maintenance time averaging about five hours per week, plus approximately one-half day for the bimonthly process of loading and tweaking Serials Solutions data. Print journals were not included in the E-journal Finder database; the project had an e-journal focus due partly to the fact that it was developed in the Distance Learning Services Department of the Libraries. The institution is now in the process of implementing SFX linking. That service will provide usage data and the question of how the E-journal Finder will be incorporated is still uncertain. Thus, the session ended on an interesting note. The innovative E-journal Finder may become obsolete, but the information gleaned by the researchers adds to librarians' knowledge of users' search strategies and full-text title access.

NOTE

1. The researchers wish to thank Tim Mori for his assistance with the data-gathering portion of the project.

CONTRIBUTORS' NOTES

Joanna Duy is chemistry and Physics Librarian at Concordia University. Eric Pauley is Computing Consultant at North Carolina State University Libraries. Wendy Highby is Acquisitions/Serials Librarian at the University of Northern Colorado.

Using the Library's OPAC to Dynamically Generate Webpages for E-Journals

Kathryn Paul
Elena Romaniuk
Workshop Leaders

Daisy T. Cheng
Recorder

SUMMARY. Electronic journals are being added to library collections at exponential rates. Kathryn Paul and Elena Romaniuk shared their experiences with the audience on how to provide electronic journal access to the users of their libraries. The workshop included a brief introduction of the University of Victoria and its libraries, the context of the project, its rationale, and a detailed explanation of the methodologies with emphases on planning, policies, processes, and systems. They then examined the challenges they faced and will still be facing. They concluded that their users loved the easy access to the electronic journals. An online demonstration was given at the end of the presentation. *[Article copies available for a fee from The Haworth Document Delivery Service: 1-800-HAWORTH. E-mail address: <docdelivery@haworthpress.com> Website: <http://www.HaworthPress.com>]*

[Haworth co-indexing entry note]: "Using the Library's OPAC to Dynamically Generate Webpages for E-Journals." Cheng, Daisy T. Co-published simultaneously in *The Serials Librarian* (The Haworth Information Press, an imprint of The Haworth Press, Inc.) Vol. 46, No. 3/4, 2004, pp. 301-308; and: *Serials in the Park* (ed: Patricia S. French, and Richard Worthing) The Haworth Information Press, an imprint of The Haworth Press, Inc., 2004, pp. 301-308. Single or multiple copies of this article are available for a fee from The Haworth Document Delivery Service [1-800-HAWORTH, 9:00 a.m. - 5:00 p.m. (EST). E-mail address: getinfo@haworthpress.com].

http://www.haworthpress.com/web/SER
Digital Object Identifier: 10.1300/J123v46n03_17

INTRODUCTION

Kathryn Paul opened the workshop with a brief presentation of the background of the University of Victoria and its libraries. With 18,000 undergraduate and graduate students, the university is ranked as one of the top comprehensive universities in Canada. It is located in suburban Victoria, the capital of British Columbia, on Canada's west coast. Endeavor Voyager is the integrated library system for the libraries. At the present time, the libraries hold 35,000 serial titles, of which 10,000 are active journals and 5,000 are electronic journals, including titles with both print and online versions. Except for the Law Library, all technical services are centralized.

Like most libraries, the libraries at the University of Victoria maintained an HTML list of electronic journals which was created by the public services librarians and manually updated by them as well. With the increasing volumes of e-journals added to the collections, the librarians at the University of Victoria felt the urgent need to automate the process in order to improve efficiency, to reduce workload in public services, and to improve service to the users.

PLANNING

Paul remarked that the team consisted of herself as a public services librarian, Romaniuk as a serials librarian/cataloger, one systems programmer, one Web designer, two additional catalogers, and one serials acquisitions assistant. Romaniuk then talked about the scope of the project. Because the scope of the periodicals collection was consistent with the HTML list already manually maintained at the University of Victoria, the team decided to limit the effort to periodicals only. It would be less confusing for users. They also decided to include all full-text titles, either titles acquired individually or titles that came as part of a large collection. Related resource and titles in aggregator databases were excluded. They felt that the titles in aggregator databases were not uniform in coverage and were added and dropped frequently. Other reasons to not include these titles were the difficulty in cataloging and the large numbers of these volumes.

Once the scope was defined, Paul and Romaniuk discussed the goals of this project. They wanted their product to have a similar user interface and the same functionalities as the HTML listing system. These functionalities were: an A-Z list, a list by collections, and a list by subjects (see the Webpage screen shots, Figures 1-4, for views of these choices and of an individual record).

In addition, the team felt that it was important for users to be able to search by keywords and to see recently added titles. Thus the keyword search and the new title list were added to the functionalities. Romaniuk further examined the technical aspects of these goals. In order to avoid the tedious and time-consuming task of manual maintenance, the data-

FIGURE 1. E-Journals–by Subjects

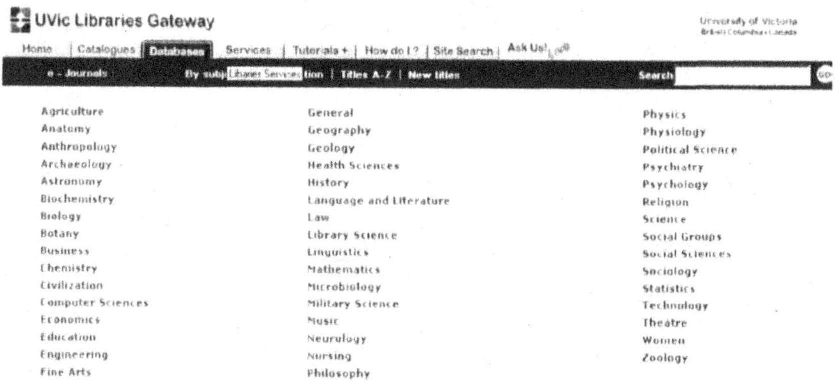

FIGURE 2. E-Journals–by Collections

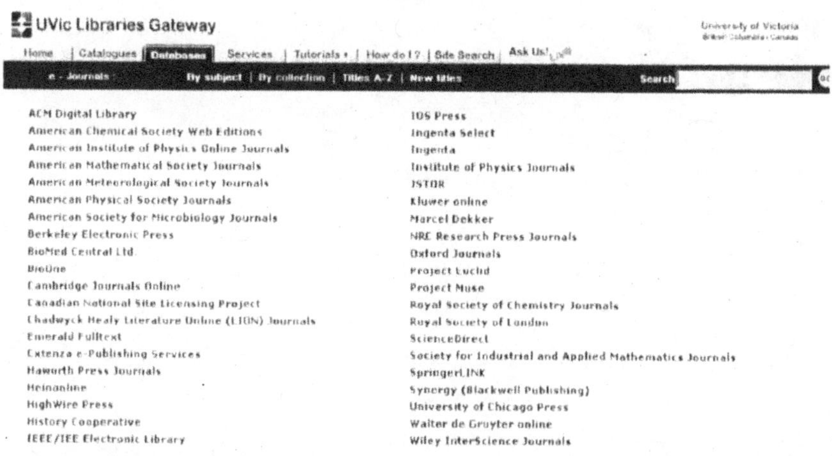

FIGURE 3. E-Journals–A-Z List by Titles

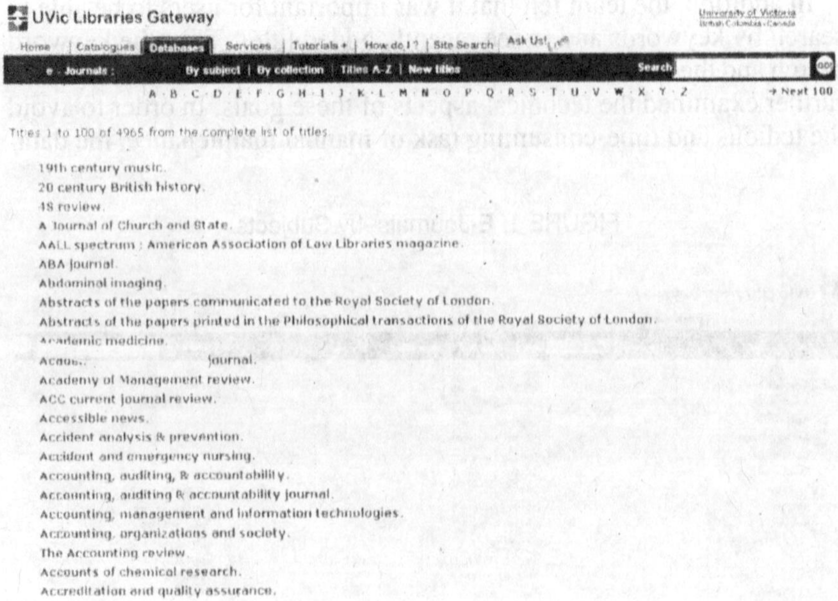

FIGURE 4. E-Journals–Individual Record

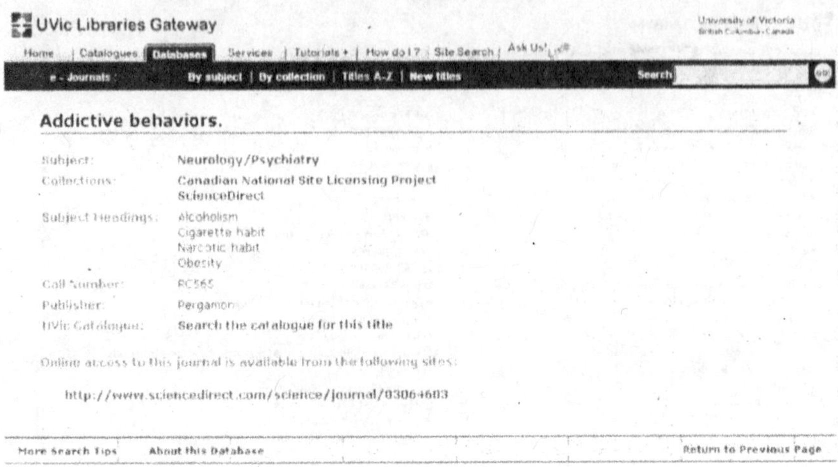

base had to be automatically generated and updated on a regular basis. They also wanted the system to be a database-driven model that would separate the programming of the user interface from the e-journal database. They felt that it was important that the system be scaleable so that in the future the thousands of titles in the aggregators' database could be imported without modifying the user interface. As the project continues to develop, they would like to be able to use MARC records in the library catalog.

POLICIES

The next step was to examine the policies for cataloging e-journals. Romaniuk stressed that the old policies and workflows needed to be reviewed and new ones needed to be established. The decision had to be made about who would do what and how. Catalogers worked on the electronic-only titles, and one experienced serials acquisitions assistant was trained to add URLs, notes, and updates to the existing print and other physical format records. Since they wanted to be able to identify records by collection, the 730 uniform title field was added to the records. If it was an individual title, the provider's name was added in the 710 field. Speed and consistency were important factors in setting up the policies. They used the single record approach if a title was already held in a physical format. Otherwise, they cataloged the electronic-only version. In order to be able to map the subject to each record, an LC classification number was assigned to each title. It was assigned to the 050 field instead of 090 in order to be consistent with the records that had a call number in the 050 field at the beginning of their library's online system in 1971. Finally, the URL and notes were added to records. As a cataloger, Romaniuk would prefer to see the format itself on the e-journal Webpage. As a public services librarian, however, Paul did not see the need to identify the format of the record. This was one of the compromises they had to make in this project.

PROCESSES

In order to provide subject access on the e-journal Webpage, they wanted to have a general overview of broad subject categories. Paul explained how they mapped LC classification numbers to subject categories. Table 1 shows the actual mapping they did. For example, if an e-

TABLE 1. Classification Mapping

LC class	Subject area	LC class	Subject area
A	General	QA 75-76	Computer Science
B-BD	Philosophy	All other QA	Mathematics
BF	Psychology	QB	Astronomy
BH	Philosophy	QC	Physics
BL-BX	Religion	QD	Chemistry
C	Archaeology/Civilization	QE	Geology
D-F	History	QH	Biology
G-GF	Geography	QK	Botany
GN-GF	Anthropology	QL	Zoology
GV	Geography	QM	Anatomy/Physiology
H	Social Sciences	QP 501	Biochemistry
HA-HJ	Business/Economics/Statistics	All other QP	Anatomy/Physiology
HM-HN	Sociology	QR	Microbiology
HQ	Women/Social Groups	R-RB	Health Sciences
HS-HX	Sociology	RC 346-571	Neurology
J	Political Science	All other RC	Health Sciences
K	Law	RT	Nursing
L	Education	RV-RZ	Health Sciences
M	Music	S	Agriculture
N	Fine Arts/Theatre	T	Technology
P	Linguistics	TA-TN	Engineering
PA-PM	Language and Literature	TP	Technology
PN	Fine Arts/Theatre	U-V	Military Science
PQ-PZ	Language and Literature	Z	Library Science
Q	Science		

journal were cataloged with an RT classification number, the subject category would be nursing based on the mapping chart. The subject categories were loosely based on the 46 academic departments at the University of Victoria.

Romaniuk went on to identify the general parameters for retrieving MARC records: bibliographical level would have to be "s" for serials; type of serials would have to be "p" for periodicals; bibliographical record would have to contain the subfield "a" in 050 field; and the record would have to have an 856 field. The records would have to be unsuppressed (in their system records to be cataloged or deleted were suppressed). She further identified specific parameters for mapping titles to collections. In order to map each title to a specific collection or even more than one collection, the bibliographical record would have to contain the particular name of the collection, for example, JSTOR or Literature Online. In some cases, a portion of the URL would have to be specified in addition to an added entry.

SYSTEMS

After the parameters were identified, the programmer used these parameters to run the initial record extraction from the MARC database. Error reports were generated to identify records without subject headings, records missing 050 fields, and records missed in the mapping of LC classification to subject categories. All records from error reports were fixed. These records were extracted from Voyager. The programmer wrote the Perl scripts to manage mapping and the loading of new or changed records into MySQL. Another Perl script was written to manage the deletions. These were run separately. The controlling script ran all processes. The content of the MySQL database is updated on an overnight basis.

Paul discussed the Web development at the front end of the systems. They developed the interface using the PHP Web system. Basically, they used keywords or phrases combined with titles or subject headings. In order to have a standardized look and feel throughout the library's Website, the Boolean search, truncation features, and cascade display were applied.

CHALLENGES

They called the challenges they faced "the never ending story." Romaniuk commented that it was a real challenge to keep up with new titles and new changes. Some of the never-ending challenges facing the personnel in the technical services were new collections continuously being added, outdated collections needing to be deleted, and new cataloging rules needing to be applied. Paul expounded on dealing with change. One of the issues was to expand the parameters to include all serials, and to add analytic records and government statistics to the database. In addition, issues concerning EZproxy were examined. She commented that electronic journals were constantly evolving, and that the changes that would lie ahead were beyond even their imagination. Some known challenges that she foresees are to incorporate titles in aggregator databases, to investigate new technology, and to make the OPAC as easy to use as Google.

CONCLUSION

The users at the University of Victoria did not just like the new electronic journals database the team designed; they loved it. The e-journal statistics showed over 50,000 hits during the peak month of the school year, which was a sound proof of the users' preference. Paul and Romaniuk concluded their portion of the workshop with an online demonstration through the electronic journal database Website (http://gateway.uvic.ca).

During the discussion following the presentation, the audience was enthusiastic about the project and applauded the innovative approach to provide better access to the electronic journals collection. The issue of steering the users away from the main catalog was raised. Romaniuk acknowledged that it was not their intention but it was what happened. The users definitely saw this as their source for serials materials. That was part of the reason that the team also linked the record back to their catalog. Romaniuk hoped that this would steer users back to the main catalog. One participant suggested that those who were comfortable with the online catalog could take that path, and those who were comfortable with the Web interface could use the other path. These were not necessarily contradictory outcomes. The meaning of the word "dynamically" in the presentation title was discussed. Romaniuk stressed that they were looking at the dynamic interaction between the user interaction and the system, in which the system pulled information from the database and assembled it into the format of the unified interface.

CONTRIBUTORS' NOTES

Kathryn Paul is Reference Librarian at the University of Victoria. Elena Romaniuk is Serials Librarian at the University of Victoria. Daisy T. Cheng is Catalog Librarian at the University of Mississippi.

Keeping the Connection: Maintaining E-Journal Subscriptions

Bill Kara
Christine Stamison
Workshop Leaders

Sarah E. George
Recorder

SUMMARY. Electronic journal management has many requirements and processes similar to traditional print serials management. This presentation highlights the skills and information needed for successful e-journal management. Libraries and subscription agents can work together to simplify and expedite the management process. Communication among all parties involved is essential. *[Article copies available for a fee from The Haworth Document Delivery Service: 1-800-HAWORTH. E-mail address: <docdelivery@haworthpress.com> Website: <http://www.HaworthPress.com>]*

The challenges of managing electronic journals have stretched the time, understanding, and patience of serials librarians for years. Libraries, subscription agents, and publishers have created various ways to track e-journals, but most are not satisfied with the complexity of the current situation. Bill Kara and Christine Stamison presented ways to

[Haworth co-indexing entry note]: 'Keeping the Connection: Maintaining E-Journal Subscriptions." George, Sarah E. Co-published simultaneously in *The Serials Librarian* (The Haworth Information Press, an imprint of The Haworth Press, Inc.) Vol. 46, No. 3/4, 2004, pp. 309-313; and: *Serials in the Park* (ed: Patricia S. French, and Richard Worthing) The Haworth Information Press, an imprint of The Haworth Press, Inc., 2004, pp. 309-313. Single or multiple copies of this article are available for a fee from The Haworth Document Delivery Service [1-800-HAWORTH, 9:00 a.m. - 5:00 p.m. (EST). E-mail address: getinfo@haworthpress.com].

http://www.haworthpress.com/web/SER
Digital Object Identifier: 10.1300/J123v46n03_18

simplify the process by using complimentary data sources. Kara focused on steps that individual libraries can follow that mimic procedures already in place for print journals. Stamison then discussed how subscription agents facilitate subscription management, and in some cases take over certain processes.

Four keys to successful e-journal management are licensing, good records, good notes, and staffing. Licensing is critical for placing the initial order. Order and bibliographic records with accompanying notes facilitate problem solving. Serials staff need to have a good understanding of the entire cycle of serials subscriptions to aid in troubleshooting their particular part of the process. Currently Cornell has not yet cancelled print subscriptions when adding electronic access; therefore, e-journal work is an additional responsibility for all involved. Furthermore, more time is spent on maintaining the current e-journal collection than adding new titles to it.

The staff skills needed to successfully manage print subscriptions are also needed for e-journals. Specifically, managers need a knowledge of serials, an understanding of the cycle of serials processing (i.e., order, renew, etc.), business skills for contacting publishers or vendors, and problem solving skills as titles change or cease. Additionally, new skills are needed. These skills include an understanding of new terminology, knowledge of changes in the industry, and tenacity in troubleshooting. Staff often work on reactive troubleshooting as soon as they are notified of an existing problem. Proactive troubleshooting occurs when staff check titles that were problems in a previous year or titles with changes in their subscriptions. Cornell uses a library staff listserv to notify staff of possible trouble; this technology allows the Systems and Reference Departments to check for technical causes at the same time that Technical Services is checking subscription details.

Yet these skills alone are not sufficient. Librarians and support staff will benefit from further training in using and managing e-journals. Additional experience will increase confidence in troubleshooting. Improved communication among librarians, publishers, and vendors could ease e-journal management for all parties involved. Most importantly, flexibility is essential because management does not consistently follow a sequential process that is easily documented.

Moreover, subscription changes in the electronic world have features different from print subscriptions. Changes occur more frequently, and midyear changes are particularly bad. Subscription prices can fluctuate, with some online access no longer coming free with a print subscription, changes in the content of package deals, or cancellations of some journals. Many vendors now have grace periods to assist in continuous online access while subscription renewals are being processed; however, these extensions are useless if the vendor does not notify the library that such a grace period has begun. Additionally, changes in publishers or access can affect URLs and license agreements, negatively impacting user access to the journals.

From Kara's perspective as an academic librarian, the subscription agent provides valuable information for troubleshooting. A customer representative assigned to the account provides knowledge of the library's account and assistance for troubleshooting. Agents also collate and pass along notifications from vendors and publishers via online newsletters or listservs.

Stamison picked up on Kara's last point regarding the role of subscription agents and expanded the topic to explain how vendors handle subscriptions. Ultimately, vendors would like to identify best practices for managing e-journals; currently, though, most vendors are treating e-journals like print, but with a twist. They provide traditional subscription services, address the overwhelming effects of the e-resources explosion, and track e-journal information. Overall, subscription agents can do more if they receive greater cooperation from libraries and publishers.

Subscription agents have provided value-added services for print subscriptions for years, and many of these traditional services can be applied to handling electronic subscriptions. One existing best practice for e-journals that come with a print component is to count the two formats as separate subscriptions. This method results in the establishment of online access more quickly because two letters are mailed to the publisher, one to the ordering department and one to the electronic department. In the first year that this routine has been used, there have been fewer problems with subscriptions processed this way. Subscription agents have also negotiated with publishers to extend grace periods for e-journals as they do with print. Many of the top one hundred publishers have agreed to at least a one-month grace period.

Furthermore, subscription agents track a number of different data for electronic journals. Pricing includes costs for print only, print and online, electronic only, and free with print subscriptions; special rates that may be leftovers from previous aggregate deals (e.g., old IDEAL rates for Academic Press titles); site licenses; and consortial pricing. One of the most difficult aspects of tracking consortial pricing is tracking participant status, which publishers do not always share with agents. Some consortia are beginning to include statements that allow for or require the use of subscription agents to handle the subscriptions.

Pricing is not the only type of data agents track, however. For each journal, the URL for the publisher's Website and the direct link for the journal are recorded. If the publisher incorporates digital object identifier (DOI) syntax for articles, this information is included. The requirement of a license is noted, as well as the URL for the license agreement if available. If the publisher provides reference numbers for the subscriptions, the database will include these numbers for both print and electronic subscriptions. The agent's business system maintains a record of the customer's IP range(s) and domain name(s). Definitions of "site" are included both for the publisher and the customer. Names of technical contacts are listed to facilitate troubleshooting. Some publishers have separate print and electronic departments, and contact information for both are included where necessary. The method of order transmittal, via paper or electronically, is also recorded.

Stamison identified five key benefits to libraries of this information tracking. The first is notification of which titles are available electronically. These reports can be arranged by titles that are available for no additional cost with a print subscription, for an extra fee, or through an aggregator service (e.g., Ingenta). These reports can also be customized to a library's current list of print subscriptions. Agents can set a library's profile so that free electronic access with a print subscription is automatically established. Many agents are compiling a database of license agreements, which can easily be mailed to customers as soon as a new order is placed. Finally, agents can provide to customers notification of changes in URLs.

The expansion of services for electronic journals has placed new demands on subscription agents. A different type of expertise is needed to handle new subscriptions and troubleshooting, especially in terms of technical and legal understanding. The variety of pricing models used for electronic journals requires a flexible database that can store and calculate costs based on multiple variables. To use such flexibility, more information must be tracked for both publishers and customers. Customers in the online environment now expect immediate response and resolution to problems. As a result of these demands, operating costs have increased due to a constant need for new technology and continuous training. Agents must make a solid commitment to technology if they want to succeed with these additional demands.

Subscription agencies are service-oriented businesses that can provide greater and more effective service if libraries and publishers work together. For example, some European publishers allow agents to set up online access for libraries. If libraries want this type of service, they need to insist to publishers that this is how they want to work.

This presentation was initially designed to be an informal discussion of how libraries and subscription agents can work together on e-journal management. The size of the audience imposed some formality to Kara's and Stamison's presentations; however, discussion after the presentations was lively and centered on exploring the intermediary role of subscription agents in e-journal management. One person questioned the advantage to publishers of involving agents in the purchasing process; the primary benefit is the lessening of an administrative burden because agents will track what libraries subscribe to. Several questions were related to making it easier to establish the online access that comes free with print subscriptions. The ironic need to keep large paper files for customer numbers needed to establish such access can be alleviated by asking subscription agents for the publisher reference numbers stored in their databases, and by storing such numbers in the serials record system as part of the check-in record. There was also a word of caution that "free" does not always mean the same thing among publishers and may be something that you do not want in your collection because of accompanying license restrictions. A concern that remained unanswered was the decreasing number of fixed, published prices. When each customer must negotiate a price individually, the ordering process suffers delays.

CONTRIBUTORS' NOTES

Bill Kara is Head of Technical Services at Cornell University. Christine Stamison is Academic Sales Manager at Swets Blackwell. Sarah E. George is Serials Librarian at Illinois Wesleyan University.

Providing a Table-of-Contents Service to Faculty

Madeleine Bombeld
Lynn R. Shay
Workshop Leaders

Rebecca Sheffield
Recorder

SUMMARY. Madeleine Bombeld, Access Services Librarian, and Lynn Shay, Serials Coordinator, described the procedures and benefits of implementing a table of contents delivery service at the William Madison Randall Library at the University of North Carolina at Wilmington. The TOC delivery service underwent a rethinking after a major budget cut at UNCW. The impact of the budget cut on the TOC delivery service and resulting reorganization of positions and workflow were also discussed. *[Article copies available for a fee from The Haworth Document Delivery Service: 1-800-HAWORTH. E-mail address: <docdelivery@haworthpress.com> Website: <http://www.HaworthPress.com>]*

INTRODUCTION

With 434 full-time faculty and 10,500 students, the University of North Carolina at Wilmington is growing rapidly. UNCW offers

[Haworth co-indexing entry note]: "Providing a Table-of-Contents Service to Faculty." Sheffield, Rebecca. Co-published simultaneously in *The Serials Librarian* (The Haworth Information Press, an imprint of The Haworth Press, Inc.) Vol. 46, No. 3/4, 2004, pp. 315-320; and: *Serials in the Park* (ed: Patricia S. French, and Richard Worthing) The Haworth Information Press, an imprint of The Haworth Press, Inc., 2004, pp. 315-320. Single or multiple copies of this article are available for a fee from The Haworth Document Delivery Service [1-800-HAWORTH, 9:00 a.m. - 5:00 p.m. (EST). E-mail address: getinfo@haworthpress.com].

http://www.haworthpress.com/web/SER
Digital Object Identifier: 10.1300/J123v46n03_19

twenty-six graduate programs, with its first doctoral program being offered this year in Marine Biology. *U.S. News & World Report* ranks UNCW in the top ten public universities in the South. Eighteen librarians and twenty-three support staff work in William Madison Randall Library. When the University Librarian was hired at UNCW five years ago, a table of contents (TOC) delivery service was implemented for UNCW's faculty that would regularly alert faculty to current literature of possible interest in their field.

TOC TO GO

Two of the goals of the TOC delivery service were to increase the use of the serial collection by enticing more people into the area and to add value to the library service offered to faculty by making their lives a little easier. One of the biggest obstacles to this new service was removed when the library and UNCW's Printing Services each agreed to pay half of the printing costs for the service. While current literature is the focus of the service, older items are provided upon request.

MANAGEMENT OF TOC

UNCW currently holds 2,321 serial subscriptions, with 328 titles available only electronically. About 40 percent of the titles are available both in print and online. Records for all formats are included in the OPAC, with locations such as "Current periodicals," "Rec. reading," or "Gov Docs" designated. Graduate assistants and faculty may check out bound periodicals.

When the TOC service began, three librarians identified potential faculty to be offered the service and made appointments with the faculty in order to arrange a personal visit. A list of titles that would be of particular interest to the faculty member was sent prior to the meeting. The library representative then met with the faculty member and signed up the individual for the service in print or online if desired.

This became a good public relations tool, and it was hoped that the faculty would then encourage their students to visit the library. During the first year that the service was offered, 169 faculty members took part. By the end of 2002, 226 faculty members were participating in the service. There were 1,117 titles that were routed to at least one faculty member. Library faculty members continue to identify and enroll new faculty members in the service.

When an issue of a TOC title is checked in, a route list is produced and the issue is placed on a designated table. Interlibrary Loan personnel retrieve routed issues on a daily basis and photocopy the table of contents. TOC photocopies are then placed into the appropriate faculty's folder and are mailed to each faculty member once a month. The colleges on campus are divided into four groups, and each college's faculty receives its table of contents package every four weeks, with a different group receiving its TOC photocopies each week. Upon receipt of the TOC, the faculty member highlights the article(s) he wants photocopied and returns the list to the library. Library personnel photocopy the appropriate article, generally within a week, and send it to the faculty member. During the first year that the TOC delivery service was offered, 52,000 pages were photocopied. The number of pages photocopied increased to 63,000 during the second year of the service.

BUDGET CUTS AND CHANGING FORMATS

The TOC delivery service was impacted by state budget problems, which cut UNCW's serials budget by 21 percent. During the resulting 2003 serials reduction project, 706 print titles were cancelled and 137 print titles were converted to electronic access only. Two hundred ninety-one titles were available in aggregated databases to which UNCW subscribed. Of the titles cancelled, 284 were titles that had TOC routing. Of those 284 titles, 139 had two or more faculty on the route list.

In order to assist with the cancellation project, academic departments were encouraged to cancel titles. If a department cancelled more than the required 21 percent, it could get a new title. The caveat was that if the new title was available electronically, the library would not purchase the print. As a result, 27 new titles were added.

With the formats of some titles changing, a change in the library's workflow and routines was needed. It became clear that the Serials Librarian and the Access Services Librarian needed to determine who had what, to communicate thoroughly with each other, and to check and double-check the lists. The Serials Librarian maintained the cancellation list and ensured that cancelled title records were closed and properly annotated. She communicated cancelled title information to the Access Services Librarian who maintained the TOC route lists. The serial paraprofessional who performs serial check-in will become more involved with the online titles in the future.

There was also the concern of keeping the TOC service going even through the budget cuts, and this involved keeping track of what was available electronically in cases where the print journal was cancelled. The Serials Coordinator and the Access Services Librarian identified journals routed for TOC treatment and began looking for vendors who could provide an electronic TOC alerting service that would include titles that had been cancelled. They concentrated on vendors that offered broad subject coverage, and kept the difficulty of having to use many different interfaces in mind. They selected Ingenta because the library already had a site license and the majority of cancelled titles were available. The print TOC project is still ongoing for available titles, and the faculty continues to be happy with the current TOC procedures.

TOC ACTION PLAN

Notifying faculty of all the changes was then necessary. A notice was sent to all enrolled faculty and a follow-up message will be sent to faculty with two or more routed titles. This second notice will be sent in the fall after the faculty has returned for the academic year. The first notice emphasized the continued access to titles and maintained a positive tone. Faculty members were invited to contact the Serials Coordinator or the Access Services Librarian with comments and questions. Numerous responses were received to the first group of notices. Faculty wanted to receive their TOC in a variety of ways. Some wanted to move all titles to electronic only TOC, some felt overwhelmed with the way the TOC were going to be provided and decided to drop their TOC routings, and some wanted to add more titles. These responses have provided some additional work for the Outreach Librarians who are now also working with the faculty.

WHAT WE LEARNED

Public Services staff at UNCW learned the importance of marketing. They also learned to be open and receptive to reviewing and changing or adding to their programs. And, as would be expected, they learned to always be helpful to faculty and patrons.

Technical Services staff learned that they were not as good at keeping up with title changes as they needed to be, that access to the public is only as good as the catalog, and that database maintenance is of utmost importance. They discovered that the cancelled titles are still used and recognized that it is their responsibility to continue to provide access to those titles even though the titles were cancelled. One satisfying result is that the paraprofessional in the serials area now wants to learn more about what is in the databases rather than just being aware that the databases are available.

TRENDS

The workshop presenters feel that libraries will continue to add more e-journal subscriptions and that there will be more interest in TOC delivery services and more TOC conversions. Librarians will need to be more creative and will have to adapt to changing job roles and duties if the budget continues to be tight. Librarians also will need to find and provide alternative ways of accessing information. The last slide at this presentation displayed the coffee bar that is housed within Randall Library. The advent of coffee shops located within libraries also appears to be a trend.

QUESTIONS AND DISCUSSION

One of the questions asked was whether UNCW had tried to get extra money such as a grant to support document delivery. The answer was that UNCW had not gone that route. Throughout the cancellation project, faculty members were assured that interlibrary loan would provide the necessary articles. In the coming year, ILL activity will be monitored to see if cancelled titles are being heavily borrowed through ILL. UNCW is looking for ways to keep faculty informed without mediation by librarians. Of course, if the faculty desires the mediation, the library will continue to provide it.

Another question was what were considered to be the benefits of this particular TOC delivery service. The answer was that a great deal of goodwill had been generated by it. Faculty have become much more familiar with library individuals, faculty come into the library more, and the print journals are receiving heavier use. In an unrelated survey that was conducted among the faculty, the TOC delivery service was mentioned in a positive light numerous times. Another benefit is that the yearly follow-up that is part of the program has provided a necessary and desired structured self-assessment for the program and related areas.

There was also substantial discussion about the impact of the installation of a coffee bar within the library. The library gate count has gone up 9 percent since the coffee bar was opened, and it has proven to be the most heavily used coffee shop on campus even though there is another coffee shop in close proximity to the library. The opening of the coffee bar was a positive experience for the library. The library provided substantial input and even vetoed one proposal that was not considered to positively reflect the library's atmosphere.

CONTRIBUTORS' NOTES

Madeleine Bombeld is Access Services Librarian at the William Madison Randall Library at the University of North Carolina at Wilmington. Lynn Shay is Serials Coordinator at the William Madison Randall Library at the University of North Carolina at Wilmington. Rebecca Sheffield is Head of Acquisitions Services, Ball State University.

Poster Sessions

Accessing Serials: A Reliable Guide to Finding Your Serials

Karlene Patricia Robinson

University of the West Indies, Mona Campus

Technology has made it possible for information to be produced, stored, and disseminated in a variety of ways. Today serials are available in a variety of formats. Thousands of journals are published internationally in print and an increasing number, in a variety of subject areas, by electronic means. A burgeoning number of students and faculty members in all disciplines who are not information literate seek after journal articles and, in some cases, with limited success. They are simply ignorant of the many ways available to them to access these articles and do their evaluation in the minimum of time.

This poster presents and analyzes the usefulness of secondary and tertiary lead-in tools in locating journal articles. It examines secondary sources like indexes, citation indexes, abstracts, databases and the many services attached to these, as well as tertiary sources like bibliographies and catalogues. The illustrations used in the poster come primarily from the science and medical disciplines.

[Haworth co-indexing entry note]: "Poster Sessions." French, Patricia S. and Richard Worthing. Co-published simultaneously in *The Serials Librarian* (The Haworth Information Press, an imprint of The Haworth Press, Inc.) Vol. 46, No. 3/4, 2004, pp. 321-328; and: *Serials in the Park* (ed: Patricia S. French, and Richard Worthing) The Haworth Information Press, an imprint of The Haworth Press, Inc., 2004, pp. 321-328. Single or multiple copies of this article are available for a fee from The Haworth Document Delivery Service [1-800-HAWORTH, 9:00 a.m. - 5:00 p.m. (EST). E-mail address: getinfo@haworthpress.com].

http://www.haworthpress.com/web/SER
Digital Object Identifier: 10.1300/J123v46n03_20

Administrative Metadata for Continuing Resources

Dalene Hawthorne

Stanford University Libraries

What is administrative metadata? How are libraries handling administrative metadata for continuing resources? What ILS vendors have products available? Are there other solutions out there? This session covers the presenter's research into administrative metadata solutions and includes information obtained from interviews with libraries that have developed solutions and information gathered from interviews with major ILS vendors.

An Alternative Funding Model for a University Library's Serials Budget

Joe Becker

New Mexico State University

Over the last decade, most university libraries have faced the task of managing serials budgets characterized by rapidly increasing costs and static funding allocations. There is a great deal of information in the (library) literature on the nature of this serials "crisis," the inevitable reaction in terms of serials cancellations, and the possible effect on scholarly communication. There is also debate on the possibilities of alternative publication models and alternative pricing models, based on electronic access. The topic of cost-sharing is generally described only in the context of consortia buying options.

This presentation describes how New Mexico State University, in an effort to deal with an ongoing budget shortfall, developed a local cost-sharing plan and acquired a significant alternative fund source to augment its typical budget. The library won approval for a recurring allocation of a percentage of all research grant funding awarded to the university. This poster outlines the typical nature of the problem in budget terms and describes short-term fixes such as serials.

Collaborative Selection of New Science Journal Subscriptions

Anne Christie
Laurel Kristick
Oregon State University

Science and engineering faculty and students need access to new journals because science changes and evolves, resulting in shifting emphases in research and teaching programs. This poster session describes an efficient, effective and collaborative process developed at Oregon State University to facilitate the purchase of new journals. Faculty members and librarians make recommendations about new journals needed to support OSU's teaching and research programs. Recommendations must include justification addressing the journal's importance. Librarians and acquisitions staff work together to gather data about each journal. Each librarian uses these data and other qualitative selection criteria to prioritize the journal requests for their subject areas, which are then discussed and ranked at a group meeting. Final selections are made when the amount of money available for new subscriptions is known. The information needed by acquisitions staff to place orders is already complete.

With this process, the science librarians consider the collection and the university's programs from a broader perspective than just their own subject areas, fostering their awareness of interdisciplinary research and teaching on campus. The science librarians work as a team and trust each other's judgment. Selection decisions are not made in isolation so that available funds are spent effectively to achieve a balanced collection that serves the university's research strengths. This practical method accomplishes several objectives:

- It creates a mechanism for faculty participation in journal selection
- It establishes a process for collecting data on which to base purchase decisions
- It establishes a timeline to ensure the completion of the process
- It creates a predictable workflow for faculty, librarians and acquisitions staff

It can be easily adapted for making journal selections in subject areas other than science. It can also be applied in libraries where selection decisions are made either by an individual librarian or by several librarians sharing collection development work.

Counting Serials for Surveys: How the Questions Have Changed and the Problem of Peer Comparison

Gail C. Anderson
Medical College of Georgia

This poster describes the problem of accurately identifying and counting print and in-scope online serials for annual statistical data collection. It focuses upon the Medical College of Georgia, a free-standing academic health sciences university that is also a part of a state-wide consortium, currently providing over 2300 links to full text titles (including duplicate titles from alternate providers)–most of which are serials–but could provide a lot more from Georgia's Virtual Library, GALILEO. Peer institutions from other states may be included for comparison. It presents an analysis of the serials data questions asked over the past five years for the Annual Statistics of Medical School Libraries in the United States and Canada and for the Integrated Postsecondary Education Data System. It is expected that the results will show that planning for statistical counting may be time ill spent unless there is flexibility in the way numbers are gathered. The question will still remain–Are your peer institutions counting the same way you are?

Disaster Preparedness in the Portland Area

Kris Kern
Portland State University

PORTALS is a multi-type and multi-state library consortium dedicated to meeting the research and education needs of people in the greater Portland area through cooperative access to information resources and services. Two years ago, PORTALS identified the value of extending our cooperation to disaster prevention and recovery. The Disaster Recovery Group (DIRG) was formed to look at some of the problems facing our institutions:

- Our librarians need continuing education in disaster preparedness
- Our librarians do not have plans for disasters
- Our libraries do not have quick access to disaster supplies when they are needed

This poster documents the work the DIRG has done in the past two years on disaster preparedness including development of a disaster plan template, helping members with disaster barrel content, mentoring, training and ongoing discussion of relevant topics.

DOLLeR, or Managing E-Resources at UIC Library

Laurentiu Mircea Stefancu

University of Illinois at Chicago

The poster session presents the results the author and his colleagues at the UIC Library obtained working toward building and perfecting a tool to help them manage the rich data related to the UIC Library's steadily increasing number of electronic resources. DOLLeR (Database Of Library Licensed Electronic Resources) has been designed as a management system for the use of the different departments of the UIC Library dealing with various aspects of the electronic resources information flow (such as administration, collections development, acquisitions, systems, catalog, and reference), so that each and all of them could have a better control over, and understanding of, the current issues surrounding the electronic resources the Library subscribes, or is in course of subscribing, to. It is thought of as a multi-tiered, one-stop shopping place for all those involved in the many aspects and stages of the information flow in this area of increasing interest for all libraries. DOLLeR is a relational database built using FileMaker Pro, a relatively cheap piece of commercial software by FileMaker Inc. With a simple yet robust architecture, DOLLeR offers a user-friendly environment, both in the application interface and over the Web. This poster presents various aspects of the DOLLeR design and functionality.

Fine-Tuning the Claiming Process

Michele Pope
Loyola University Law Library

This poster presents a fine-tuning of the serials claiming process. The claiming process has been reduced to the mundane task of printing out and mailing claim forms. However, there are several reasons why, in the computer age, the automated claiming process has become inadequate in dealing with outstanding materials. Librarians are used to relying on their computer systems to generate claims, but what is often needed is human interaction and follow-through. Automated systems may not accurately reflect the current publisher address or what is shelved. Explanations range from a lack of time for updating the automated system, to inadequately performed check-in tasks, and system errors during check-in procedures, particularly when there is a high turnover rate in the paraprofessional position. Thinking that a claim is in process when we have claimed it six times over the course of years is really brushing off the more tedious task of taking responsibility for the claiming process.

Several additional tasks can be added to the automated claiming process that may increase the potential for receiving materials and gathering updated information:

- Assess the check-in record, type of material and publisher: What was paid for? Was material bought on standing order or prepay?
- The number of claims will indicate what steps to take.
- Research titles and publishers on the Internet.
- Compile a directory of regularly contacted vendors with company name, contact, order and/or customer number, telephone number and email address: Should claims be mailed, phoned-in or e-mailed? Follow through and share responsibilities with paraprofessionals.

Impact of Electronic Resources on Serials Acquisitions

Xiaoyin Zhang
Michaelyn Haslam
University of Nevada, Las Vegas

In the process of integrating electronic resources into library collections, new workflow paths emerge. Because electronic resources differ in selection, purchase, implementation, and maintenance from other materials, information gathering, decision-making, and workflows are affected by incorporating them. This poster displays charts that illustrate the points at which library serials functions are affected by electronic resources. In some cases, new methods or procedures have to be introduced. Sometimes traditional procedures are paralleled, and in other cases older methods are replaced. All of these outcomes need to be accommodated with changes in workload. The following examples point to areas affected:

- *Workload Changes*. Implementation of new procedures, staff development, reallocation of staff time
- *Selection*. Initiating trials, license conditions, group decision, information gathering for order
- *Ordering*. Product description, license terms, consortia purchase, vendor/consortia contacts, product producer contacts
- *Payment*. Knowledge of payment terms–price options such as print + electronic, electronic only, site license, access fee, maintenance fee, platform fee
- *Product Receiving (Check-in)*. URL supplied by vendor, check links, confirm access, track content changes
- *Maintenance*. System capabilities, claiming cycle, troubleshoot technical problems relating to connectivity
- *Statistics*. Product use, workload
- *Renewal*. Frequent reviews–not automatically renewed, changes of vendor/consortia

As libraries deal with these issues, an overview of how workflows are impacted illustrates where changes occur. By analyzing these points, ways to regroup and reorganize can be identified in order to accommodate change in an efficient way.

A Small College Solution to Big Serials Problems

Ruth Richardson Scales

Guilford College

In August of 2002, the staff at Guilford College in North Carolina became frustrated with how increasingly difficult it was to handle journal access. The staff wanted a solution that would provide them with access to their print holdings, electronic holdings through aggregators or other means, OpenURL technology to go from one database to another, document delivery options, and flexibility to add local information. Since UNCG had a tool that could do all these things, Guilford College decided to partner with them. This partnership with UNCG's Journal Finder afforded this small college the opportunity to provide their students, staff and faculty with journal access just like schools with three to four times the staff and budget.

This poster session shows how Guilford College uses Journal Finder's features, including:

- A sophisticated https database administration module, for use in maintaining data and generating reports
- Integration with our OPAC, allowing the library catalog to be used to find all electronic and print journal titles, while eliminating the need to ever populate or maintain MARC 856 fields for any serials in the catalog
- Direct links to the journal title level for over 95% of our e-titles
- The ability to link from a citation in one commercial database directly to the full text article in another database (just as SFX does, but using locally written scripts)
- Local customization for specific community needs and local library abilities
- The effects on Hege Library's librarians and patrons

18th Annual NASIG Conference Registrants

Conference Registrants	*Organization/Institution*
Acreman, Bev	Taylor & Francis
Acton, Deena S.	National Library of Medicine
Aiello, Helen M.	Wesleyan University-Middletown, CT
Aitchison, Jada	University of Arkansas, Little Rock
Aladebumoye, Shade	Auburn University
Alexander, Kathryn J.	OCLC
Anderson, Gail C.	Medical College of Georgia
Anderson, Marcia L.	Arizona State University
Anderson, Rick	Univ. of Nevada, Reno
Andrews (CN), Susan	University of British Columbia
Andrews (US), Susan	Texas A&M University-Commerce
Antonucci-Durgan, Dana E.	Queens College–Graduate School of LIS
Arnold, Teresa	Free Library of Philadelphia
Arthur, Michael A.	Ball State University
Aschmann, Althea	Virginia Tech
Ashton-Pritting, Randi	University of Hartford
Ayling, Laura L.	Lewis & Clark College
Badics, Joe	Eastern Michigan University
Baia, Wendy	University of Colorado at Boulder
Bailey, Mary E.	Kansas State University Libraries
Baker, Jeanne	Univ. of Maryland
Baker, Mary Ellen	Cal Poly State Univ.
Bakke, Celia	San Jose State University Library
Balhorn, Kathy	LLNL
Ballard, Rochelle R.	Princeton University
Barrow, Charlotte M.	Boeing Company
Barstow, Sandra	University of Wyoming
Basch, Buzzy	Basch Subscriptions Inc.
Bazin, Paul	Providence College
Beasley, Sarah	Portland State University
Beck, Roger N.	Portland State University
Becker, Joe	New Mexico State University
Beehler, Sandra	Lewis & Clark College

http://www.haworthpress.com/web/SER
Digital Object Identifier: 10.1300/J123v46n03_21

Bell, Carole R.	Temple University
Bellinger, Christina	University of New Hampshire
Bernards, Dennis L.	Brigham Young University
Bianchi, Marcia	Reed College
Bielavitz, Tom	Blackwell
Blackburn, Joseph	Texas Tech University
Blackwell, Lisa S.	Children's Hospital Library
Blosser, John	Northwestern University
Bombeld, Madeleine	UNC Wilmington
Bonadio, Sylvia	Kluwer Academic Publishers
Born, Kathleen	EBSCO Information Services
Bosch, Stephen J.	University of Arizona
Bothmann, Robert	Minnesota State University, Mankato
Bowman, Lisa	Emporia State University
Boyce, Peter B.	PBoyce Associates
Boyd, Morag	Illinois State University
Bracken, Lee	Northeastern University
Bradford, Michael L.	University of Notre Dame
Branche Brown, Lynne	Innovative Interfaces
Branham, Janie	Southeastern Louisiana University
Brannon, Kathy	Swets Blackwell
Brass, Evelyn	University of Houston
Breed, Luellen L.	University of Wisconsin-Parkside
Broadwater, Deborah H.	Vanderbilt University
Brooks, Kay M.	Portland State University
Bross, Valerie	UCLA
Brown, Elizabeth	Project Muse
Brown, Jerry R.	Central Missouri State University
Brown, Margaret M.	Kwantlen University
Brubaker, Jana	Northern Illinois University
Bruner, David L.	Northern Arizona University
Bull, Greg	University of St. Thomas
Bullington, Jeff	University of Kansas
Burk, Martha	Babson College
Burke, David M.	Villanova University
Burke, Leslie D.	EBSCO
Bussell, Jody A.	Univ. of California at Berkeley
Buttner, Mary	Stanford Univ. School of Medicine
Bynog, David M.	Rice University
Byunn, Kit	University of Memphis
Callahan, Patricia	Massachusetts General Hospital
Campbell, Susan M.	York College of Pennsylvania

Capuano, Robert G.	Washington University in St. Louis
Caraway, Bea L.	Trinity University
Carey, Ronadin	University of Wisconsin
Carlson, Amy J.	University of Hawaii at Manoa
Carmichael, Christine	Univ. of Oregon
Carrasco Renteria, Pablo	UNAM–Univ. Nacional Autonoma de Mexico
Carroll, Diane	OHSU
Cascio, Diane D.	Santa Clara Univ. Law Library
Casetta, Prima	Getty Research Institute
Castrataro, James P.	Indiana University Libraries
Castro, Steve	Annual Reviews
Cernichiari, Andrea J.	Cambridge University Press
Chamberlain, Clinton K.	Trinity University
Champagne, Thomas E.	University of Michigan
Chandler, Sarah	Cornell University
Chang FitzGibbon, Hoong	Richard Stockton College of NJ
Cheng, Daisy T.	University of Mississippi
Chesler, Adam	
Chin, Renee	UCSD
Christean, Margaret	UCSD
Christensen, John	Brigham Young University
Christie, Anne	Oregon State University
Christoffersson, Rea	Lao Tse Press
Cipkowski, Pamela J.	University of Wisconsin-Milwaukee
Cleavenger, Patricia	Hanford Technical Library
Cochenour, Donnice	Colorado State University
Cohen, Joan G.	Bergen Community College
Collins, Jill M.	Boise State University
Conger, Joan E.	University of Georgia
Congleton, Robert	Rider University
Cook, Eleanor	Appalachian State University
Corvene, Sarah	Harvard College Library
Courtney, Keith	Taylor & Francis
Cousineau, Marie	University of Ottawa
Coyoy, Edwin	IMF
Creech, Anna	Eastern Kentucky University
Croft, Rosie	Royal Roads University Library
Culbertson, Becky	UC San Diego
Cunningham, Cynthia R.	OHSU Library
Cunningham, Nancy	Roswell Park Cancer Institute
Curtis, Donnelyn	University of Nevada, Reno
Dabkowski, Charles T.	Niagara University

Dailey, Anne J.	EBSCO Information Services
Darling, Karen	University of Missouri-Columbia
Davis, Jennifer K.	U.S. Government Printing Office
Davis, Susan	University at Buffalo (SUNY)
Day, Nancy	Linda Hall Library
Dazey, Megan	U of O
DeBlois, Lillian N.	Arizona Health Sciences Library
deBruijn, Deb	University of Ottawa
Defosset, Noel L.	USAFA
Degener, Christie T.	UNC-Chapel Hill Health Sciences Library
Del Baglivo, Megan	University of Maryland, Baltimore
DeShazo, Kristina	Oregon Health & Science University Library
Devlin, Mary	Paraquest Group
Deyoe, Nancy	Wichita State Univ.
Diez, George	National Library of Education/SCSC
Diven, Yvette	R.R. Bowker LLC
Dorn, Knut	Harrassowitz
Douglas, Myrna A.	University of the West Indies, Mona Campus
Dowdy, Beverly	Univ. of Central Oklahoma
Doyle, Anne S.	University of Kentucky
Draper, Ann	National Library of Canada
Drewes, Jeanne	Michigan State University
Duncan, Jennifer R.	Columbia University
Durden, Iris B.	Georgia Southern University
Duy, Joanna	Concordia University
Dyer, Sandra Y.	Washington State Law Library
Dygert, Claire	American University
Easton, Christa	Stanford University
Edwards, Jennifer L.	MIT Libraries
Ellison, Suzanne	Memorial University
Elteto, Sharon	Portland State University
Emery, Jill	University of Houston Libraries
Endres, Ellen E.	Brill Academic Publishers/de Gruyter Publishers
England, Deberah	Wright State University
Ercelawn, Ann	Vanderbilt University
Erlandson, Rene	University of Illinois at Urbana-Champaign
Essency, Janet E.	Bridgewater State College
Evans, Tom	Canisius College
Eyler, Carol E.	Carleton College Library
Fahey, Barbara J.	University of Wisconsin Oshkosh
Fegles, Gina	Northwest College

Feick, Tina	Swets Blackwell
Feis, Nathaniel	Art Institute of Chicago
Fenton, Eileen	JSTOR
Fields, Cheryl A.	National Library of Medicine
Finder, Lisa	Hunter College
Fitchett, Christine	Vassar College Libraries
Fleck, Nancy W.	Michigan State University
Fletcher, Marilyn P.	University of New Mexico
Fletcher, Peter V.	Tulane University
Flodin, Susanna	Oregon Institute of Technology
Flohr, Donita G.	OCLC
Folsom, Sandy L.	Central Michigan University
Fons, Theodore	Innovative Interfaces
Forshaw, Natalie C.	University of Alaska Fairbanks
Fortney, Lynn	EBSCO Info. Services
Foster, Connie	Western Kentucky University
Foti, Jim	
Fowler, Angie	Swets Blackwell
Frade, Pat	Brigham Young University
Frank, Donald G.	PSU
Frederiksen, Linda J.	Washington State University Vancouver
French, Pat	University of California, Davis
Frick, Rachel L.	University of Richmond
Frohlich, Anne M.	McNeese State University
Gallilee, Patty	Simon Fraser Univ. Library
Gao, Fang	University of Illinois at Urbana-Champaign
Gardner, Gene	University of Colorado Health Sciences Center
Gaswick, Carolyn	Albion College
Gatti, Timothy	SUNY-Albany
Geckle, Beverly	University of Baltimore Law Library
Geller, Marilyn	
Genereux, Cecilia	University of Minnesota
George, Sarah E.	Illinois Wesleyan University
Gerry, Nancy S.	Blackwell Publishing Ltd.
Gibson, Jessica	Illinois Library Computer Systems Office
Gilbert, Miriam	Marcel Dekker, Inc.
Gillespie, E. Gaele	University of Kansas
Gimmi, Robert D.	Shippensburg University
Gin, Marion	University of San Francisco
Ginanni, Katy	EBSCO Information Services
Ginn, Claire	Publishers Communication Group

Gordon, Martin	Franklin & Marshall College
Goude, Pamela K.	EBSCO
Graves, Tonia L.	Old Dominion University
Green, Carol	The University of Southern Mississippi
Greene, Phil	EBSCO
Grenci, Mary	University of Oregon
Grieme, Fariha	University of Minnesota Libraries
Griensven, Gina van	Kluwer Academic Publishers
Griffin, Linda Smith	Louisiana State University Libraries
Grover, Diane B.	University of Washington
Guajardo, Richard R.	University of Houston
Gurevich, Konstantin	University of Rochester
Haas, Diane	University of Oregon
Hagan, Timothy	Northwestern University
Hamilton, Fred	Louisiana Tech University
Hamilton, Gloria	University of Chicago
Ha'o, Kimberly A.	Brigham Young University
Hardy, Ronald K.	Central College
Harris, Jay	Lister Hill Library
Hartley, Melissa	Oregon State University
Harvell, Tony	University of California, San Diego
Haslam, Michaelyn	University of Nevada
Hawthorne, Dalene	Stanford University
Headley, Stephen K.	Public Library of Cincinnati & Hamilton Co.
Healy, Leigh Watson	Outsell, Inc.
Heitman, Herrick	Washington State Library
Heminger, Sharon	JSTOR
Hendricks, Arthur	PSU
Hepfer, Cindy	University at Buffalo
Hiatt, Derrik	Brigham Young University
Highby, Wendy	University of Northern Colorado
Hill, Thomas W.	Self Regional Healthcare
Hinger, Joseph	St. John's University Law Library
Hirons, Jean L.	Library of Congress
Hirsch, Elaine	Lewis & Clark College
Hodgin, Linda	University of Oregon
Holley, Beth R.	University of Alabama
Hollis, Rachel	CSU, Monterey Bay
Hood, Anna	Kent State University
Hood, Kelly	Allen Press, Inc.
Hooss, Annette	Harrassowitz

Hopkins, Sandra	Harvard Law School
Horn, Marguerite	SUNY OLIS
Howard, Mykie A.	George Washington University
Hoyer, Craig	Swets Blackwell
Hsiung, Lai-Ying	University of California, Santa Cruz
Hudson, Patricia Bowers	Oxford University Press
Hulbert, Linda	University of St. Thomas
Hunt, Maria S.	University of Utah
Irvin, Judy C.	Louisiana Tech University
Ives, Gary W.	Texas A&M University Libraries
Ivins, October	Digital Content & Access Solutions
Jacobs, Mark	Washington State University
Jacobsen, Bruce F.	Bridgeport National Bindery
Jacobsen, LaVonne	San Francisco State University
Jaeger, Don	Alfred Jaeger Inc.
Jaeger, Glenn	Absolute Backorder Service
Jander, Karen	University of Wisconsin-Milwaukee
Jenkins, Vince	Maricopa County (Ariz.) Community Colleges
Jenner, Margaret	University of Washington
Jerose, Terese M.	Southeastern Bapt. Theol. Sem.
Joanisse, Line	NLC
Johansen, Kathleen D.	Brigham Young University
John, Sarah	UC Davis
Johnson, Judy L.	Univ. of Nebraska-Lincoln
Johnson, Kathleen	Portland Community College
Johnson, Steve	Clemson University
Johnson, Wilma	Swets Blackwell
Jones, Cathy	Sirsi
Jones, Ed	National University Library
Jones, Rebecca Soltys	University of North Carolina
Joshipura, Smita	Arizona State University West
Julian, Gail	Clemson University
Julian, Suzanne	Southern Utah University
Kapic, Hana	Phoenix Public Library
Kaplan, Michael	Ex Libris
Kara, Bill	Cornell University
Kasprowski, Rafael	University of Houston
Kawasaki, Jodee	Montana State University
Kawecki, Barbara	EBSCO
Kazzimir, Edward	OCLC
Keane, Megan	University of California Berkeley Library
Kenreich, Mary Ellen	Portland State University

Kern, Kristen T.	Portland State University
Kessinger, Pam	Portland Community College
Kimball, Susan J.	Amherst College
King, Donald W.	University of Pittsburgh
King, Paula	Scripps Research Institute
Klemperer, Katharina E.	Harrassowitz
Kniesner, Dan L.	OHSU
Kobyljanec, Kathy	John Carroll University
Koller, Rita M.	Lake Forest College
Kraemer, Alfred	Medical College of Wisconsin
Kremer, Julie	Stanford Law School
Krieger, Lee A.	University of Miami
Kristick, Laurel	Oregon State University
Krueger, Janice M.	UOP Library
Laird, David	Phoenix College
Lamborn, Joan	University of Northern Colorado
Lamoureux, Selden Durgom	UNC–Chapel Hill
Landesman, Betty	University of the District of Columbia
Lang, Jennifer	University of Cincinnati
Lange, Holley	Colorado State University
Langendorfer, Jeanne	Bowling Green State University
LaRooy, Pauline	Victoria University
Lauer, Peggy A.	Maryville University
Lawlor, Rod	Dumbarton Oaks
Leadem, Ellen	Natl. Inst. Environ. Health Sci.
Lee, Angela	Washington County Coop. Library Services
Lee, Sheila	Louisiana State University
Legg, Chris	Annual Reviews
Lehman, Lisa M.	University of Alaska Fairbanks
Lenville, Jean	Harvard
Lesher, Marcella	St. Mary
Lewis, Linda	University of New Mexico
Li, Xiaoli	University of Washington
Lin, Weina	Business Library of Brooklyn Public Library
Lindquist, Janice L.	Rice University
Lippert, Flora	Portland Community College
Llewellyn, Tony	CABI Publishing
Loghry, Patricia	University of Notre Dame
Lopez, Andrea	Annual Reviews
Lord, Jonathon	University of Virginia
Lu, Wen-ying	Michigan State University
Lyandres, Natasha	University of Notre Dame

MacAdam, Carol L.	JSTOR
Macklin, Lisa	Georgia Tech
MacLennan, Birdie	University of Vermont
Magenau, Carol	Dartmouth College Library
Malinowski, Teresa M.	Calif. State Univ. Fullerton
Malone, Deborah	University of San Francisco
Manuel, Kate	New Mexico State University
Markley, Susan B.	Villanova University
Markwith, Michael	TD Net Inc.
Marshall, Sue	Montana State University
Martin, Charity K.	University of Nebraska-Lincoln
Martin, Marcia A.E.	University of Florida
Martonik, Renee	University of Chicago
Mason, Rose	St. Edward
Matthews, Karen	Dana Medical Library
Matthews, Kathleen	University of Victoria
Maxwell, Kimberly A.	Massachusetts Institute of Technology
McBurney, Melissa	Pacific Northwest National Laboratory
McClamroch, Jo	Indiana University
McClary, Maryon L.	University of Alberta
McCracken, Peter	Serials Solutions
McCutcheon, Dianne	Library of Congress
McDanold, Shana L.	Saint Louis University
McElroy, Emily	Loyola University
McGrath, Kat	University of British Columbia
McHugo, Ann	Dartmouth College
McKee, Anne E.	Greater Western Library Alliance
McKee, Eileen L.	Brooklyn Public Library
McKendry, Yusuf	Canadian Institute for STI
McLeod, William	National Academies
McManus, Jean	University of Notre Dame
McVay-Lynch, Maggie	Portland State University
Medeiros, Carolyn	LLNL
Meneely, Kathleen	Cleveland Health Sciences Library
Menefee, Daviess	Elsevier
Mercante, Mary Ann	Maryville University
Mering, Meg	University of Nebraska-Lincoln
Meyer, Carol A.	Maxwell Publishing Consultants
Meyer, Patricia L.	National University
Miller, Heather	SUNY-Albany
Miller, Judith K.	Valparaiso University
Mitchell, Anne M.	University of Houston

Moeller, Paul	University of Colorado
Moeller, Ulrike	Harrassowitz
Moles, Jean Ann	U. of Arkansas Medical Sciences
Molto, Mavis	Utah State University
Montgomery, Carol H.	Drexel University
Moran, Sheila E.	Massachusetts General Hospital
Morrison, Laura S.	Clemson University
Morse, Carol	Walla Walla College Library
Murden, Steven H.	
Murphy, Sandra	Harvard University
Myers, Myrtle	OCLC
Narayanan, Kamala S.	Queen's University
Nauman, Matt	Blackwell
Nelson, Catherine R.	University of California
Nelson, Stacy C.	University of California, San Diego
Neville, Shelley	Dynix
Newsome, Nancy	Western Carolina University
Ng, Marilyn	University of California
Nicholas, Pamela J.	University of Notre Dame
Nobles, Steven J.	University of Tulsa
Norman, Michael	University of Illinois
Norton, Judith	OHSU
Novak, Denise D.	Carnegie Mellon University
Noyes, J.C.	Bridgeport National Bindery
Oberg, Steve	Taylor University
O'Connell, Jennifer S.	EBSCO Information Services
Oliver, Jenna L.	The Boeing Company
Oliver, Marina G.	Texas Tech University Libraries
Ono, Shigeharu	Kinokuniya Publications
Orr, Terri	Swets Blackwell
O'Sullivan, Donal	Univ. of California, San Diego
Owen, Berniece M.	Portland Community College
Packer, Donna	Western Washington University Libraries
Page, Mary	Rutgers University
Paldan, Diane N.	Wayne State University
Palmer, Joy J.	Mayo Medical Library
Palmiter, Sherry	Seattle University
Parang, Elizabeth	Pepperdine University
Paratore, Amy	Swets Blackwell
Parkhe, Smita	Arizona State University
Parks, Bonnie	Oregon State University
Paul, Kathryn	University of Victoria

Pauley, Eric F.	North Carolina State University
Paulis, Robert	SAGE Publications
Perry, Danielle	Swets Blackwell
Persing, Robert D.	Univ. of Pennsylvania
Person, Matthew A.	MBL/WHOI Library
Pesch, Oliver	EBSCO Publishing
Peters, Victoria M.	Swets Blackwell
Petsche, Kevin	IUPU University Library
Phillips, Linda	Blackwell
Picerno, Peter V.	Nova Southeastern University
Pilkinton, Carole	Univ. of Notre Dame
Pitts, Linda M.	University of Washington Libraries
Polgar, Linda C.	Stanford University
Powers, Susanna S.	Tulane University
Pribyl, Althea L.	Blackwell
Rabner, Lanell	Brigham Young University
Rais, Shirley M.	Loma Linda University
Raley, Sarah	EBSCO
Randall, Kevin M.	Northwestern University Library
Randall, Mike	UCLA
Regan, Nancy S.	Abbott Laboratories
Resco, Carol S.	OGI School of Science & Engineering at OHSU
Reynolds, Regina Romano	Library of Congress
Rhoades, Alice	Rice University
Ricker, Karina	SUNY-Albany
Riggio, Angela	UCLA
Riley, Cheryl A.	Central Missouri State Univ.
Rioux, Margaret A.	Woods Hole Oceanographic Institutiion
Ripley, Erika B.	SMU
Roach, Dani	Macalester College
Roberts, Constance F.	Hamilton College
Robinson, Karlene K.	University of the West Indies, Mona Campus
Robischon, Rose	United States Military Academy Library
Roche, Matilda	University of Alberta
Rodgers, Pat	Harrassowitz
Roepke, Greg	
Rogers, Marilyn	University of Arkansas
Romaine, Siôn	University of Washington Libraries
Romaniuk, Elena	University of Victoria
Rosati, Karen T.	USC School of Medicine
Rosenberg, Frieda B.	UNC-Chapel Hill

Roth, Alison E.	Swets Blackwell
Roush, Barbara	University of California Hastings Law
Ruelle, Barbara	Emory University
Rumph, Virginia A.	Butler University
Rupp, Nathan A.	Cornell University
Ryan, Noelle	Harvard Medical School
Salt, David P.	University of Saskatchewan
Savage, Stephen M.	San Diego State University
Saxe, Christoph	OCLC
Saxton, Elna	Univ. of Cincinnati
Scales, Ruth Richard	Guilford College
Schatz, Bob	Franklin Book Co., Inc.
Schmitt, Stephanie C.	Yale Law Library
Schneider, Chris	Elsevier
Schneider, Janet	Schoolcraft College Library
Schoen, Dena	Harrassowitz
Schwartz, Marla J.	American University Law Library
Schwartzkopf, Becky	Minnesota State Univ., Mankato
Seamans, Marsha	University of Kentucky
Selness, Sushila S.	Univ. of San Diego
Sercan, Cecilia	Cornell University
Sexton, Lonni	University of Oregon
Shadle, Steve	University of Washington Libraries
Shay, Lynn R.	UNC-Wilmington
Sheffield, Becky	Ball State University
Shpilevaya, Lyudmila	New York Public Library
Shrader, Tina	Johns Hopkins University
Shroyer, Andrew	CSULA
Silvas, Manli	CIA
Silvera, Paula	AstraZeneca
Simser, Charlene	Kansas State University
Sinha, Reeta	UNLV
Skinner, Debra G.	Georgia Southern University
Slagell, Jeff	Delta State University
Slaughter, Gloria	Hope College
Slaughter, Philenese	Austin Peay State University
Slight-Gibney, Nancy	University of Oregon
Smith, Abby	Council on Library & Information Resources
Smith, Merrill	EBSCO Information Services
Smith, Scott A.	Blackwell
Smith, Susan P.	University of Connecticut

Snider, Jacqueline	ACT Information Resource Center
Sonka, Bud	National University
Sorensen, Charlene	CISTI
Sorensen, Sally	Texas Christian University
Spagnolo, Lisa C.	University of Washington
Spight, Benita L.	Gale Group
Spoon, Jacalyn C.	Ithaca College
Sprehe, Nancy	Samuel Roberts Noble Foundation
Spring, Martha	Loyola University Chicago
Springer, Fran	Thunderbird
Srivastava, Sandhya D.	Hofstra University
Stachiw, Pat	Columbia Health Sciences
Stamison, Christine	Swets Blackwell
Stanton, Vicki	University of North Florida
Steeves, Merle	York University
Stefancu, Laurentiu M.	University of Illinois at Chicago
Stewart, Wendy A.	Portland State University
Stickman, Jim	University of Washington
Stockton, Barbara	Southern Methodist University
Sullenger, Paula	Auburn University
Sullivan, Sharon	H. W. Wilson
Sutherland, Laurie	University of Washington
Sutton, Sarah	Texas A&M University-Corpus Christi
Swenson, Jennifer	Marriott Library
Taffurelli, Virginia	Science, Industry & Business Library/NYPL
Takatani, Grace	Hastings College of the Law
Talley, Kaye	University of Central Arkansas
Tarango, Adolfo R.	University of California, San Diego
Taylor, Marit	Auraria Library
Teaster, Gail	Winthrop University
Teel, Kay	Stanford University
Tenney, Joyce	University of MD Baltimore County
Tenopir, Carol	University of Tennessee
Thomas, Molly R.	Temple University
Thomas, Rosella	University of Oregon
Thompson, Sandra	Wellesley College
Thorne, Patti	University of Alaska Anchorage Consortium Library
Tong, Dieu V.	Univ. of Alabama, Birmingham
Tonkery, Dan	EBSCO Information Services
Trish, Margaret E.	University of Missouri-Rolla

Tucker, Alice M.	U.S. Geological Survey
Tumlin, Markel D.	San Diego State University
Tusa, Sarah	Lamar University
VanAuken, Gayle J.	Linda Hall Library
Vent, Marilyn	University of Nevada, Las Vegas
Vukas, Rachel R.	EBSCO Information Services
Wadeborn, Germaine	UCLA
Waite, Carolyn	MIT Lincoln Laboratory
Wakeling, William M.	Northeastern University
Walker, Dana M.	University of Georgia Libraries
Wallas, Philip	EBSCO Information Services
Walmsley, Michael	Franklin Book Company
Walravens, Hartmut	State Library, Germany
Wang, Cheng-yee	University of Scranton
Wang, Jian	Portland State University
Wang, Jue	Cal State Northridge
Warren, Tommye	Montana State University
Waters, Daisy	University at Buffalo
Watson, Virginia	Brigham Young University
Weigel, Friedmann	Harrasowitz
Weislogel, Judy	Elsevier
Weiss, Paul J.	University of California, San Diego
Wesley, Kathryn	Clemson University
Westman, Janice	AstraZeneca Pharmaceuticals
Weston, Beth	National Library of Medicine
Weston, Claudia V.	Portland State University
Whipple, Heather H.	Reed College
Whisenant, Dave	College Center for Library Automation
Whiting, Peter	University of Southern Indiana
Wiggins, John W.	Drexel University
Wilkinson, Fran	University of New Mexico
Williams, Mary	Minot State University
Williams, Sheryl L.	University of Nebraska Medical Center
Williams, Sue	Univ. of Colorado-Boulder
Willman, Carrie	OHSU Library
Wills, Faedra	University of Texas at Arlington
Willson-St. Clair, Kimberly	Portland State University
Wilson, Jenni	Swets Blackwell
Winchester, David	Washburn University
Wineburgh-Freed, Maggie	USC
Winward, Kyle	Southwest Missouri State University

Wishnetsky, Susan	Northwestern Univ., Feinberg School of Medicine
Wood, Ross	Wellesley College Library
Worthing, Richard	California State Library
Worthington, Michele	National Library of Education/SCSC
Young, Jennifer	Northwestern University
Yu, Ying C.	Gallaudet University
Yue, Paoshan	University of Nevada, Reno
Zeigen, Laura	OHSU
Zeter, Mary Jo	Michigan State University
Zhang, Xiaoyin	UNLV
Zhang, Yvonne	Cal Poly Pomona

Index

A lower case n following a page number refers to a note or bibliography entry. A lower case f refers to a figure. Titles are italicized.

AAS *See* American Astronomical Society
AAUP *See* American Association of University Professors
Academic Book Center, 194
Acquisitions
  Auditors, 273
  Budget, 10,29-30
  Change in Dept., 270-271
  Consortial agreements, 49,100,163
  Dartmouth College Library example, 269-273
  Direct purchase plans, 185-186
  Firm orders, 271
  Fund allocation models, 9-12
  Impact of electronic resources on, 326-327
  Reinventing, 269-273
  Standing orders, 271
  System, developing, 155-159
  Time and costs, 290f
ACRL *See* Association of College and Research Libraries
Adams, John, 246,248f,251n
ADS *See* Astrophysics Data System
Airlie House Meeting, 71
ALA *See* American Library Association
Alabama Virtual Library, 279
Aldana, Lynda, 86,95,96n
ALEPH500, 70,71,72,89
American Association of University Professors, 254
American Astronomical Society, 123,132
American Council on Education, 233
American Law Reports, 260
American Libraries, 254
American Library Association, 234, 244,278
  Association of Specialized and Cooperative Library Agencies, 234
Americans with Disabilities Act of 1990, 234
Anderson, Gail, 324
Anderson, Rick, 39,41,54-55,56n, 272,273n
Andrew W. Mellon Foundation, 265
Anglo-American Cataloging Rules 2nd ed. (AACR2), 17,223,224,226
Apple (software Company), 31
Arthur, Michael A., 263,267n
ArXiv.org, 122,134
Aschmann, Althea, 245,248,249, 250,151n
Association of College and Research Libraries, 254,256
Association of Research Libraries, 122
Astrophysics Data System (ADS), 123, 132
Auburn University Library, 275-280

Bailey, Charles W., Jr., 122,140n
Barriers to clients with disabilities, 233-240
Barstow, Sandra, 257,262n
Beasley, Sarah, 9,12,15

Becker, Joe, 322
Benchmarking, 196
  Time and Costs, 287-293
Bevis, Mary D., 85,95n
Big Picture: Opportunities for Potential Areas for Closer Collaboration among the New Zealand University Libraries, 168
BioMedCentral, 49
BioOne, 49
Blackboard, 31
Blackwell, Lisa S., 287,293n
Blackwell North America, 194
Blackwell's Books, 194
Blackwell's Cost and Coverage Studies, 12, 15n2
Blackwell's Information Services, 193-194
Bobby (Web-accessibility assessment tool), 234
Bombeld, Madeleine, 315,320n
Bombing, Yale Law Library, 259-260
Bosch, Stephen, 173,179,190n
Bowman, V., 238,240n
Boyce, Peter, 121,141n
Bright Futures, 165
Briscoe, Georgia, 86,95,96n
Broadcast searching, 152f-153
Brown, Jerry R., 33,38n,191,199n
Budget, Acquisitions, 10,29-30
Bundling pricing, 31
Burke, David, 221,226n
Bussell, Jodi, 198

Calhoun, Karen S., 85,95n
California Digital Library, 69,71,75
Callahan, Ewa, 122,140n
Canada, home of University of Victoria, 302
Canadian National Site Licensing Project, 163
Cancerlit, 238
Casey, Carol, 59,67n
Cataloging, 17-23,221-225
  Aggregator-neutral records, 203-207
  Catalogs, 54,61-62
  Education, 221-226
  Electronic resources, 83-98, 275-280
  Electronic serials, 203-207
  Finite resources, 19
  Integrating resources, 203-207
  LC Classification mapping, 306f
  MARC fields for access and license data, 275-280
  MARC record, 223,224,226, 275-280
  Materials processing and conservation unit time and cost, 291f
  Metadata librarians, 222
  Multiple versions, 69-81f
  Ontologist, 221-222
  Policies for electronic, 305
  Serials time and cost, 292f
  Title changes for electronic resources, 203,207
Cataloging & Classification Quarterly, 226
CAUL *See* Council of Australian University Librarians
CDL *See* California Digital Library
Center for Research Libraries (CRL), 263,264,265
Challenges to clients with disabilities, 233-240
Champion, Robbie, 246,251n
Change, 41
  Acquisitions Dept., 270-271
  Job description, 45
  Managing, 245-251
  Models, 245-251
  Work, 50
  Workflow, 47
Cheng, Daisy T.,301,308n
Chesler, Adam, 39,47,56n
Christie, Anne, 323

CI *See* Contextual Inquiry
CIC *See* Committee for Institutional Cooperation
CIC/CRL Reference Books Archive, 265
CIRP *See* Cooperative Institutional Research Program, 233
Clark, Stephen, 34
Clients with "differabilities," 233-239
CLIR *See* Council on Library and Information Resources
Coalition of Australian University Libraries example, 122-131
Collection development, 10-12,126-132
  Coalition of Australian University Library example, 122
  Drexel University Library example, 122-131
  E-resource policy, 122
College & Research Libraries News, 222
Collegiality, 255
Collocated access, 72-81f
Committee for Institutional Cooperation, 264,265
  Midwest Big Ten Conference, 265
  University of Chicago, 265
Competition, 156,196,197
Conference dates, 35
Conferences (list of), 243
Conferencing, 211
Conger, Joan, 39,50,55,56n
Congleton, Robert J., 281,286n
CONSER *See* Cooperative Online Serials Program
Consolidation, 193,196
Consolidation of Information Content Industry, 29
Consortia agreements, 49,100,163
Content Industry, 27-31
Content integration, 30-31
Content-spaghetti, 29
Contextual Inquiry, 155-159
Continuing education, 36
Continuing resources, 19
  Administrative data for, 322
CONZUL *See* Council of New Zealand University Librarians
Cook, Eleanor, 5-6,195,197
Cooperative Institutional Research Program, 233
Cooperative Online Serials Program, 103,203-204,207
Coopetition, 193
Copying by Libraries, 228
Copyright Law, 227-231
Core competencies, 192
Council of Australian University Librarians, 163
Council of New Zealand University Librarians, 168
Council on Library and Information Resources, 122,140n
Count Online Usage of Networked Electronic Resources (COUNTER), 49,147,149,154
COUNTER *See* Count Online Usage of Networked Electronic Resources
Courtney, Keith, 191,192,193,197, 198n
Cornell University Library example, 225,310
Corps of discovery, 1
CRL *See* Center for Research Libraries
CrossRef (Reference-linking project), 49
Customer-centered, 53
Customer requirements, 156
Customization, 40-41

Darling, Karen, 17,18-22,23n
Dartmouth College Library, 270
  Acquisitions Dept., 269-273
Database Of Library Licensed Electronic Resources, 325
Davis, Susan, 241,244n
Devlin, Mary, 3n

Dig Your Well Before You're Thirsty, 211
Digital Library Degree, 225
Digital Library Foundation, 101
Digital Library Federation Electronic Resource Management Initiative, 41,280
Digital Millennium Copyright Act, 230
Digital preservation, 107-120
  Content paradox, 108-109
  Federal agencies, 112
  Infrastructure, 118-119
  Institutions, 112
  JSTOR, 112,115
  Legal/regulatory paradox, 110-111
  Organizational paradox, 109-110
  User paradox, 111
Direct purchase plans, 185-186
Disabilities, Clients with, 233-240
Disaster preparedness, 324-325
Discrimination, 259
Dissertation Abstracts, 299
Distance learning, 216
Diversify, 196
D-Lib, 123,226
Documentation, lack of, causing problems, 259
DOLLeR *See* Database Of Library Licensed Electronic Resources
Douglas, Michael, 210
Drewes, Jeanne, 263,264,267n
Drexel University Library collection development example, 122, 123,126,127,129,130,131
Drucker, Peter, 143
Dublin Core, 223
Duy, Joanna, 295,296,297,298,299,300n
Dygert, Claire, 253,255,256n
DYNIX, 155-159

"e", 28
E-Archive *See* Electronic-Archiving Initiative
E-journal Finder, 295-300
E-journals. *See* Electronic journals
E-Metrics (with figs.), 143-153
  Summary of ARL E-Metrics, 149f
  Summary of ICOLC Guidelines, 149f
  Summary of NISO Z39.7, 150f
  Summary of Project COUNTER initiative, 151f
Easton, Christa, 33,36,37, 38n
EBSCO, 50,194,195,217
  EBSCOhost, 235,236,237,238
ECO *See* OCLC's FirstSearch Electronic Collections Online
Electronic access and repositories, 265
Electronic-Archiving Initiative, 115
Electronic communication tools, 215, 217-219
  Ask a Librarian, 217
  Camtasia, 217
  Chat sessions, 219
  Discussion board, 217-219
  SMARTboard, 217
  Web-based trails, 215-217
  WebCT, 215-217
Electronic Content, 233-240
Electronic journals, 39, 83-97,99-105, 173-189
  A-Z lists, 302,303f,304f
  Access, 301-308
  Agents, 173-177, 310,311-313
    Benefits to libraries, 177
  Branding, 129
  Cataloging, 203-207,305,306f
  Content access, 104-105
  Managing, 39-57,101
  OPAC access, 85-95
  Print began with note (MARC 362), 206
  Provider note, 206-207
  Subscriptions, Maintaining, 309-313
  Tracking status of the collection, 103-104,311-312
  Uniform title, 205
  Usage patterns, 121-141, 295-299
  Usage statistics, 144-151

Web page access, 301-308
Electric Library Plus, 238
Electronic Resource Management, 173-189,275-280
Access and integration, 175
Identify, 174
Negotiate and license, 174-175
Order, 175
Payment, 175
Registration, 175
Electronic resources, 50
Access to full-text databases, 295-300
And disabled clients, 234
Bundling pricing, 31
Challenges, 148f
Consortial agreements, 49,100,163
ICOLC Guidelines for Statistical Measures, 149f
Impact on serials acquisitions, 326-327
Items examined, 147f
Licenses, 48,84,101,104,163
Life cycle, 102f
Logins, 145f
Metasearching, 152-154
Numbers of E-resources, 144f
Philosophy towards, 276
Provide access, 103f
Purchasing, 169
Searches, 146f
Turnaways, 145f
Electronic serials cataloging, 203-207
Elteto, Sharon, 215,216,217,219n
Emery, Jill, 39,40,56n,99,100,105n
Encyclopedia of Education, 254
Enlightened leadership, 53
ERIC, 299
ERIL-L (electronic discussion list), 243
Erlandson, Rene J., 281,286n
ERLIC (Electronic Resources Licensing and Information Center), 277
Everetts (vendor), 194
Ex Libris, 70,152
Metalib, 152
Excel (software), 31
Extenza, 50
EZproxy, 307

Factiva, 31,122
Fair Use Doctrine, 228
Faxon/RoweCom, 194,195
Federated searching, 152f-153
Fenton, Eileen Gifford, 107,113, 115-119
Fifth discipline, 53
Finite resources, 19
Firm orders, 271
First sale doctrine, 228
Fitzpatrick, Jack, 276
*Five Absolutes That Get Results,*250,251n
Follett, Mary, 53
Fons, Ted, 39,54,56
Ford, Simon, 211
Forget To Do List, 269-73
Frank, Don, 9,14,15
FRBR *See* Functional Requirements for the Bibliographic Record
French, Patricia Sheldahl, 1-3
Functional Requirements for the Bibliographic Record, 70, 76
Fund allocation models, 9
Factors in, 11-12
Linfield model,10

Gatti, Timothy, 83,98n
Geac ADVANCE System, 89
Gekko, Gordon, 210
Geller, Marilyn, 197,198
George, Sarah E., 309,313
German KOBV Consortium, 70
Gilbert, Miriam, 191,192,196,198n
Ginanni, Katy, 195
Ginn, Claire, 99,100,105n

Goldratt, Eliyahu, 246,247f
Google, 31
Gordon, Marty, 196
Gorman, Michael, 60,66n,254,256n
Graham, John-Bauer, 85,95n
Greene, Phil, 197
Grenci, Mary, 287,293n
Guilford College Library example, 327-328

Hagler, Ronald, 65,66n
Hamaker, Chuck, 85,95n
Harrassowitz (vendor), 194,195
Haslam, Michaelyn, 326-327
Hawthorne, Dalene, 322
Hazardous Substances, 238
Healy, Leigh Watson, 2,27-32, 32n,192,193
Herrera, Gail, 86,95,96n
Herrin, Barbara, 249
Herring, Mark, 254,256n
Highby, Wendy, 295,300n
HighWire, 49
HOLLIS system, 72f,73f
Hot Topics, 191-199
Hotels, 33-35
Howard, Mykie, 209,213n
HTML *See* Hypertext mark-up language
Hypertext mark-up language (HTML), 236,238

IBM, 31
ICT *See* Information and communication technology
IFLA, 70
ILS *See* Integrated Library System
Industry trends, 27-32
Information content industry, 28-32
Information environment, 61-64
Information Resource Matrix, 59-67
Information retrieval, 46
Information Science programs, 221-227
InfoTrac, 122,297
    InfoTrac Web Business & Company Profile ASAP, 235, 236,237,238
Integrated Library System software development, 155-159
    See also Specific system
Integrating resources, 19-20,203-204
Interoperability, 133
IRM *See* Information Resource Matrix
iTune, 31

Jacobs, Mark, 59,67n
James C. Kirkpatrick Library example, 235
JASIST *See Journal of the American Society for Information Science and Technology*
JAWS for Windows 3.7, 235,236,238
Jefferson, Thomas, 1
Johns Hopkins University library example, 225
Journal articles, locating, 321
Journal Finder, 327-328
Journal of Biological Inorganic Chemistry, 298-299
Journal of Internet Cataloging, 226
Journal of the American Society for Information Science and Technology, 226
Journal subscriptions, new, 323
JSTOR, 90,112,115,265,276,307
    Electronic-Archiving Initiative, 115
Julian, Gail, 245,251n

Kanter, Rosabeth Moss, 246-249f,251n
Kaplan, Michael, 69-81
Kara, Bill, 309,310,311,313n
Kara, William J., 85,95n
Kaufman, Paula T., 242,244n

Kenreich, Mary Ellen, 9,10,13-14,15
Kern, Kris, 324
King, Donald W., 121,122,140n,141n
Kling, Rob, 122,140n
Kluwer's STM content, 31 (double list)
Knowledgebases, 102
Kristick, Laurel, 323
Krueger, Janice M., 227, 232n
Kurzweil *See* L&H Kurzweil

L&H Kurzweil 1000, 235
L&H Kurzweil 3000, 235
La Rooy, Pauline, 161,171n
Lamoureux, Selden Durgom, 173, 241-244n
Lange, Holley R., 203,208n
Langendorfer, Jeanne M., 269,273
Latest entry cataloging, 20
LC Bicentennial Conference on Bibliographic Control for the New Millennium, 69-70
  Confronting the Challenge of Networked Resources and the Web, 69
Lesher, Marcella, 9
Leung, Shirley W., 86,96n
Lewis, Meriwether, 1
Lexis-Nexis, 238
Li, Yiu-On, 86,96n
LIANZA *See* Library and Information Association of New Zealand Aotearoa
LIBQUALL, 290
Libraries Serving Special Populations, 234
Library and Information Association of New Zealand Aotearoa, 161-171
Library and Information Policy Summit, 165
Library Association Record, 211
Library branding, 129
Library cooperation, nationwide, 161-171
Library Hi Tech, 235
Library Journal, 12, 15n3
Library of Congress MARCMaker, 90
Library school education, 221-226,241-244
Library Services for People with Disabilities Policy, 234
Library Systems Analyst, 157
Library websites for specific courses, 216
Library workshops for faculty, 216
Licenses, 48,84,101,104,163
Lilly, E.B., 235,240n
Linfield model, 10
LIPS *See* Library and Information Policy Summit
Listserv *See* specific lists
Literature Online, 307
LOEX of the West, 216
Longenecker, Clinton O., 250,251n
Loose tight organization, 53
Los Alamos e-print service, 134
Lowry, Charles, 11, 15n1
Loyola University Law Library claiming process example, 326
LSA *See* Library Systems Analyst
LSSP *See* Libraries Serving Special Populations, 234

Mackay, Harvey, 211
Magenau, Carol, 269,271,273n
Maori Library and Information Workers' Group, 164
MARC Record, 223,224,226, 275-280
Marcel Dekker, 197
Market requirements, 156
Marketing skills, 31,32
Markwith, Michael, 191,192,195, 196,198n
Martinez-Mienhoff International, 194
Matthews, Karen, 227,232n
Maxwell, Kim, 191,193,194,199n

McCord, S., 238,240n
McCurley, Henry, 276
McHugo, Ann, 269,271,273n
McKee, Anne, 191,195,196,197, 198,199n
McVay-Lynch, Maggie, 215,216,217,219n
Medical College of Georgia Library example, 324
Medline Plus, 238,239,240
Melvyn Union Catalog, 70,71,75
Mental disabilities, 239
Merger trends, 192
METADEX, 279
Metapress, 50
Metasearching, 152f-153
Microsoft, 31
Migration, retaining data in, 277
Miller, Heather S., 83,98n
MIT subscription example, 193,194
Mitchell, Anne, 275, 280n
Montgomery, Carol, 121,141n
MSDS, 238
Multiple version problem, 71,73
Mulver *See* Multiple version problem
MySQL, 307

Napster, 31
NASA, 132
  Astrophysics Data System, 123,132
NASIG, 33-38,243-244,278
  Conference 2002, 86
  Conference dates, 34-35
  Conference hotels, 33-35
  Conference Student Grant, 243
  Continuing education, 36,225,243
  Dues, 35-36
  Library School student education, 242
  Office Space, 35
  Paid Staff, 35
  Website, 36-37

National Information Standards Organization (NISO), 147, 153,239,
National information strategy, 161-171
  Knowledge access, 165-166
  Knowledge content, 166
  Knowledge equity, 166
  Library and Information Commission, 166
National Library of New Zealand, 162,164
National Science Foundation, 132
National Serial Data Program, 204
National Union Catalog, 70
Nationwide approach to library cooperation,161-171
NCSU Libraries *See* North Carolina State University Libraries
Negotiating, 47
Networking in a Library, 209-213
  Keep track and maintain contacts, 212
  Quality networking with fewer people, 212
Neville, Shelley, 155,159n
New Mexico State University library, 322
New State, The, 53
New Zealand
  Connecting Communities Strategy, 167,170
  CONZULSys, 169
  E-government Strategy, 167,170
  Heritage Information Strategy, 168
  Information and communication technology in Schools Strategy, 167,170
  Intellectual Property and National Consortia Information Strategy, 168
  National Library Act, 162
  National Library Bill, 166
  Public Library Standards, 166
Newtonian management, 51-53
NISO standard, 239
NISO Z39.7, 147,153

North American Serials Interest Group
See NASIG
North Carolina Serials Conference, 36
North Carolina State University
Libraries, 295-300
Northwest Center for Technology
Access, 239
NSDP *See* National Serial Data
Program

Oak Ridge National Laboratory, 123
Oberlander, Cyril, 9,12-13,15
OCLC, 70,152,204,222,223
FirstSearch Electronic Collections
Online, 235,236,237,238
Web-Z, 152
*Online Educator, The,*216
Online Public Access Catalog, 86-95
Used to generate web pages for
e-journals, 301-308
See also OPAC access under
Electronic journals
OPAC *See* Online Public Access
Catalog
Open Archives Initiative, 122,196-197
OpenBook 5.0, 235,238
OpenURL, 150
OpenURL Resolver, 151
Oregon State University, 239, 323
Oregon University System, 13
Outsell, Inc., 27-28
Ovid, 31,122,238

Page, Mary, 197
Parang, Elizabeth, 215,219n
Partners,Strategic, 32
Partnerships, 49,193,215-219
Paul, Kathryn, 301,302,305,307,308n
Pauley, Eric 295,296,297,299,300n
Penn State University, 277
Perfection, 46,54-55
Performance standards, 194
Pesch, Oliver, 143,154n
Petsche, Kevin, 99,105n
Planning for Serialists, 241-243
Policies and Procedures Manuals in
Technical Services, 257-261
Political culture, 256
Pope, Michele, 326
PORTALS Consortium, Disaster
Recovery Group, 324-325
Portland State University Library,
9-15,215-219,324-325
Preservation
Digital, 117-118
Print, 116-117
Pricing models, 48
Print preservation, 116-117
Print Repositories, 263-267
Problem solver, 42-47
Procedure follower, 42-47
Processing, materials time and cost, 291f
Professional survival, 209-213
Program for Cooperative Cataloging,
71,73,204
See also Cooperative Online Serials
Program
Project Muse, 90
ProQuest, 122,297
ProQuest Research Library, 238
PSU *See* Portland State University
Library
Public Library of Science initiatives, 49
Publications and tenure, 254,255
Publishers
Goals, 49-50
Information systems, 48
Services to Libraries, 183-185
View, 47-50
PubMed, 238
*Purchasing Electronic Resources: A
National Approach,* 163

Quantum management, 51-53
Reading patterns, 122-126

Advanced phase, 123-126
Amount of, 128f-129f
Astronomers, 132-136
Early phase, 123-126
Evolving phase, 123-126
Factors affecting journal use, 136-139
Finding articles, 125f
Identification of articles, 124
Preprint servers, 134-135
Scientists, 127-132
Source used, 124f
Readmore Academic and Blackwell's Periodicals, 193
Reinventing acquisitions, 269-273
Repositories, print, 263-267
Electronic formats and, 263-267
Light and dark, 265-266
National system, 266-267
Storage, 263-267
Richard Abel, 195
Riley, Cheryl, 198,233,240n
Robinson, Karlene Patricia, 321
Romaine, Siôn, 17
Romaniuk, Elena, 301,302,303,305, 306,307,308n
Rupp, Nathan, 221-226n

Scales, Ruth Richardson, 327
Schmetzke, A., 234, 240n
Schmitt, Stephanie, 257-262n
Schoen, Dena, 195,198
Scholarly Communications Report, 192,193
School of Library and Information Science, 234
ScienceDirect, 90
Screen readers, 235-238
Seamans, Marsha, 253,256n
Self-assessment, 32
Self-serve behavior of end users, 30
Serial aggregations, 69-82
SERIALIST (electronic discussion list), 243
Serialists,
developing of, 241-243
Tenure, 253-255
Serials
Acquisitions, impact of electronic resources on, 326-327
Budget, 322
Cataloging time and costs, 292f
Check-in, 271,272
Claiming, 271,326
Counting on surveys, 324
Funding model, 322
Operations,
benchmarking, 287-293
Time and costs, 287-293
Renewals processing, 157-158
Selection of, new, 323
Serials vendors *See* Vendors
Serials Solution, 73,85,87,296
Service and tenure, 254,255
Seventy Percent Solution, 9-15
SFX, 73,125,300
Shadle, Steve, 203,202,205,207, 208n
Sharing (Networking), 210
Shay, Lynn R., 315,320n
Sheffield, Rebecca, 315,320n
SIAM Journal on Matrix, 75,77f-81f
Simonetti, Jack L., 250,251n
Sinha, Reeta, 27,32n,197
Six sigma, 53
Skinner, Debra, 39
Slagell, Jeff, 209-213n
Slight-Gibney, Nancy, 287,293n
SLIS *See* School of Library and Information Science
Smith, Abby, 107,113n,115,116, 117,118
Software development, 155-159
Storyboards, 158
Space limitations, 264
SPARC, 49

Spencer, Sabina, 246,248f,251n
Stamison, Christine, 309,311,312,313n
Standards, 40-41, 42-47
  E-metrics, 147-150
Standing orders, 271
State University of New York Library example, 71
  Albany Library example, 83
  Office of Library Information Services example, 69
Stefancu, Laurentiu Mircea, 325
Stewart, Ron, 239
Storage,
  Facilities, 264
  Repositories, 263-267
Storyboards, 158
Subject clusters, 12
Subscription Agents,173-177, 310,311-313
Successive entry cataloging, 20
Sullenger, Paula, 275-280n
SUNYConnect Union Catalog, 71,75
Survival of the profession, 209-213
Swets, 50
Swets Blackwell, 194
Swets Subscription Services, 194

Table of Contents Service, 315-320
  Budget cuts, 317
  Changing formats, 317
  Goodwill, 319
  Management, 316-317
  Marketing, 318
  Notifying faculty, 318
  Trends, 319
Taylor & Francis, 197
Te Ropu Whakahau, 164
Teach Act, 230-231
Team-based, 53
Technical Services librarians, 221-226
Technical Services, policy and procedure manuals, 257-261
  Appealing certain work assignments, 260
  Discrimination, 259
  Emergency contact list, 259
  Personnel policies for involuntary leave, 260
  Prohibition of censorship by staff, 260
TELSIG *See* Tertiary Education Libraries Special Interest Group, 169
Tenney, Joyce, 34
Tenopir, Carol, 121,122,140n,141n
Tenure process, 253-256
Time and Costs for Serials Operations, 287-293
Title changes, 20-21
TOC *See* Table of Contents service
Tonkery, Dan, 99,101-103,105n
Tools for Change Workshops, 246,250n
Towards a National Information Strategy, 162
Toxline, 238
TQM, 53
Training, 281-285
  Alternatives, 286
  Analysis, 286
  Assessment and evaluation, 282-284
  Design, 284-285
  Implementation, 285
  Ongoing, 286
Treaty of Waitangi (1840), 164
Tumlin, Markel, 253,255,256n
Tuttle, Marcia, 243

UCLA Graduate School of Education and Information Studies (cosponsor), 234
Ulrich's Periodical Directory, 121
United Kingdom. Keystone for the Information Age Conference, 165
United Kingdom. National Information Policy, 165
U. S. News & World Report, 316

University of California Melvyl Union Catalog, 70
University of Chicago Press (codeveloper), 132
University of Illinois at Chicago (developer of DOLLeR), 325
University of North Carolina at Chapel Hill Alumni Association mentor program, 242
University of North Carolina at Wilmington, William Madison Randall Library example, 315-320
University of Oregon Libraries, 288
  Acquisitions and Cataloging Depts,. 287-293
University of Pittsburgh Library example, 126,139
University of Tennessee survey, 86,123,126,129,131
University of Victoria libraries example, 301-308
University of Wisconsin System web page example, 234
Usage patterns, 121-141, 295-299
Usage statistics, 143-153

Van Fleet, C., 235,240n
Vendor's priorities, 156
Vendors, 179-190
  Changing roles, 186-189
  Merges, 194
  Performance standards, 194
  Services offered, 180-183
  See also specific vendors
Victoria University of Wellington Library example, 168-169
Virtual Union Catalog, 69-82
Visually impaired users, 236
Voyager System, 278,302,307

W3C *See* World Wide Web Consortium
WAI *See* Web Access Initiative
Wall Street (movie), 210
Wallas, Philip, 173,177n
WatchThatPage, 271
Web Access Initiative, 235
Web-based Trails, 215-219
Web of Science, 297
Web-Z, 152
WebFeat, 152
WebFountain, 31
Webpages, 234,301-308
WebSPIRS, 297
Weston, Claudia, 9,10,11-12,15
Wilder, Stanley, 242,244
WindowEye, 238
Word, 31
Workflow, 156,157-158
World Wide Web Consortium, 235, 240
Worthing, Richard, 1-3

Yahoo, 31
Yale Law Library, bombing example, 259-260

Zeter, Mary Jo, 263,264,267n
Zhang, Xiaoyin, 326
Zhu, Lihong, 59-67
Zink, Steven D., 272,273n
ZoomText 7.0, 235,237-238